REINING

The Art
of Performance
in Horses

by Bob Loomis
with Kathy Kadash

REINING
The Art of Performance in Horses
by BOB LOOMIS
with KATHY KADASH

Published by
EquiMedia

REINING

THE ART OF PERFORMANCE IN HORSES

Bob Loomis	***Author***
Kathy Kadash	***Editor***
Robert Feinberg	***Production Mgr.***
Kathy Kadash	***Photographer***
John Hillenbrand	***Graphic Designer/ Illustrator***

Fourth Printing, 1996

Published by
EquiMedia Corporation
P.O. Box 90519
Austin, Texas 78709-0519
Tel: 512-288-1676

Library of Congress Catalog Card Number: 90-81845

ISBN 0-9625898-8-8

Printed in Singapore

I dedicate this book
to the memory of George Phillips
for the many hours he spent with me
as a young man and for the all things
he taught me about horses,
mentally and physically.

Contents

Preface

BY KATHY KADASH

Any good builder is sure of his foundation. It is impossible to construct something which will stand the test of time without laying down a solid foundation first. Only after the groundwork is laid, can the rest of the structure be built brick by brick.

In "Reining, the Art of Performance in Horses," Bob Loomis is such a builder, a master craftsman, if you will. His horses are his creation. He starts with a flawless pedigree, then molds and shapes his material until he has created a solid performing animal.

This book follows a blueprint from start to finish. It, too, has its own foundation. To understand the concepts and techniques which have taken Loomis a quarter of a century to perfect, it is necessary that the reader start at the beginning of this book and follow Loomis' thought pattern throughout. It would be difficult, indeed, to read Chapter 12 "Rollbacks and Turn Arounds" without having read the first 11 chapters. How Loomis has arrived at his procedures and philosophies is as important to understand as the training maneuvers themselves.

But learning about reining and how to accomplish maneuvers is only part of the knowledge to be gained in reading this book. The "soul" of this text is Loomis' love for his horses and his desire to understand and communicate with them. These lessons can be the hardest to learn.

Foreword

BY DICK PIEPER

Reining, in the truest sense of the word, is far more than a particular class in the spectrum of Western riding. It is a communication between horse and rider employing the principles of classical horsemanship to create an art form that is pleasing and exciting to watch.

Bob Loomis, one of the premier reining trainers of all time, has put together in this volume a lifetime of experience and knowledge that is beneficial for any horseman, whether his chosen event is Western pleasure, cutting, reining, roping, English events or trail riding.

The basic suppling exercises that a reining horse must know have their foundation in classical dressage and are essential for any horse, regardless of the direction that his training and career take him.

This book is a necessary addition to the library of anyone seriously interested in the art of horsemanship.

My hat is off to Bob Loomis for a job well done!

Acknowledgements

My thanks to the following people and organizations for their help in the preparation of this book.

American Quarter Horse Association, breed registry and governing body of Quarter Horse activities, for cooperating in the chapter on the development of reining and for permission to reprint AQHA reining patterns.

Don Burt, one of the nation's leading horsemen, show judges and lecturers, for allowing us to reprint his views on the trapezoid theory as it relates to conformation.

Greg Darnall, master bit maker, for his help on the theories and construction of bits.

Pat Feuerstein, editor of the Reiner magazine and NRHA Historian, for her additions in the chapter on the history and development of reining as a sport and the National Reining Horse Association.

Rich McDonald, farrier, for all of the information regarding tips on shoeing reining horses.

Dr. Jim Morgan, equine veterinarian and NRHA non professional rider, for his assistance with technical matters concerning veterinary topics.

National Reining Horse Association, an organization dedicated to the promotion of the reining horse, for cooperation when I asked for it and for permission to reprint parts of the NRHA Handbook and Judge's Guide.

John Snobelen, NRHA board member and Chairman of the Judge's Committee, for his assistance in the chapter on judging reining.

Kathy Kadash

Profile

Animals touched Bob Loomis' life at an early age and, no doubt, were largely responsible for the path he has taken.

Born in Lincoln, Nebraska in 1943 to Leslie and Juanita Loomis, Bob grew up surrounded by horses, dogs and other four-footed friends.

His father, now deceased, was the Midwest director for the American Humane Society. Besides supervising the regional offices of the Society, he often acted as their representative to the motion picture industry. His father was asked to be present during animal scenes to make sure no cruelty took place.

Bob's mother raised pedigreed dogs. She still lives in Lincoln as does Ed, Bob's brother who is older by six years. The eldest son, Leslie E., is also deceased.

The Loomis family was quite active in the world of gaited horses and hunter/jumpers. In 1948, Bob showed his first horse, a three-gaited American Saddlebred named Mystery Of Rhythm. He won the first class he entered, one of many to follow in his life-long career in the saddle.

While his brothers were content to post to the trot, Bob needed a faster pace. All he wanted to do was match race the neighbor's children. When his father gave him Fancy Pants, the three-gaited pony Ed had done so well on, his father pulled off the pony's shoes and exasperatingly said if Bob wanted to be a cowboy so much, he could.

His parents' divorce when he was 10 changed Bob's life dramatically. He and his mother moved to town. That ended his involvement with horses until he was 16 years old. He quit school at 16, held several odd jobs, followed the local rodeo circuit and drove fast cars.

As a teenager, Bob dated a girl named Bonnie Sherwood, whose father, George, trained reining horses. The Sherwoods owned Magnolia Denny, the world champion reining horse in 1960. When he would visit Bonnie, Bob always ended up in the barn watching Bonnie's father with his horses. One night Sherwood put Bob up on an old mare called Shady Pecos. She had a feathery light mouth, could really stop, turn around and run backwards. That lit a spark in Bob. From that day on, he knew he wanted to train horses for a living and reining horses would be his first choice.

Back in the '60s though, there were few places in the Midwest to learn his chosen trade. Most of the serious reining horse activity was east of the Mississippi.

Bob never had any formal riding instruction. He did, however, have an excellent mentor in George Phillips, the man he credits with much of his success. Phillips was a teamster and horse trader. In his construction business, Phillips drove horse and mule hitches, as many as 20 to a team. He was one of the largest horse buyers in the United States. He bought them by the boxcar load for resale.

Bob is pictured here winning his first horse show when he was five years old. His family had American Saddlebreds at the time. He is here on the three gaited Saddlebred, Mystery Of Rhythm. Bob's father, Leslie, is also in the photo.

Phillips taught Bob to read a horse. According to Bob, Phillips could look at a 2-year-old's head and tell him what it would be like to break, how smart it was and how good it would be when it was trained. Phillips was like a father to Bob. They spent a lot of time together and Bob learned from the great horseman.

Phillips' wife died when Bob was 23. Bob went to live with his friend and worked at a nearby packing plant. He still went to rodeos on the weekend, riding bareback broncs.

Although Phillips didn't ride, he could make a horse do anything with a set of driving lines. It is from Phillips that Bob learned how and why horses move the way they do. Phillips taught Bob how to watch them while standing on the ground.

Phillips would hand Bob a set of driving lines that were attached to a horse with a piece of ordinary string. He then expected Bob to drive the animal without breaking the string. If Bob broke the string, Phillips would have a fit. He would say "Feel a horse, don't force him." Phillips was a kind man, but blunt.

Bob had a quick temper as a young man. He was hot-headed and would fly off the handle. If Phillips caught Bob losing his temper with a horse, he would chastise him unmercifully. "Whenever a man loses his temper with a horse, all he is doing is displaying a lack of knowledge." In no uncertain terms, Phillips let Bob know what he thought of his temper.

Phillips made powerful impressions upon Bob that have shaped Bob's philosophies and methods of riding horses. From the old teamster, Bob learned how a horse thinks and moves and how to get along with a horse. But most of all, he learned how to have a good mental attitude and provide a slow, solid foundation for training.

Bob hung out his shingle as a horse trainer in 1966 when he was 23. He started campaigning the winter livestock show circuit during the mid-'60s, concentrating on reining horse classes in the Quarter Horse shows. In 1966, he was fifth at Denver and Fort Worth. He lost in Houston and dropped a rein in Chicago, but he was learning. He trained his first NRHA Futurity horse that year, made the semi-finals, but didn't place in the finals. He returned to the stock shows in 1967 and started placing better with seconds and thirds.

In 1969, he was lucky enough to campaign Monika, a horse that changed everything for him. The pair won wherever they went: the Nebraska Futurity, Denver, Fort Worth, Houston, San Antonio and Odessa. Along with Monika, he campaigned Janice Jo Leo, who won all the senior reining classes. Bob was off and running and he has never looked back. He was in the top ten in the NRHA Futurity for the first time in 1969 and has been in the top ten every year but one since.

Bob Loomis has had many career achievements in the 25 years he has been in the saddle. He has captured the prestigious NRHA Futurity six times, more than any other rider. He is the only rider to win the event three times in succession. No one else has won it twice in a row. His chronicle of futurity wins began in 1976 with Benito Paprika. He dominated the scene from 1978 through 1980 on Lady Eldorado, Cassandra Cody and Topsail Cody respectively. In 1984, he captured the futurity on Miss Della Doc. In 1986, the first year the futurity moved to Oklahoma City, he won on Sophie Oak.

Loomis has won the AQHA World Show in reining seven times and once in working cowhorse. He won both the junior and the senior reining at all the major stock shows. At the All American Quarter Horse Congress, Bob won the Open reining and the Futurity the same year twice. He has been the NRHA's top money earning futurity rider for many years running.

Bob is an internationally known horseman who has been invited to give numerous clinics and seminars on reining in Europe, Canada, South America and Australia.

He married Joyce Shelly, a former Miss Rodeo America and world champion barrel racer, in 1975. Their daughter, Bobbie Jo, is both an avid reiner and barrel racer. Bob and Joyce have children by previous marriages. Bob's son is Joseph Scott Loomis and Joyce's son is Opie Burk. Bob and Joyce moved to Marietta, Oklahoma, from Bee, Nebraska, in 1986. There they run a commercial horse breeding and training operation on 400 acres.

(above) *Early in his career, Bob won the junior and senior reinings at all the major stock shows. In those days, reining was the highlight event and entries of 50 and 60 in a class were not uncommon. He is pictured here with Britton Princess (left) and Monika (right) winning the 1973 Houston Livestock Show.*

(below) *The Loomis family, (left to right) Topsail Cody, Bob, Joyce and daughter Bobbie Jo.*

Introduction

BY BOB LOOMIS

All of my life, I've wanted to know why. What causes things in horsemanship to happen the way they do? What body position does a horse have to be in to perform a certain maneuver? I couldn't just accept that it worked. I wanted to know the reason why. If the person riding couldn't explain the logic to me and tell me what mechanical thing you have to do to cause something to happen, I wasn't interested. I've never been partial to gimmicks or anything that mystically fixed the problem. To me, there is nothing mystical about training a horse. It is factual. It is scientific.

In the science of riding, we deal with a live animal with a bone structure, muscles, tendons, ligaments and a brain. A good performance horse has correct conformation, proper muscling, good attitude and a sound mind. All are crucial. When all these things are in place, I know I have a trainable animal. Then in training, everything has to be logical and explainable. If I can't fully understand what I am doing and how to apply it, I won't do it.

As you learn to ride, try to understand everything about what it is you are trying to do. Don't do something just because someone tells you it is supposed to work. Supposed to doesn't cut it. Facts are what makes a good horseman.

I don't care what kind of horsemen you learn from. If you go to a good dressage teacher, hunter/ jumper instructor, reiner, cutting horse rider, pleasure horse rider or polo player, correct horsemanship is correct horsemanship. We teach our horses different maneuvers for different events. However, if there is correct horsemanship, there should not be a big difference in the way we approach riding and training horses.

The chapters of this book are filled with my life's work — breeding, training and riding horses. Although reining horses are my specialty, my experience and theories can be applied to any field of horsemanship. When we learn about riding, your object and mine should be to become a better horseman.

1

How a Horse Thinks and How a Horseman Should Think

Horses are much more intelligent than people give them credit. However, their intelligence and logic are different from human standards. They learn and understand through repetition. Their form of intelligence does not necessarily allow them to pick up on something the first time it is shown to them. However, they understand if it is repeated. A horse relates to repetition, not just in being ridden, but in everything in its life. Watch a horse play. Nine times out of 10, a stalled horse turned out to play follows a set routine. Horses are comfortable with repetition.

The first time you do anything to a horse, you plant a seed; after several times, you've created a habit. Since a horse understands repetition, if you let him do something wrong repeatedly, he will develop that bad habit. If you figure out a way to make him do it right more than once, then he will have a good habit.

Repetition is a horse's logic. Handle a horse with repetition and train with it. Your mannerisms are as much a part of training as are your techniques. If you are repetitiously loud, rough and abrupt, the horse will get spooky, scared and wild. If you are consistently quiet, soft, but firm, he will be responsive and alert to your commands.

When I was young, I worked with an experienced teamster and horseman, George Phillips. I had quite a temper back then. Sometimes I'd get angry and rough with his horses. He would stop me and tell me that "temper is a display of lack of knowledge." When training horses, there is no room for temper or a bad attitude. As soon as you lose your temper, it shows you don't know the right way to handle the situation. You might as well hang out a neon sign that says you are incompetent. That has nothing to do with

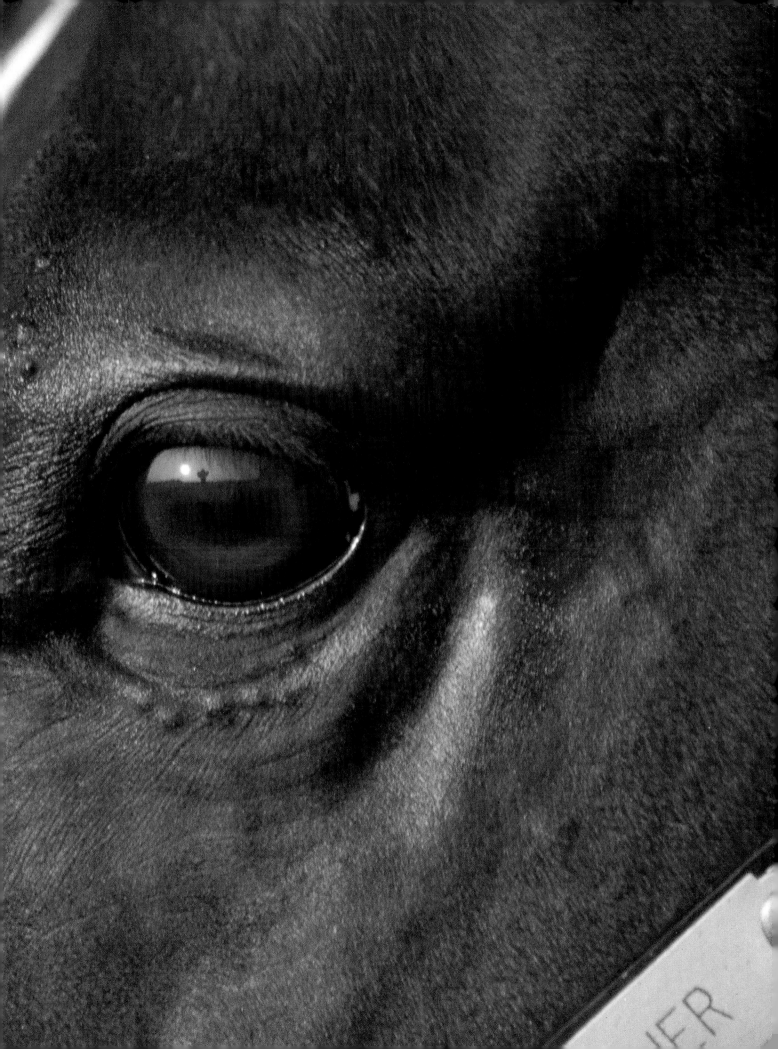

horsemanship. Handling a horse properly and being a horseman is being a thinker and knowing how a horse thinks.

A successful horseman must eliminate bad attitudes and turn temper into a concern and desire to fix problems correctly. This is probably the most important lesson a rider can learn. There is no such person as a great horse trainer with a bad temper.

When handling a horse, a true horseman always puts the animal in situations where the easiest way out is the rider's way out. If he wants a horse to do one thing and it wants to do another, the horseman makes the escape route suit his purposes. For example, if the horse does not want to back up, the rider shouldn't fight him. Rather the rider should walk the horse into a corner, lift the slack out of the reins and bump him with his legs to encourage the horse to move. The only exit the horse has out of that corner is reverse. The rider has made the easy way out his way out.

The days of forcing a horse to yield are gone. If you want to win, you'd better be a horseman. You'd better be a deep thinker. A deep thinker is a person who, when confronted with a problem, doesn't rush in and try to knock things into shape. A deep thinker backs off. When a real horseman encounters a serious problem in training and isn't sure how to deal with it, he'll stop, put the reins down, sit there or walk around until he figures out the correct way to confront the situation. Then he'll come back with a slow, quiet program and work it out.

The man who jerks and spurs won't turn out many good horses. He may get lucky once in a while, but he'd have to be on a particular kind of horse, one that is cold-blooded and lazy. If he got on a good horse with a lot of feel and sensitivity, he'd better learn to do some thinking. That kind of horse won't tolerate abuse. In the late 60's, early 70's, we had quite a few rough trainers who had a large influence on newcomers. That era is finished. Now, talented trainers are deep thinkers who go about things slowly and correctly.

There are horsemen and there are intimidation artists. To get a point across, a horseman thinks. An intimidation artist uses fear. There is room for a certain form of mental intimidation in training and I use it carefully. I think every good trainer does. However, I don't use it in a rough, crude way. I use it in a quiet, non-aggressive way. I never intimidate a horse through pain, fear or lack of air. By lack of air I mean riding a horse until he is exhausted and unable to catch his breath. My form of intimidation shows horses that the easiest way out is the way I want to go.

When you think about it, you intimidate a horse throughout the training process. The horse learns that responding to your requests is the easiest way out because if he doesn't respond, you make it hard work for him not to respond. If he responds to your requests, that is the end of it. The horse, which is basically a lazy animal, finds it easier to comply with your requests than fight them.

For example, speed control is a form of intimidation. In speed control, you teach a horse to look forward to going

(previous pages) *A good horseman tries to look through a horse's eyes to see how he perceives the world around him.*

(opposite) *Speed control is a form of intimidation. The rider teaches the horse to look forward to going slow instead of going fast.*

You can read a horse by watching his body language. This horse is cooperative and paying attention to his rider. The horse's muscles are relaxed, eyes calm and ears pointed in the direction of his rider.

slow instead of looking forward to going fast. When you gallop a horse and teach him to want to slow down, you have intimidated him to a degree. You've shown him that slowing down is the easiest way out.

The intimidation artists I referred to use physical intimidation to get their points across in training. A horse that is afraid because he has been physically intimidated does not cooperate the way a horse who respects his rider does. The two forms of training produce very different results. On the one hand, an intimidation artist has an equine adversary he has to deal with when he rides. On the other hand, a good trainer has a partner to share his work.

One of the best ways to learn how horses think is to watch how they relate to each other in their own environment. Spend some time in the breeding barn or out in the pasture observing herd psychology. Learn what makes horses tick.

You can learn to read a horse by watching his body language. A horse is like a bad boxer. He advertises what he is going to do by giving you a warning before he does anything.

A lot of equine body language involves facial expressions and use of the ears.

Horses' eyes tell you a lot about their moods. A soft, languid look indicates a horse is quiet, calm, serene; everything about his world is okay with him. A wide-eyed, wild or alert look shows a scared horse or at least one that is intensely curious about what is going to happen to him next.

Watch a horse's ears. They express what he is thinking. If you are trying to catch a horse that is boxed into a corner and he drops his ear to the left, he is going to run past you on the right.

Also, a horse usually doesn't spook until he has pointed

an ear in the direction of the scary object.

Especially watch those ears when you get on a colt for the first time. If his ears start turning around towards you and start shaking, he is thinking about bucking. You'd better get his head pulled around and do something to get his mind off bucking. When his ears finally come together and actually touch, that horse will be bucking. A horse doesn't do anything without telling you first.

When you approach a horse in a stall, be careful if he turns and runs to the other side of the stall with his hind-quarters facing you. He may tip his head around to see where you are and snort to show his fear. He is scared. If you press him too quickly, he may defend himself with a well-placed kick.

On the other hand, if you open the stall door and the horse charges at you with ears pinned back and teeth bared, you have an aggressive horse on your hands and one that is not afraid to fight facing you.

For the most part, horses are not mean. But if they are unhappy with something, they always let you know by pinning their ears back. Respect that. Try to figure out what is going wrong to make the horse unhappy. He is trying to communicate with you the only way he knows how.

A horse that is not scared should come to you or at least not move away when you approach. Often a curious horse stretches out his neck to sniff you. Horses' sense of smell is a strong identifying factor for them.

Flared nostrils are another sign. The horse wants to take in as much air as he can to identify his surroundings. He is scared or excited and ready to take flight if he thinks an enemy or harm is present.

There is no reason to get into a fight with a horse when all you have to do is read the signs. Most people aren't aware of the signs. They run right into problems after the horse has already told them it didn't understand or didn't want to do something. If you read the signs, you can stop, back off and return to slow preparation in training or handling the horse in any manner.

Through their innate sensitivity, horses learn to read people. I can plan to stop 40 feet away and my horse already knows it. I can think about turning and it seems my horse turns just a second before I ask. Your own body language tips a horse off. If you do the same thing the same way every time, horses are going to wire in on it.

Personalities, the horse and the rider's, play a large part in the training process. A person can learn as much about riding and training techniques as he wants. He uses the mechanics, the methods and the strategies he learned, but the mental approach is his own. Personality is the deciding factor in the way a rider applies all the things he has learned. A radical person uses techniques radically. A gentle person uses them gently. A rider's personality surfaces when he rides horses.

Knowing how a horse thinks, what makes him react the way he does and recognizing our own personalities are pre-requisites to successful training.

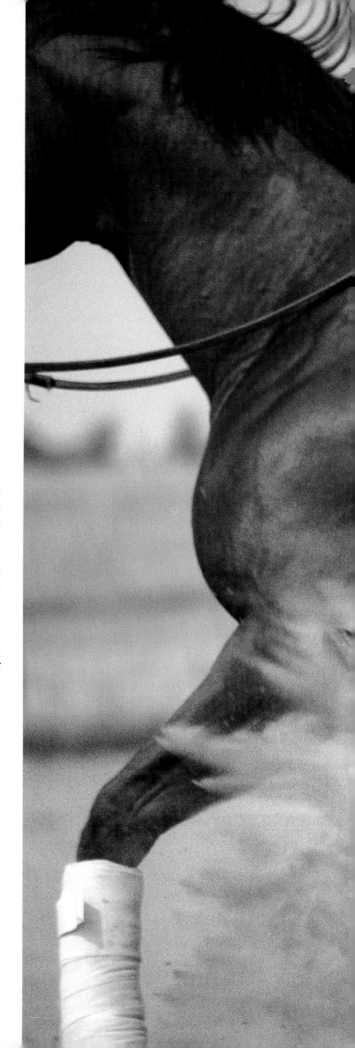

2

What Is
a Reining Horse?

A reining horse is a horse that is extremely broke. It is a horse that allows a rider to handle it, to move all of its working parts effortlessly. Just as significantly, however, it must have a good frame of mind and a good attitude.

There is a big difference in a horse that performs at a rider's command and one that works an object or another animal. The latter is a horse with more of a desire to work something. Cutting horses are a good example. When you ride a cutting horse and it does something wrong, you can correct it. But then you must turn it loose to do its job. That is vastly different than telling a reining horse "Do what I ask you to do and only that." A reining horse has that type of mind.

The true mixture of a great reining horse is one with a golden mind, athletic ability, a huge heart and lots of guts.

A good mind is probably the most important quality a reining horse can have. To me, a good-minded horse is one that has a lot of give. It is willing to give its entire body to the rider. I don't necessarily mean from the beginning. Some horses are stiff when you start to train them. They can be a little hard to train, but they never want to fight. I don't mind teaching a stiff horse to be soft and supple. But I do mind a horse that wants to fight. There are horses that might be good in other events, but won't be good reiners because they have tempers.

A horse that doesn't want to fight and doesn't have a bad temper usually falls into line quickly. Most often, these horses come from certain families. I can tell which horses are going to fight and which have the kind of mind I need for a reiner by the way they are bred. Dispositions are strong in families. I think mind and mental attitude are definitely in-

(previous pages) *A good reining horse allows its rider to move all of its working parts effortlessly.*

(above) *An early photo of Bob on the great Okie Leo, sire of Okie's Bamboo, the first reining horse Bob exhibited.*

herited traits in horses.

I can usually determine what kind of mind a horse has within the first 60 days of training. By the end of that time, I know whether or not he will make a reining horse, but not how good a reining horse. I know if he is has the mental capacity and physical ability to perform the required maneuvers. What I can't tell is how big a heart the horse has or how much guts. That I don't know until I put the finishing touches to the training program. A lot of horses feel as if they are going to be good reining horses, but when the pressure is on, they don't have enough guts or a big enough heart to carry them through.

I can tell more about a horse faster if I know what family the horse comes from. In many cases, I have ridden the mothers, fathers, grandparents and even the great grandparents of a lot of my horses. With them, I know how good they are going to be in the first 30 days.

Bad minds run in families just as good minds do. I've ridden horses that were built beautifully. You couldn't fault them conformationally. Yet they had bad attitudes, would fight and not allow training to take place. That type of horse never reaches over 20 to 25 percent of its capabilities. If you push him beyond that point, he blows up. You could spend years on that kind of horse and never get anywhere with him. You could use gimmicks and make him resemble what it is you want him to be. Eventually, though, his true nature shows through and lets you down. In the end, you aren't going to beat anyone with him.

Most bad-minded horses have a sour attitude toward life because their mothers and fathers did. You can't take a good-minded stallion and breed it to a bad-minded mare and hope to raise good horses. A winner has to be good on both sides of his pedigree. With one bad cross, you can easily breed out the good mind and athletic ability of a horse in one generation.

A good reining horse has a certain feel. It is difficult for a rider who has never ridden one to understand that quality. One of the best things that happened to me as a young trainer was being able to ride a mare named Okie's Bamboo. She was the first reining horse I exhibited. Unbelievably talented and with an extremely light touch, she was a truly great horse born 20 years ahead of her time. She inspired me to go on and do what I have done.

Okie's Bamboo was sired by Okie Leo. It was because of her that I found myself searching for other horses with that pedigree. I had nothing to do with training her. She was trained by a friend of mine, Bob Bassinger. Her nickname was Brown.

I knew nothing about training a reining horse at the time. Brown showed me what a reining horse should feel like. She was the ultimate in lightness and control. I rode her in 1964 and 1965 and started training professionally in 1966. When I did, I tried to make every horse I rode feel like her. I wanted them to stop like her, turn like her, change leads like her. Brown was my first teacher. She taught me what a reining horse is.

3

Breeding for Reining Horses

Since I was a child, my dream and life's ambition was to raise horses. When I started specializing in reining horses in 1965, it was hard to find suitable prospects. Everyone was breeding halter and pleasure horses at the time. No one was breeding for reiners, which prompted me to go into the breeding business. If I couldn't buy the kind of horses I wanted, I knew I would have to breed my own.

I started with the intention of creating a powerful broodmare band. That's the rock I built my program on. When their show careers were through, I bought many of the great mares I rode and those I showed against. I crossed them on my two reining stallions, Topsail Cody and Boss Nowata Star.

I have ridden many of the sires and dams of the horses I ride now. Their offspring are what I would expect them to be, good reining horses. Because I know their families so well, I see a lot of similarities between them and their parents.

I'm such a family man. I know that good minds and athletic ability are inherent in strong families. Of the six times that I won the NRHA Futurity, all six have been on horses with Joe Cody or Doc Bar in their pedigrees or they were Joe Cody-Doc Bar crosses. Topsail is a good example. He is by Joe Cody and out of Doc Bar Linda, a Doc Bar daughter. A NRHA Futurity winner and AQHA World Champion that has never been beaten in competition, Topsail is now passing on his superior genetics. He has established himself as a leading sire of reining futurity horses.

When it comes to reining horses, King P234 is the foundation. King-bred horses inherit strong bone, correct body structure and good hard, black feet. They are mentally

and physically sound horses. Good minds and sound bodies are characteristic in King families. Joe Cody's pedigree is full of foundation. He traces to King through his dam Taboo, one of the great horse's daughters. Joe Cody's sire is Bill Cody, by Wimpy P1, who traces to Old Sorrel on both his sire and dam's side.

Doc Bar horses in a breeding program add refinement and a tremendous amount of athletic ability. They are classy, modern looking and have plenty of ability. They have a lot of "sting," that extra snap to movement which is so electrifying in a reining pattern. I love the Doc Bars. I feel a lot better when a reining horse I am riding has a little Doc Bar blood.

However, not all Doc Bar lines produce the kind of mind necessary in reining horses. Doc Bar was bred to be a racehorse. His is by Lightning Bars by Three Bars (TB) and out of Dandy Bell by Texas Dandy. History recognizes Doc Bar to be the progenitor of the modern day cutting horse. The kind of mind that makes a good cutting horse does not necessarily make a good reining horse. Some Doc Bar families are too hot; they want to fight you. Put them on a cow, turn their heads loose and they are phenomenal. But you take hold of them, try to handle them and they won't accept it.

Most of the Doc Bar-bred horses that have been good

(previous page) **This Topsail Cody foal, out of an Okie Leo daughter, is a product of crossing two performance pedigrees.**

(below) **King P-234 is the foundation sire of many top performance horse bloodlines.**

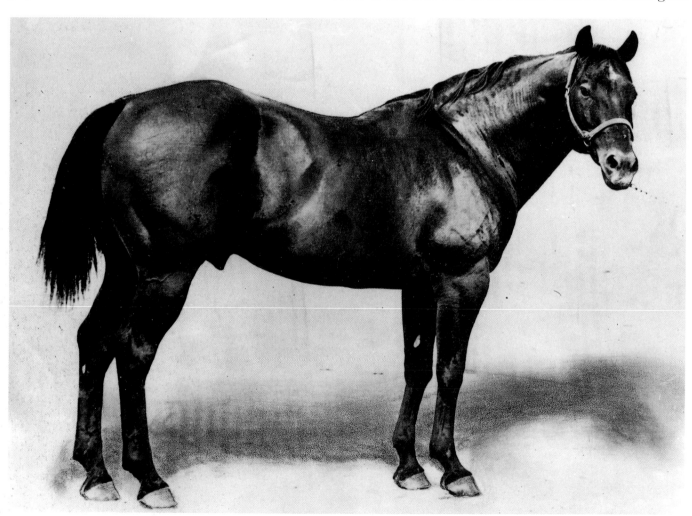

(top) ***Horses sired by Okie Leo helped start Bob's career in reining.***

(bottom) ***Doc Bar horses in a breeding program add refinement and a tremendous amount of athletic ability.***

(below left) *Joe Cody was a top sire of performance horses. His foundation pedigree traces to King P-234 and Old Sorrel.*

(below right) *Doc Bar Linda is the only Doc Bar mare ever bred to Joe Cody.*

(bottom) *Topsail Cody is a cross between two performance horse bloodlines: King P-234 and Doc Bar.*

reiners have King somewhere in their backgrounds. Doc's Eldorado sired only two foal crops, but each one of them counted. From each there have been many good reining horses. I never rode a Doc's Eldorado which didn't have a good mind and wouldn't make a reining horse. I have four of his daughters in my broodmare band. Doc's Eldorado was out of a daughter of Hollywood Gold.

Doc Bar breeding crossed on a foundation-bred mare is always a good bet. I have had good luck with the Sugar Bars,

Okie Leos and Joe Codys crossed on Doc Bar lines.

Topsail Cody mares in the Loomis broodmare band. (front) Sailwin Sally (back) Mizzen Topsail.

The best way to find out which Doc Bar stallions would make good reining horse sires is to talk to the people who have ridden them. Ask about their minds. Were they quiet and good-minded?

Many people make the mistake of not breeding like to like. They breed halter horses to performance horses and expect to end up with something. If you want to raise winners, keep your blood pure. If you have a halter mare, breed her to a halter stallion. Reining horses come from other great reining horses. When you mix your bloodlines, you are in trouble.

There are exceptions. A shot of Thoroughbred in a breeding program can be fantastic, but you have to be selective. The right Thoroughbred has to have the proper conformation combined with a golden mind, one that is quiet and responsive to being handled. Thoroughbreds typically have the heart you need for giving the utmost in performance. They generally have a gorgeous way of moving, fluid and agile. They have a lot of guts, a lot of try in them. If you can find all of that and the mind too, it is great to bring it to a breeding program.

In order for a stallion to sire well, he must be crossed on good mares. However, it is equally as important that he have an outstanding mare for a mother. I am a fanatic on dams. I've bred stallions for myself and my customers for the past

NRHA Futurity and Derby winner and AQHA World Champion Lady Eldorado is one of the top Loomis broodmares.

25 years and ridden a lot of them. The great ones had great mothers, the average ones had average mothers and the poor ones had poor mothers. I can go back through all of them, without exception, and the dam influences the way the colt turned out as a riding and siring animal.

A stallion can do a lot to improve his offspring, especially in passing on his good mind and athletic ability. However, he can't do enough to overcome a broodmare with a bad mind and limited ability. It might take 10 crosses to breed those traits out. Still, the cross would never be pure and the traits would probably pop up again down the line.

There are two ways for a broodmare to prove herself. One is in the show ring. Mares that were good show horses are less of a gamble. They have displayed their athletic ability and trainability. The chances of such a mare becoming a good broodmare are strong if she is bred to the right kind of stallion.

The other way a broodmare proves herself is in the quality of her produce. You can't evaluate a broodmare adequately unless you have seen three of her foals. When you breed a mare to the best stallion you can find and look at her produce, you will know what kind of broodmare she is. If she has one good one, one average one and one poor one, she is an average mare. If she has three outstanding foals, she is a great broodmare. If she has two outstanding foals and one average one, she is a good broodmare, but not a great one. Great broodmares don't miss often. There are few such mares around.

Ready Sugar Bars is a good example of such a mare. When I purchased her, I did so for several reasons. I had ridden two colts out of her by average stallions. They had fabulous minds and lots of ability. When I checked into the mare's pedigree, I found that her mother was a full sister to one of the greatest mares I ever rode, Monika, and her sire was a son of Sugar Bars. The mare herself had never done anything in the show ring. I didn't know anything about her sire, but I never rode a Sugar Bars that couldn't stop. I decided to give her a try. The mare turned out to be a good gamble. She is a leading producing mare of reining horses. She produced Ready To Star, who placed sixth in the NRHA Futurity, won the Pre-Futurity, the Select Futurity and numerous open reinings. Another of her foals is Boss Sugar Bars, third in the NRHA Futurity and an AQHA World Champion Reining horse. Yet another is Kathleens Boss, fourth in the NRHA Futurity and Register of Merit in reining. That is a great broodmare. She has proved that she is through her produce.

Even though the sire and dam contribute their genes equally, 50-50, to an offspring, I think the dam accounts for 65 percent. A horse gets a lot of its attitude from its mother. The mare has more environmental influence on her produce than does a stallion. She is with her foal from day one until it is weaned.

Pay attention to the mare line when buying prospects for any event, reining, cutting, barrel racing or for the racetrack. If you spend the money it takes to get six nice horses and buy one great horse, that horse will buy many more for you. If you choose horses from good families, you will have more winners, make more money and have a lot fewer disappointments.

(above) ***Okleos Sail Win is out of the first Topsail Cody foal crop. The bay stallion went on to become the 1984 AQHA World Champion Junior Reining Horse and an NRHA Futurity finalist. He now stands at stud in Switzerland. He is shown here with Bob and owner, H. P. Reiss. The Swiss Alps are in the background.***

(below) ***Monika holds a special place in the development of the Loomis broodmare band.***

*"A PERFORMANCE HORSE HAS TO HAVE
A CORRECT TRAPEZOID."*

4

Selecting the Reining Prospect

Selecting prospects for reining, or any other performance event, is not an exact science. It is partly what the eye can see and partly what it cannot. It is knowing what physical characteristics to look for and what mental attitude is necessary to make that body perform.

Because mental and physical attributes are equally important in performance horses, I base my selection process heavily on those factors.

When I look at a reining prospect, whether it is a weanling or a 2 or 3-year-old, there are certain questions that cross my mind. First, how is the horse bred? I want to know who his sire is and what the stallion's accomplishments are. Also, I want to know who his dam is and what her accomplishments are and/or those of her family. There are some good broodmares that never had the chance to prove themselves in the arena, but yet come from strong performance pedigrees. Or maybe the mares have had produce that competed successfully.

Second, I look hard at conformation. Does this horse have a balanced body structure? I am interested in the horse having a correct trapezoid, which is explained later in this chapter. Also, does he have the type of legs that will stay sound through a training program?

Since many of my prospects are born on my ranch, I am familiar with them from the day they are born. Knowing their parents takes the work out of researching their bloodlines. Also, for the past 25 years, I have been culling my herd for conformation and mental attitude. When I look at a foal from good parents, I know that two years down the road, I'll be riding a good one.

(previous pages) *Watch herd behavior to find out about a particular horse's personality. This dominant mare puts a young upstart in his place in no uncertain terms.*

(above) *These three Topsail Cody fillies are what the Loomis breeding program is all about. Bay Cody Oak (left) is out of AQHA World and Reserve World Champion Rosetta Oak, Topsail Sophie (middle) is out of NRHA Futurity winner Sophie Oak and Topsail Desire (right) is out of Ready Sugar Bars, producer of four NRHA Futurity finalists that placed sixth or better.*

MENTAL CHARACTERISTICS

I find attitude to be extremely inheritable. I would even go so far as to say that attitude and trainability are more inheritable than conformation. In other words, horses pass on their dispositions as easily as they do their looks. The good-minded horses I have ridden have come from good-minded horses. There are exceptions to every rule, of course. I must say that I have ridden some poorly bred horses that made relatively good reining horses, but they usually didn't reproduce their abilities in the breeding shed.

Trainability is a function of attitude. A horse will only perform as well as his attitude allows him. There is a difference between trainability and personality. Trainability is the willingness to accept training, a desire to obey. Personality is a horse's outlook on life. A horse may be cranky or sweet and many variations in between. He may be disagreeable about some things, but pleasant about others. For example, a horse may lay his ears back when you feed him, but at other times follow you anywhere with a bright and cheery attitude.

I know a horse gets much of its personality or outlook on life from its mother. This is not to say that the horse will be a good or bad performance horse. It is simply an indication of the type of personality you will have to deal with when you handle the horse.

If you have the opportunity, study mares and foals in the pasture and you'll see what I mean. There are always dominant and subordinate mares. By the time their foals are 30 days old, they take after their mothers.

You can see a good example of this by watching horses at a watering tank. When the dominant female comes to drink, she lays her ears back and the rest of the herd scatters until she is through drinking. Before you know it, her colt starts laying its ears back too and the mare backs him up. If other horses bother that colt, the mare goes after them. When that colt is an adult, he'll have the same disposition. If you have a mare that is timid and shy, her colt will take after her. Some of his personality is inherited, but a lot is picked up from the dam.

Personality doesn't necessarily dictate the type of riding animal the horse makes. As far as riding aggressive or timid horses, I've had both extremes and had great horses with either type of personality. By aggressive horse, I don't mean rank or unmanageable. An aggressive horse is one that doesn't need much encouragement to go forward. He's gutsy. He's already confident in himself, but you must control his confidence if you want him to perform for you. A timid horse needs confidence and encouragement. You have to develop his faith in you as his master. Once you have it, a timid horse is quite dependable.

When it comes to riding, don't rely on a horse's attitude towards other horses. Some of the best-minded horses I've ridden have been absolutely cranky with other horses, but sweet with people. I make my judgement about a horse when I handle it.

I can tell a tremendous amount about a colt when I halter

break it. In a weanling, I look for a horse that has a natural willingness to cooperate. That tells me it will accept training later on. I don't want one that puts up a big fight, drags me around and won't give me its head. I prefer the one that looks at me and pays attention to what I ask it. I don't mind if it is scared at first and wants to leave as long as it returns to me when I ask. Since I do nothing to hurt the colt, his confidence in me comes quickly.

In handling young horses, you must be quiet, slow moving, firm, but gentle (see Chapter 5 "A Foundation for Riding: Early Ground Work"). Fast action and loud noises rattle horses. They are not used to communicating on that level and don't know how to perceive it when humans act that way. The confusion frightens them and communication between horse and human is blocked.

Being handled in a rough or loud manner horrifies even the best of colts. If you want to evaluate a horse's potential, don't scare him. A person who treats horses in a way foreign to them is not going to be able to tell anything about a horse after he scares it. When an uneducated handler frightens a horse, the animal's true personality can't come to the surface. The only thing that does surface is fear and the desire to get away from the human. The horse's natural instinct for self preservation is to flee.

Sometimes a good horse can appear to be difficult because it was improperly handled as a young horse. Its owners must have been rough, gruff and generally loud and

It is easy to evaluate horses as prospects when they are raised on the ranch and handled for two years before they are broke to ride.

offensive. Any horse, handled incorrectly, feels threatened by humans. It is difficult to evaluate such a horse's mentality. You have to overcome its past and develop its confidence in man before you can tell what kind of a riding horse it will be.

PROSPECT EVALUATION

With horses that are raised on my ranch, I have the advantage of handling them for the first two years of their lives. That gives me sufficient time to evaluate them as riding prospects, both mentally and physically. After they are weaned and halter broken, they are put out to pasture to grow until their 2-year-old year. However, during those two years, they are brought up every 60 days for veterinary and farriery care. I have an honest appraisal of each horse long before I get in the saddle.

I don't have that luxury with horses that are brought to me as 2 or 3-year-olds. I look for the same things I do in a weanling; although, I have a much shorter time to classify the horse's mental and physical characteristics.

When I look at a 2 or 3-year-old prospect that I didn't have the chance to watch grow, I go over its breeding and conformation thoroughly first. I look for the horse that is bred right top and bottom. I don't want any holes in the pedigree. If there is a bad cross in the pedigree, I'm not interested. I'll go back three generations to be sure.

A horse with a hole in his pedigree is a horse that does not fit the type or family of horses in the rest of the pedigree. For example, say you are looking for a racehorse prospect. In the second generation of the pedigree of the horse you are evaluating, there is a horse with no performance record. That horse either didn't or couldn't run. Therefore, he probably had no running ability to pass on. I consider that a hole. What you want is strong racehorse performance on both sides of the pedigree.

The same goes for other types of horses. If you want a good halter horse, look for strong halter horse bloodlines in the pedigree. If you want a good reining horse, look for strong reining horse families. It doesn't make sense to mix up bloodlines, such as breeding halter and reining horse families to get a horse that can stand Grand Champion at halter and then win the reining. More than likely you will breed out the qualities for both halter and performance. The animal won't be good enough for either event.

I believe in genetic principles and keeping bloodlines pure. I especially don't want out-crosses that dilute the strength of the last three generations. Reining horses should have a strong performance background.

When I am sent a horse that is two or three years old, I assume that they have been handled extensively. But how they have been handled is something I don't know. I need to have the horse approximately 30 days before I can get a true evaluation of his mental attitude. I've had colts come to me for training that seemed a little rank. After I handled them for a month, it was evident that they had been scared as young horses. After careful handling, they would mellow, gain confidence and turn into good horses.

I've also had horses that had been handled correctly and were pleasant at first. Then after 30 days, I could tell that when ˙I applied any pressure at all, by that I mean the simplest of basic cues, they actually had bad attitudes. Their true personalities surfaced when they were asked for more than they cared to give. That's usually a hint of things to come. But even then, there are exceptions. I've ridden some cranky, bull-headed horses for several months before I liked them. It just took them longer to get with the training program. Horses' personalities and attitudes are as variable as people's. We shouldn't forget that.

After that 30-day period of consistent handling, which includes veterinary care, farriery work and riding, I have a good picture of what kind of horse I am dealing with. I spend the first month quietly with the basics. I like to do a lot of walking, bending the horse's neck both ways, asking for the horse's head in either direction. I soften the body with simple suppling exercises (see Chapter 7 "The 2-Year-Old: Basic Training"). I keep the horse relaxed and build his confidence in me as a rider. At the end of 30 days of the basics, such as walk, trot, lope, turn and stop, I can learn a tremendous amount about a horse's temperament. The things I would have learned had I halter broke the colt become obvious in that time. Is the horse willing to accept training? Or does he want to fight? Is he slow to understand and need more time? Or is he bright and need challenges to keep from being bored?

After this 30-day evaluation process of the 2 or 3-year-olds that are brought in to me, I can tell which horses have the mentality and trainability to make reining horses. At this point, I'd cull any horses that don't have the attitudes to accept training. What I have left to work with are horses that have all the prerequisites: breeding, conformation (see below), ability and attitude.

The next big cut comes after approximately six months of riding in the horses' 3-year-old year. The young horses are well broke by this time. This is when I ask for more advanced maneuvers (see Chapters 9 through 13) and when horses with guts start standing out. It may have taken me six months, but now I find out which horses' mental attitudes can stand the rigors of the training program. I realize which horses are capable of giving me 100 percent when I ask for it. I find out if they will go the extra mile it takes to be winners. I categorize the horses at this point into average reining horses, nice ones and ones that have the ability to be great.

Eight times out of 10, those that show me potential for greatness are the ones that had great fathers and mothers. Their good breeding shows. Again, it all goes back to the breeding shed. Without superior genetics, you can't expect superior performance. I can't stress this enough.

Mental attitude is intangible. You can't put your hands on it. It takes a knowledgeable horseman to recognize the signs of cooperation in a horse, no matter what age the horse is. While a horse's mentality is not visible, conformation is.

However, it still takes a horseman with a trained eye to recognize good conformation and unacceptable faults in the horse's mechanical structure.

PHYSICAL CHARACTERISTICS

When it comes to conformation, I'm a mathematician. I want a horse to have a correct trapezoid in its body structure. Without a mathematically correct trapezoid, a horse won't have the athletic ability to perform all of the required maneuvers of a reining horse.

Trapezoid Theory

A correct trapezoid is balance, pure and simple. Most horsemen can see it, but they can't describe it. In this case, a trapezoid has to do with angulation of the horse's bone structure.

One of the finest horse show judges in the country and a long-time friend of mine, Don Burt, described the trapezoid theory in a speech he gave at a seminar. He explained how to look at a horse's body and draw a trapezoid on it with the mind's eye.

The following is an excerpt from his speech.

"The first step is to look at the body only. Divide it into thirds. The first third is from the point of the shoulder to the girth line, which is the line drawn between the back of the withers down under the chest behind the foreleg. The middle third is from the girth line to a line drawn from the top of the croup down the flank. The rear third is from the last line described to the point of the buttocks. The horse should divide equally (see illustration 4 A).

"Step two. While observing the body, draw an imaginary line starting at the point of the shoulder. Make a straight line to the point of the buttocks. From there, draw a line to the top of the croup. From the top of the croup, draw a line to the withers and from the withers draw a line to the point of the shoulder. This figure is a trapezoid (see illustration 4 B).

"The front sloping line from the point of the shoulders to the withers is an indication of the horse's speed and endurance. The line from the point of the buttocks to the top of the croup is an indication of the horse's power. The line from the top of the croup to the withers is an indication of topline strength.

"The key to this trapezoid and the usefulness of the horse is the bottom line, the longer the better. A horse that is divided evenly into thirds will have a short topline and a long bottom line. The matching angles are all important for balance. Angles that are equal are better than angles that are mismatched.

"Most horses are unbalanced. Those that have correct balance happen to be the champions. Angles are the key to performance. Secretariat had perfect angles for both speed and power. That is why he could run like he did. When artist Jim Reno sculpted his bronze of the famous horse, he discovered a trapezoid of immense proportions."

One day, Don and I went through my barn and actually took a tape measure to the horses. Every horse on my ranch

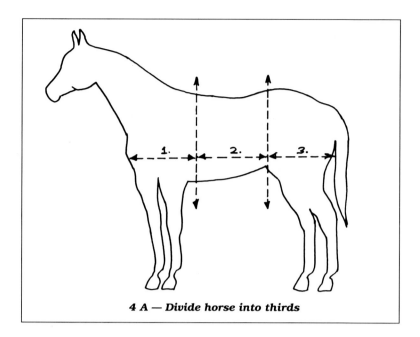

4 A — Divide horse into thirds

(4 A upper right) **To determine a horse's body measurements, first divide the body into thirds, from the point of the shoulder to the girth, from the girth to the flank and from the flank to the point of the buttock.**

(4 B lower right) **In a structurally correct trapezoid, the horse's shoulder and hip angles are equal and his bottom line is longer than his top line.**

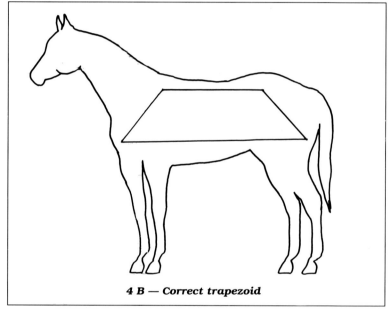

4 B — Correct trapezoid

that was a winner had a correct trapezoid. Every horse that had been giving me problems didn't. The trapezoid theory is based on physical fact and good horses prove it with their ability to perform. The better ones measured correctly and the limited ones had unequal angles.

I am a stickler on correct conformation. Horses that are off anywhere in their trapezoids are not acceptable for training. When a horse has a correct trapezoid, he is in balance to do all the maneuvers effortlessly and with comfort. If the trapezoid is off in any area, that causes a strain. Strains cause soreness and soreness causes horses to quit, go lame or both (see illustrations 4 C and 4 D).

Winners have correct trapezoids and losers don't. It's a fact of life. Unfortunately, there are a lot more horses without correct trapezoids than those with them and there are a lot more losers than winners. That is just the way it is.

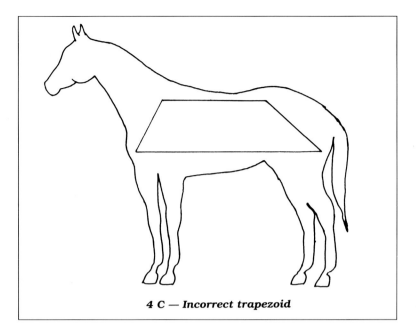

4 C — Incorrect trapezoid

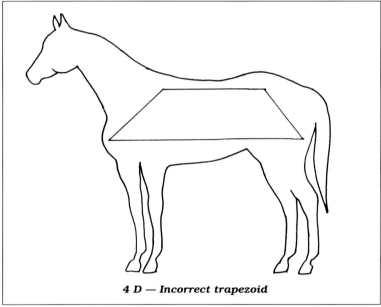

4 D — Incorrect trapezoid

(4 C upper left) **This horse's steep shoulder angle does not match his elongated hip angle.**

(4 D lower left) **This horse is unbalanced with a long, sloping shoulder and short hip.**

Horses with lopsided trapezoids may place, but rarely do they win anything.

I accept only horses with correct trapezoids for training. You can go through my broodmare band and you won't find a mare without a correct trapezoid. You can go through my barn and you won't find a show horse without one either. For the past 25 years, I have eliminated everything out of my breeding and riding program that didn't measure correctly.

Having horses with balanced conformation is one sure way to cut down on your work load. You won't have unsuitable horses to ride and train or waste your time on.

If you have a horse that doesn't measure correctly, it is not going to be easy for him to perform. I had to learn the hard way with horses that didn't measure up. It got to be a strain on them and they quit. It's a chain link reaction.

But, as I said earlier, a horse with correct conformation

This mare's good breeding shows in her balanced conformation, which is a good example of a trapezoid. Her shoulder and hip angles are equal. Her bottom line in much longer than her top line.

has to have a good mental attitude to use that body to its fullest. Conformation has to go hand in hand with a good mind. For example, one year I started with 14 futurity prospects. Ten went on to become good reining horses. The other four had good conformation, but they didn't have the desire to mentally extend themselves in training. Their minds limited their abilities. However, the point is that 10 out of 14 were good horses. Those are exceptional odds. Riders who don't pay attention to the mental and physical details of selecting prospects might get only one out of 14.

I wrap my entire breeding and training operation around correct trapezoids and good mental attitudes. I may go to a sale with 100 horses and see only one or two that I would take home. Sometimes, I see none. I go to shows and see horses entered that I wouldn't have accepted for training. Yet other riders took the chance on bad-minded and poorly built animals.

POINTS OF CONFORMATION

When it comes to conformation, there are certain characteristics I look for in a prospect. Those physical traits usually coincide with balanced, well-structured bodies.

Head

Good heads have wide-set eyes, which indicate plenty of

room for brain capacity as well as visual capability. Large nostrils make it easy for the horse to take in a sufficient amount of air. Performance horses need great quantities of air to do their jobs to the maximum. A horse with small nostrils can't take in as much air as he needs. He'll get tired sooner than he should because he can't get enough air to oxygenate his blood and, therefore, his muscles (see illustration 4 E).

Neck

Necks should be moderately long and clean. A horse uses his neck to balance himself. It should come straight out of the body with a slight elevation from the withers. Medium length is best. A horse with a short neck has a tendency to move his shoulders too quickly. A horse with a long neck has a tendency to be a little too loose and it is difficult to keep his spine aligned or straight in the maneuvers.

Neck length should be in proportion to the size of the horse's body. Determining neck length takes the same practiced eye it takes to see a trapezoid on a horse's body. View the horse from the side. The neck should appear to fit the horse's body. It shouldn't be short, stubby and upright. Neither should it be extremely long and ponderous.

Guidelines for a particular horse's neck length are in his trapezoid measurements. The ideal neck would be the same length as the horse's shoulder, back and hip. The neck should measure from the poll to the withers the same as it does from the withers to the croup, from the croup to the point of the hip and from the withers to the point of the shoulder.

A slim, smooth neck should be attached to a good head by a clean throat latch. "Clean" means the neck is not thick or meaty looking. The trachea is located in the throatlatch area and is the horse's main air passage system. A horse should be able to bend or flex his poll and still not have trouble breathing.

Shoulders

The length of a horse's stride is determined by his shoulder angle. A sloping or well-angled shoulder permits a horse to reach a good distance over the ground. Straight shoulders do not allow a horse to have much reach in his stride. Also, straight-shouldered horses are extremely uncomfortable to ride because they strike the ground hard. Horses built that way aren't good movers. Without a long, flowing stride, a horse can't possibly present a pretty picture as he is moving (see illustration 4 F).

Withers

A good set of withers is important to a performance horse. A horse's center of gravity is located in the same area. Withers that are low, say lower than the croup, shift the horse's center of gravity too far forward. The horse feels as if he is moving down hill. He can't pick up his front end as well. Also, good withers help keep the saddle in place. They prevent it from slipping forward or to the side.

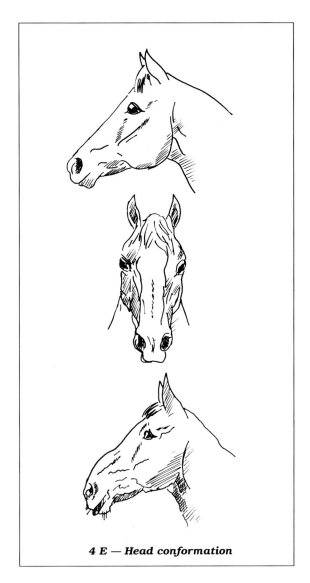

4 E — Head conformation

(4 E) **The top two illustrations are front and side views of good head conformation showing clean-cut features; large nostrils; broad forehead and wide-set eyes. The bottom illustration shows a poor quality head with small nostrils; small, close-set eyes and coarse nasal bone.**

A horse with long, sloping shoulders and high withers usually has a large heartgirth. The bigger the heartgirth, the larger the lung capacity. The more air a horse can take in, the more endurance he has and the sounder he stays.

Back and Loins

Truly athletic horses have strong backs and loins and know how to use them when they perform. Watch a horse that can stop deep and hard. He doesn't lock his hocks and skid. He drops his loins underneath himself. It is effortless for a horse with a short back, strong loin, long hip and short cannon bone to stop.

He can do it over and over again, without laboring, without getting hurt. If a horse is a little long in the back, weak in the loin, long in the cannon, stopping is hard work. Then it is going to hurt. He'll get sore and it will be hard to keep him sound. If something doesn't hurt, horses don't mind doing it.

Train your eyes to look for that correct trapezoid on a horse's body. It takes time to teach yourself. However, there is only one way to do it and that is look at lots of horses. Those with long backs, steep shoulders and short croups do not fit nicely into a correct trapezoidal figure. A horse's body that doesn't conform to a balanced trapezoid has problems with basic structure. You won't be able to compensate for that in training. Instead, you'll have to find ways to live with the structural defects. You'll probably have to resort to

This horse has a good shoulder, deep heartgirth, good withers and short back.

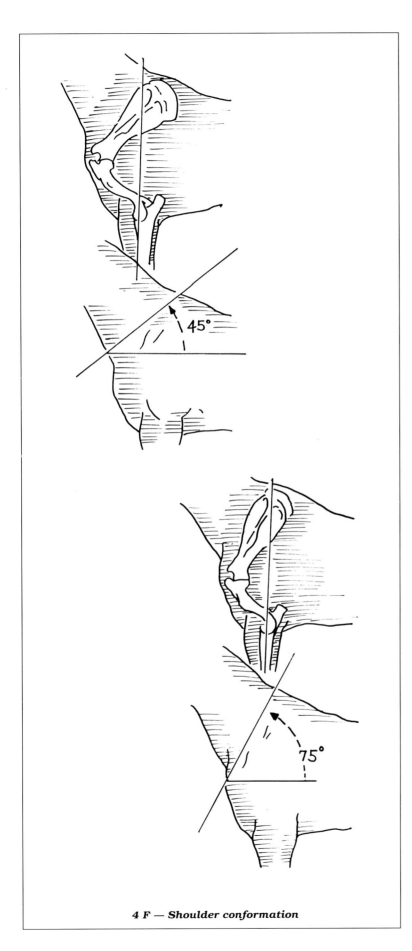

4 F — Shoulder conformation

(4 F) *These illustrations show the relationship between shoulder angles and a horse's ability to move. Long, sloping shoulders allow a horse to stride farther than do short, steep angled shoulders.*

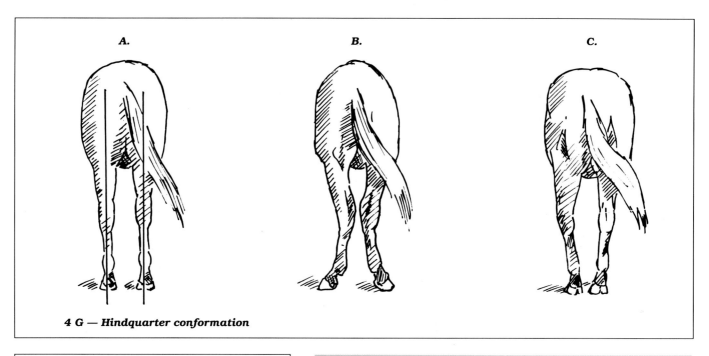

A.   **B.**   **C.**

4 G — Hindquarter conformation

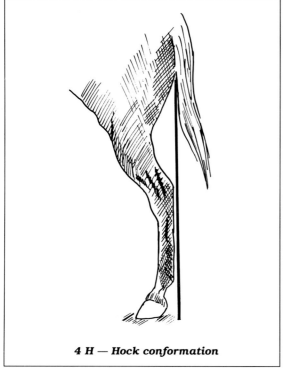

4 H — Hock conformation

(4 G top) **Hip and hindquarter alignment. Figure a. shows correct hip and hind leg conformation. Figure b. shows toe-out conformation of the hind legs, often called a cow-hocked condition. Figure c. shows toe-in conformation, where the hocks bow outward.**

(4 H above) **Hocks should be set low to the ground and in a straight line down from the hip.**

(right) **This horse has a long hip and well-set hocks.**

training gimmicks that force the horse to perform beyond his abilities. The horse will forget his training the moment you take off the gimmicks.

Hips

Hips should be long·and powerful with hocks set low to the ground in a straight line down from the hip. Power in a horse comes from his hindquarters. A reining horse has to gallop hard, stop deep and turn fast. He can't do it if his hip is inadequate (see illustrations 4 G and 4 H).

Legs

A well-structured body is useless without a good set of legs and feet to support it. Forearms should be long for plenty of length and sweep in the stride. They usually go together with long, sloping shoulders and moderately long, sloping pasterns. Pasterns should be the same angle as the shoulders. Both are the horse's shock absorption mechanism. Since a horse carries much of his weight on his forehand, it takes most of the concussion. Straight shoulders and pasterns are not able to absorb concussion. In time, the horse goes lame from the weight pounding hard on his navicular bone and other delicate structures inside his hoofs. Ring bone and side bone can also result (see illustration 4 K).

Cannon bones should be in proportion to the horse's size and short compared to the forearm. Short cannon bones are strong and increase a horse's stability. Long cannon bones are weak and interfere with the stride produced by good shoulders and forearms. A horse with long cannons is gangly and uncoordinated.

A horse's leg columns must be straight in order to stay sound. An imaginary line drawn from the forearm down through the hoof wall should dissect the leg in two. Any other configuration means there is a conformational defect somewhere. If a horse is crooked from the knee or pastern down,

(4 I) *A horse's leg column should be straight. Draw an imaginary line from the forearm down through the pastern. It should dissect the leg in two.*

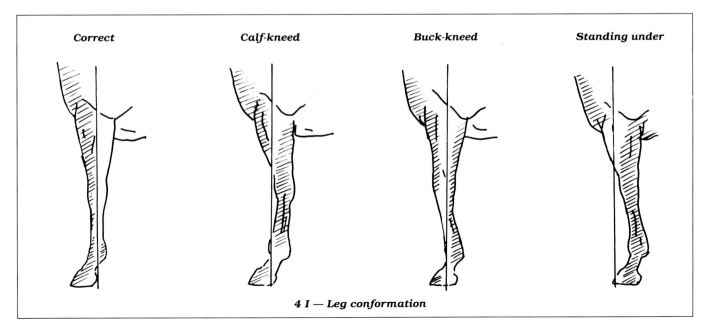

| Correct | Calf-kneed | Buck-kneed | Standing under |

4 I — Leg conformation

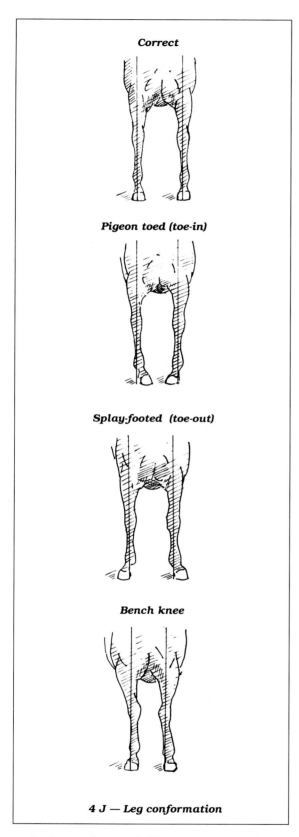

Correct

Pigeon toed (toe-in)

Splay-footed (toe-out)

Bench knee

4 J — Leg conformation

(4 J) *In correct front end alignment, you can draw a straight line down through the horse's forearm, knee, cannon, pastern and foot. Any other formation places too much stress on the leg column and eventually leads to soundness problems.*

it puts undue pressure on bones and joints. They won't hold up under stress (see illustration 4 I).

I forgive a horse for toeing out a little, but not much. When a horse toes out, his front legs point outward from his body instead of straight ahead. A horse can toe out and still have a straight column if the fault starts at the top of the forearm and goes down. In other words, if the problem with his leg column begins in the shoulder, his leg may still be straight from his shoulder down.

I won't forgive horses that are back at the knees, often called calf-kneed. When viewed from the side, horses that are back at the knee literally look that way. Instead of a straight line to the ground, the leg looks bent backwards at the knee. That places incredible stress on the leg joints and tendons. Offset knees (bench knees) are another serious fault I won't overlook. When viewed from the front, offset knees look tilted on the horse's leg or the surface of the knee is off to one side of the leg column.

Horses that toe in with their front feet are also inexcusable. With a toe in or pigeon toe condition, a horse's front legs point more toward each other than they do straight ahead. Fetlocks take a beating with the strain placed on them. Horses with any of the above leg column faults do not hold up even under mild work (see illustration 4 J).

Feet

Good, hard, well-shaped feet are essential to any performance horse. It's similar to putting only the best tires on a race car. It just can't perform without them. Good feet are large enough to support the weight of the horse. Breeders, especially of Quarter Horses, have had a tendency to breed small feet into our horse population. That's unfortunate from a soundness point of view. What once was a fad is now a crippler of many horses. Large feet are not ugly. They serve as excellent weight-bearing surfaces for a 1,000 pound animal.

In addition to sufficient size, good feet are oval-shaped and have tough horn (material that makes up the hoof wall), large heels, healthy frogs, hard soles and well-developed bars of the heels.

Heart

We often hear that a horse with a lot of guts has a big heart. While we can never actually see the size of the heart, there is physical evidence for the saying. A horse with a big heart pumps more blood. Blood and oxygen give a horse strength. Therefore, a horse with a large heart has more stamina.

There is also heart on another level, however. A horse with a big heart is worthless unless he gives it to you. That separates the great horses from the average ones. A horse's heart has a lot to do with his mental attitude. It has to do with how much they let you use them, how much of themselves they give. Lady Eldorado, one of my favorite horses and an NRHA Futurity winner, would do things in the arena that she wouldn't do at home. When we would walk into the

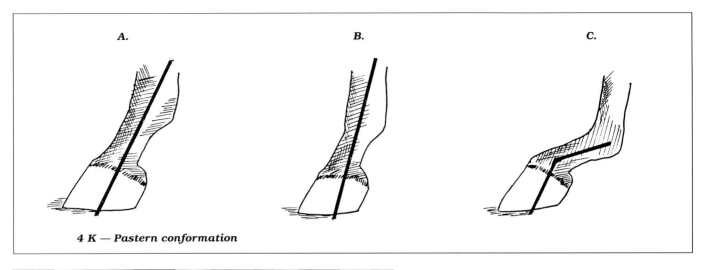

A.   B.   C.

4 K — Pastern conformation

(4 K above) **Correct pastern conformation is crucial for soundness. Figure a. is a pastern with a normal angle. Figure b. is a short, upright pastern and figure c. is an excessively long pastern.**

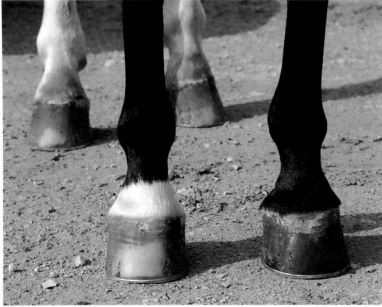

(left) **Good, hard, well-shaped (oval) feet are essential for a performance horse.**

arena, I could feel her heart pumping against my calf. That is usually a sign that a horse is nervous and may cheat you. But with her, it was a sign that she was going to try harder. She would get excited when she got into the pen, but nobody could tell it but me. She would guide better, turn faster and stop harder. That's heart and it comes from a good mind.

The magical combination in a good reining horse is one that is light and responsive when you handle it, yet extremely quiet with a calm, cool-headed personality.

Even some quiet horses, however, are extremely sensitive. Sensitivity shows an alert, intelligent mind. When a sensitive horse doesn't understand something, he jumps out of fear. With training, the rider can turn that sensitivity into the controlled, confident maneuvers of an outstanding performance horse.

In selecting a reining horse prospect, you must concern yourself with the horse's mind and body. One isn't any good without the other. Start out with good, raw material, a quiet mind, willing attitude and capable body, and you'll end up with a highly polished, finished product - a winner.

5

A Foundation for Riding: Early Ground Work

The first two years of a horse's life are formative years, a time for building a solid foundation for the future. From the time a foal is first handled to the time he is first saddled, everything that is done to the colt has a direct bearing on how he views humans and his work as a riding animal. It is up to us, his handlers, to show him the correct way.

With the horses raised on our ranch, we have a head start on breaking them even before we saddle them for the first time. They've had two years of consistent handling by that time.

When foals are weaned, we put them in a 12 foot by 12 foot box stall for two to three weeks. They receive daily handling, which includes halter and hobble breaking. Hobbles, which are restraining devices, teach the colts to stand still. It usually doesn't take more than two to three days for them to understand the hobbling lessons. Teaching a horse to hobble is helpful. Throughout the horse's entire life he'll be better off for knowing it. If his legs become caught in a fence, he won't panic. When being doctored, he'll stand motionless. Also, hobbling prevents horses from pawing. It's a great disciplinary aid.

Every 60 days we bring in the weanlings for veterinary care and farrier work. Their feet are trimmed and they are inoculated and wormed. When they are 2-year-olds, breaking them to saddle is a much faster process than with horses that were left untouched.

Early handling is a plus in any training program. I begin by working with weaned colts in the round pen about 20 minutes each day for two to three weeks. In a round pen, there isn't any place for them to go except in a circle since there aren't any corners. A colt can't develop bad habits,

(previous page) *After two years of life in a lush, green pasture, this colt will be ready to begin his life as a riding animal.*

(above) *Round pen lessons, introduced when the foals are weanlings, are repeated when horses are two years old. They learn the meaning of "whoa" with the use of body language and a lead rope.*

(below) *Learning to stand hobbled is one of the first lessons weanlings are taught.*

such as hiding with his head in the corner and his hindquarters towards me. In a small pen, say 60 feet, I get his attention easily.

One of the first lessons a colt learns is the meaning of the word "whoa." It is the only voice command I use. I use the word "whoa" every time I want the colt to stop and stand still. In the round pen, it is easy to get the meaning across. Whenever I want the colt to stop, I step in front of him, not necessarily directly in his path, but at an angle to his head. I say "whoa." Most colts will startle, stop and look at you. Since a horse learns from repetition, every time you step in front of him and say "whoa," he makes the connection that you want him to stop. Do this consistently and stopping becomes fixed in the colt's mind as the only response to the stimulus "whoa."

It's important to create a bond between you and the colt. Gain his confidence by teaching him to come to you. A horse that is not looking at you won't come to you. The confines of the round pen help the colt concentrate on you. Tap him on the rump with a rope to get his attention. The rope is simply an aid, an extension of your arm. When he turns around to look at you, go up to him and pet him, rub him. After a while, he will want to come to you first. When he takes that first step towards you, it is a sign that he is willing to work with you and is not afraid. Encourage him with more petting, rubbing and soft words.

A horse really responds to being touched. Putting a hand on a horse slowly and touching him gives him confidence that nothing is going to hurt him. When you are rubbing the colt, stand close to his shoulder. The reason for this is simple. Watch horses in a herd situation. There is a definite herd hierarchy and psychology. Horses that are friends with one another stand shoulder to shoulder, swishing flies with their tails. Each horse's tail acts as a fly swatter for the other horse's head and neck. Also, horses stand shoulder to shoulder to scratch each other's withers with their teeth. It is a gesture between friends that feels good, similar to human friends scratching each other's backs. It is a form of acceptance that horses understand. If we, as humans, perform actions that horses already understand, it is easier for them to accept us. We communicate on their level. Opening the lines of communication with horses while we are standing on the ground paves the way for them to accept us later in the saddle. They are more willing to do our bidding when we talk their language.

When the colt stops to look at you in the round pen, you have his attention. If he looks away, tap him on the rump and get his attention again. Put your hand out and encourage him to come to you. Make everything peaceful and pleasant when he does. Usually, a colt will walk forward gingerly, extend his neck and sniff your hand with his nose. Horses use their sense of smell to identify things. Watch strange horses when they meet. They greet each other by smelling their noses first. They use the same identification process for humans.

When you tap the horse, make sure he doesn't interpret it as a hit. Tapping abruptly or too hard scares a horse. A horse never gains confidence in you if you scare him. If your voice is loud and your actions quick, the horse takes it as aggression.

Don't let the colt look away from you or his attention wander. You want the colt watching you and coming to you for security. You want him to look to you when he is scared and doesn't know what to do. Again, your work with him on the ground will translate to a better working relationship in the saddle.

This is a touchy area. Think before you act. You can get too rough and destroy what you are trying to accomplish. People that are loud and move quickly frighten horses. In contrast, people that are quiet and slow, that give a horse confidence by their speech, movement and overall demeanor, draw horses to them.

Turn the youngster loose and work it at a walk, trot and lope. You want him to be familiar with the routine and being asked to do things. I don't use a longe line, but there is a halter on the horse's head.

The commands I use to control the colt's movements are a kissing, or smooching, noise to make him move forward, "whoa" to make him stop and body cues.

Whenever I make the kissing noise, it means speed up. If the horse is walking, it means trot. If the horse is trotting, it means lope. If the horse is already loping, it means gallop.

By stepping in front of the colt and using outstretched arm movements, Bob turns the colt in the opposite direction.

In this sequence of photos, Bob encourages a young horse to come to him. The wary movements of the palomino show that he is uncertain, but curious, about his handler. When the colt stretches out his neck and sniffs Bob's hands, it is a form of identification and a sign of acceptance.

The kissing noise or signal to speed up returns later on in training when I ask for more speed in advanced maneuvers. The horse is familiar with the noise and already knows it means to go faster.

Using body cues is a form of space manipulation. Some people call it free longeing, which means the horse is longed or worked without a longe line, responding only to the handler's body language. Horses, like other animals, consider the area around their bodies to be their personal space. They don't want you to invade it and they respect your own space.

When you want to teach the colt to speed up, besides using the kissing noise, move in closer to his hindquarters. When you close in on what the colt believes to be his personal space, he leaves the area he thinks you are going. In effect, you have squeezed his personal space and he bursts forward with a quicker pace.

To stop or turn the colt in the other direction, step in

towards his head and close off his personal space. He should respond by stopping and electing to go the other way rather than hitting you or invading your personal space.

Arm movements are beneficial during this type of exercise as well. Extend your arms outward from your body when you step in front of the colt or behind his hips. You increase your personal space that way and form a wall the horse doesn't want to run into.

When the colt is sufficiently halter broke and I can maneuver him around the round pen at will, I send him out to pasture with his buddies. There he stays until his 2-year-old year.

However, during those two years, the colt is handled every 60 days as I mentioned earlier. Throughout the two year period, we bring all horses out of the pasture for worming, vaccinations and farrier work. Because we handle them so often, the young horses never forget their early lessons.

"THE MOST IMPORTANT STEP A HORSE TAKES IS THE ONE HE MAKES WHEN YOU ARE ON HIS BACK FOR THE FIRST TIME."

6

The 2-Year-Old: Preparation and Breaking

High school for 2-year-old reining prospects begins January 1. We bring the young horses out of the pasture 10 at a time depending upon their birth dates and size. We start the older, larger colts first and wait to start the younger, smaller ones until later in the year. The maturity level of each young horse is important to the timing of the breaking process. Starting one too soon can do more harm than good. He may not be ready for it physically or mentally.

The youngsters are ridden a minimum of 90 days and then turned out until they are three years old. Some colts are ridden more, even up to six months. It depends on what I think each colt needs for a foundation. Some are flighty and need more work. Some are slower mentally and need time to comprehend the training program. Others are just more resistant to the program.

I keep the horses that are having problems longer. This does not mean, however, that those horses will always be problem horses. I have ridden some outstanding horses that took more than the usual length of time to break. Initial breaking time is no guarantee that the horse will turn out well. However, I will say that an average 90 day breaking period is a good sign that the horse is bright and willing to cooperate.

The typical training session for a green 2-year-old is explained in this chapter and the next. This chapter concentrates on the first two weeks, which include the first saddling and riding in the round pen and arena. Sessions on the slide track or pasture are detailed in Chapter 7, "The 2-Year-Old: Basic Training."

Each session lasts approximately 30 minutes, but what happens during that time varies somewhat during the 90

(previous pages) *By cheeking the colt before he steps on, Bob has control of the situation. This 2-year-old futurity prospect is Eldorado Cody.*

day initial training period.

The first two weeks, I start out in the round pen and arena and work the horse by free longeing him until he is rid of his excess energy. When I feel he is ready, I work with him on the ground getting him to pay attention to me and softening his nose from right to left. I soften him by attaching a lead rope to his halter and asking him to give in the direction I want. All of this takes about 15 minutes of that 30-minute session.

When the colt is in a relaxed frame of mind, I get on him. I walk and trot him around, softening his nose from left to right again. When I think he is paying attention to me and guiding reasonably well, we go to the slide track or pasture for further lessons.

At this point, I don't need to longe the horse. I ride him for the entire 30 minute training session out on the slide track. We work at a walk and trot again. We've probably started loping by this time and the colt should be quiet and comfortable with it.

About 30 days into the program, I usually start backing up the horse a little. I also work on trotting and loping in circles as well as straight lines.

Explanation of my in-depth program for 2-year-olds follows.

PREPARATION

A lot of preparation goes into the 2-year-olds before serious training begins. During the first 30 days, the young horses have their teeth checked, they are shod and the fillies are sutured.

Dental Work

Dental work is an often neglected area in horse care. All of my 2-year-olds have their teeth floated if necessary to file down any sharp points. Their wolf teeth are also pulled. Wolf teeth are small teeth that develop in front of the horse's molars. They have no function and sometimes bump the bit causing the horse to become sore and, consequently, apprehensive of what is in his mouth. The horse learns bad mouth habits which prevent him from accepting the bit quietly. If one of your main lines of communication with the horse, its mouth, hurts, training won't be effective.

Farriery Work

I don't shoe 2-year-olds during the initial breaking period unless I think they need it. Because I live on sandy soil, my 2-year-olds seldom need shoes. The only time one needs shoes is if his feet break up or crack. However, for horses that live on hard, rocky ground, shoes might be necessary. If I do have to put shoes on a 2-year-old, they usually go on the front feet only. Since a horse carries most of his weight on his forehand, his front feet tend to chip more than the hind feet.

Medical Work

Our veterinarian performs caslicks operations on all the

fillies. That is, their vulvas are sutured shut. This prevents the mares from sucking air or getting vaginal infections. If a mare gets infected, you may not be aware of it. The pain causes her to be irritable and you won't know why. A lot of people blame mares' crankiness on being in heat. Personally, I have never had a mare in heat cost me a dime. I've had mares that were in standing heat and when I got on their backs, I couldn't tell. Their attitudes towards performance were not hampered. Suturing is not only an advantage when you ride, it is a big benefit in the breeding shed. The mares are free of infection and ready to breed.

BREAKING

In the Round Pen

After this thorough preparation, the young horse is ready for his first saddle.

A crucial day in the life of any horse is the first day he is saddled and ridden. That experience leaves a lasting impression throughout his riding career. If you scare or hurt him, he'll remember it and think of riding as something to worry about. If you keep him relaxed and quiet, he'll be obedient, confident and responsive to your commands.

Bring the 2-year-old into the round pen to reintroduce him to the exercises he learned as a weanling. Let him run around and get rid of any nervous energy first. You don't want to take a colt that is fresh and full of play out of a stall and expect him to pay attention to you. You might create a problem. Work him at a walk, trot and lope using the same commands (kissing sounds, body cues and "whoa") you used in previous lessons (See Chapter 5 "A Foundation for Riding: Early Ground Work"). When he moves relaxed around the pen working gaits at your command, stops, turns in both directions and comes to you, he is ready for more advanced work.

Reintroduce the 2-year-old to the round pen lessons he learned as a weanling. Here, Bob encourages a young colt to come to him, an important aspect of gaining a horse's confidence.

The process of sacking out helps a colt get over his fears. Rub a blanket all over the horse's body.

Before you saddle a 2-year-old, sack him out with a blanket. Rub it all over him so he learns not to be frightened of it. Then put the saddle on and off several times until he gets used to it. Cinch up the saddle lightly at first, but tight enough to keep it from slipping.

Turn the horse loose in the round pen and let him run around getting acquainted with the strange feel of something on his back. For the first two or three days, you can expect the youngster to buck immediately after you turn him loose with the saddle on. Obviously, as long as the horse is crow hopping, you don't want to get on him. Wait until the colt is comfortable carrying the saddle before you attempt to mount.

I usually get on a 2-year-old the first day. I use a halter and lead rope as head gear during the first week of riding. One end of the lead rope is already attached to the halter. Tie the loose end to the same ring under the halter. This forms a set of reins. From day one, I want a horse to learn to give its nose to my hands when I use the reins I have made out of the lead rope.

The most important step a horse takes is the one he takes when you are on his back for the first time. Make that first step quiet, uneventful and easy for the colt and the rest that follows won't be hard either.

Cheek him by taking hold of the halter cheek piece and

turning his head to the side you are getting on the saddle, usually the left. If you have the horse's head the first step, you are in control of the situation and rarely have a problem. If you give a horse his head the first time and let him walk away, you are giving him a fair chance to buck or run off.

While you are cheeking the horse, step on and off the left stirrup a few times letting the horse become used to the feel of the added weight. After he is relaxed and comfortable with you stepping on and off, throw your right leg over the saddle and sit on him for a while. Don't do anything. Get on and off several more times.

When being mounted doesn't bother the horse, he is ready for his first step. I graduate from cheeking to pulling the horse's head around with a lead rope. This is his introduction to giving me his nose. I follow that by holding his nose with the left rein which has been made out of the lead rope. The colt's first step is naturally to the left as he follows the direction his nose is being pulled. I merely hold the rein taut so that the only escape for the colt is to follow the pressure placed on his nose. This is not a difficult concept for horses to understand, which is precisely why it is the first maneuver they are taught.

We move off in a left circle when I squeeze my legs on the colt's ribs. At the same time I take the slack out of the left rein, I give the horse slack in the right rein. Otherwise, his head would be in a bind when I ask him to turn to the left. Continue to tilt the horse's head towards the left and you. There is a reason for starting off on the left. Most riders are comfortable with left side mounts. Since that is the side you cheeked the horse and pulled the rope towards you, it makes sense the horse will take his first step to the left. You don't want to change directions with the first step the horse takes with a rider. If you do, you are only adding more elements to confuse the young horse.

There should be no slack in the rope. You want direct contact between your hand and the horse's nose. As you gently squeeze with both legs asking him to move, he may jump. Because you have his nose tilted, he'll move in a tight, left circle and you'll have control of the situation. It's hard for a horse to buck or run off when he can't use his head. A horse that can get his head down has a good opportunity to buck.

If your horse is frozen and won't move, this is not the time to use the kissing sound to make him go. Kissing means speed up. The horse knows that from his previous lessons; but it is too strong a cue to use at this time. You might get bucked off.

Instead, quietly nudge him forward with your legs. It may take five minutes for him to understand that moving is what you want him to do. When he does, release the pressure on his sides immediately. Be gentle and soft here. A rough kick or spur could ruin the horse for the future. Don't make any quick movements either. That may startle the colt and cause him to come unglued. Handled correctly, most well-bred horses don't buck. There is no excuse for bucking out a young horse anymore. That type of training is outdated. There is no room for muscle tactics when what you

(below) *Put the saddle on and off the horse several times until the horse gets used to it.*

(bottom) *Adjust the saddle so it is comfortable on the horse and fits on his withers.*

Cinch the saddle lightly at first, but tight enough to keep it from slipping.

are trying to achieve is a finely tuned reining machine.

Walk the horse around in a circle until he feels relaxed. When he is comfortable, lightly tug on the right rein asking for his nose to go to the right. I squeeze my legs again and we move in a right circle. I repeat this exercise around the round pen making small circles to the right and left.

When the colt begins to understand what I want, he gets lighter in the head and neck area. By that I mean, he softly and easily gives to the pressure on his halter nose strap. I don't yank the colt around. That would make him scared; he'd get stiff in his head and neck. Soft, gentle tugs on the rein achieve the response I want, a horse that quietly follows where his nose goes. As his nose softens and follows my hand, his neck naturally bends to go with it. I would never fight the colt. That would only make his neck rigid and we wouldn't go anywhere. Straighten him out and continue walking, pulling his head around in either direction. Teach the horse to guide by following his nose.

Stop the horse by taking the slack out of the reins (or rope) and saying "whoa." Don't pull back hard. That encourages the horse to pull back as well. Maintain a gentle, firm hold of the reins. If the horse gets confused as to what you mean when you ask him to stop, guide him or point his nose into the fence or wall of the round pen. He has to stop. Say "whoa" as soon as you feel the horse must stop or he'll hit his head. Make the association between "whoa" and stop that way. Because you used "whoa" in earlier lessons, asking the colt to stop and stand still, he should make the transference without much difficulty.

If on the first day a colt breaks into a trot, I let him. Also, if he breaks into a lope, I don't mind. This is not the time to fight a horse to slow down. However, walking and trotting are two relaxing gaits at which a horse can learn a lot. You accomplish more at any stage of training if you don't crowd a horse. Let him do things quietly and relaxed.

If a horse stays at a walk for that first ride, I do nothing else. During that first saddling, I may do nothing more than walk for 20 minutes. Then I step off and put him away.

The next day, if the horse wants to walk, we'll just walk. I guide him all over the round pen and make certain he is relaxed.

By the second, third or fourth day, I may trot. If the horse doesn't break into it on his own, I quietly urge him forward with my legs.

By the end of the first week, I can usually lope the horse. Again, I encourage the faster gait by squeezing him into it with my legs. The kissing noise shows up only after the colt is totally confident with a rider on his back, several weeks down the road.

Cues for lead departures are introduced when I begin loping the colt. I don't expect a 2-year-old to pick up his leads immediately. He may trot 10 steps before he breaks into a lope. I don't rush him in the beginning. This would only frustrate the colt by forcing him to grasp a concept he is not fully ready to comprehend.

I teach lead departures as I do anything else, with repetitive commands. The more consistent I am, the easier

Turn the young horse loose in the pen and let him get used to the feel of something on his back.

(right) *Bend the colt to the left by taking the slack out of the left rein and releasing any pressure on the right rein. The colt tips his nose to the left. Squeeze with your legs to encourage forward movement.*

(below) *While cheeking the horse, step on and off several times to accustom the horse to added weight in the saddle.*

it is for the youngster to understand what I am asking. Also, I help the colt by putting his body in the correct position so that it is effortless for him to pick up the lead I want.

While urging the horse forward, I tip his nose to the inside of the direction I want to go and lay my inside leg on his rib cage to lift or move it over. This frees him up to move his hip in the direction I want. When the colt has done that, I then lay my outside leg against his flank to move his hip over. That produces a hind leg first lead departure. We may take a few trotting steps before he lopes, but when we do his body is in the correct position to take the lead I asked for.

For example, if I want a right lead, I tip the colt's nose slightly to the right and I lift or move his rib over to the left by pushing with my inside or right leg on his rib cage. I then put my left leg against his flank and push his hip to the right.

The same thing for a left lead departure. I tip the horse's nose to the left, move the rib over to the right and lay my right leg against him to push his hip over. When I urge him forward with the right leg, if the nose is tipped and the rib is over, there is no way he can do anything but take a left lead.

Never make a horse lope until he is ready. At a lope, a horse can run off with you much easier than he can at a walk and a trot.

A horse is ready for the next faster gait only after he is quiet and relaxed at the one preceding it. In other words,

(left) ***To move to the right, take the slack out of the right rein and squeeze with both legs.***

(below) ***When the colt begins to understand what you want, he gets lighter in the head and neck area. This colt gives his nose easily to any pressure on the rein, in this case, lead rope.***

don't trot the horse until he is relaxed and guides well at a walk. Don't lope the horse unless he is relaxed and guides well at the trot.

Some colts take longer to relax at speed. With some that need more time, I don't care if I don't lope for the first two or three weeks of training. The main thing is not to let a horse get in trouble in the first place.

Out To The Arena and Slide Track

I find that using my system the average colt guides, walks, trots and lopes quietly after the first week. From there, we leave the small space of the round pen and go to the arena where we repeat the same procedure, only in a much larger space. I don't want the colt to think that he needs to be confined to be controlled. I want him to know from the beginning that I am the one controlling him, not a fence or wall. We spend a week in the arena repeating the same things we did in the round pen. From then on, we go to the slide track or pasture. My slide track is as big as a football field. There is no feeling of confinement riding on it.

The only thing I want to teach a horse at this level is that riding is a pleasant experience and the rider on his back is not his enemy. I definitely do not introduce hard stops or turns to 2-year-olds. Those maneuvers wait until the colt's 3-ycar-old year.

"THE FASTEST WAY TO ACCOMPLISH THE MOST IS TO GO SLOWLY."

7

The 2-Year-Old: Basic Training

Basic training usually takes three months. As I said earlier, some horses take longer because of their particular circumstances.

The fastest way to accomplish the most is to go slowly. At the end of 30 days, the colt that has been taken the slowest will be the farthest along.

For example, take two colts and start them the same day. With one colt, you insist on making him walk, trot, lope and back up on the first day. For several days after that, you keep applying the pressure. With the other, you do what he is comfortable with, just guiding him around, walking, trotting. You don't rush him. If you stop him by taking the slack out of the reins and he takes a step or two backwards, you quit. You keep the colt relaxed, quiet and calm. At the end of 30 days, that colt will be doing twice as much as the colt that has been pressured. The colt that has been forced may be doing some fancy things, but he is going to be scared. The things he is doing are not going to be dependable. Somewhere down the line, the pressure cooker is going to blow.

At the end of those first 30 days, you'll wonder how the relaxed colt came to learn so much. You really didn't think you taught him that much. It happened because you didn't scare him.

EQUIPMENT

Once a colt guides well, in other words, stopping and turning on command, he is definitely ready for a hackamore or bit. I never use a hackamore or a bit on a horse that isn't giving its nose easily in both directions with the use of a halter and lead rope. Neither do I put a bit or hackamore on one that isn't stopping from verbal commands and soft

(previous pages) **By the time they are through with their lessons as 2-year-olds, young horses should be dependable riding animals that can go cross country comfortably. Eldorado Cody is a pleasure to ride.**

(above) **Hackamores are good transitional headgear between halters and snaffles. However, they should be used by horsemen familiar with hackamore reinsmanship.**

contact when the slack is taken out of the rope. I use a mild O-ring snaffle, one with a medium diameter, jointed mouthpiece. Overly large or thin, wire mouthpieces are not appropriate for a young horse to handle in the initial stages of bitting (see Chapter 15 "Equipment and Bits"). O-ring or D-ring snaffles are true snaffles. They have no shanks, which work on the leverage principle. Shank bits, even those with jointed mouthpieces, exert pressure on the horse's jaw. That is too much bit for a 2-year-old to handle.

Although there is no harm in going right to a snaffle, a hackamore can be used as a transition between the halter and the snaffle.

I like hackamores and do use them, but recommend them only to riders who are knowledgeable in the intricacies of hackamore reinsmanship. Explaining the proper use of the hackamore is beyond the scope of this book. However, if you are interested in learning more about riding in a hackamore, I suggest you read "Hackamore Reinsman," by Ed Connell. The book was first published in 1952 and remains the bible of hackamore training. The address to order the book is listed in the Appendix.

The hackamore uses nose and jaw pressure to communicate with the horse, whereas the snaffle bit uses mouth and lip pressure. To accomplish his goals, the average horseman can be lighter with his hands using a snaffle. The contact with the young horse's soft mouth is more direct. Therefore, the rider needs only a light tug to signal to the horse. Hackamores require more firm pressure with the hands.

Whether or not you use a hackamore as a transition piece depends on your level of expertise with hackamores. If you know how to use one properly, use it. If not, go directly to a snaffle bit.

A SOLID FOUNDATION

The foundation I want to build during the months of the breaking process is a series of simple maneuvers that are the basis of all good riding. I want a 2-year-old to walk, trot, lope and back up on a loose rein. He should guide well by giving his head softly in both directions. I want him to be able to lope a pretty circle. By that I mean a round circle with his body between the bridle reins, not pulling in or out of the circle. I want him to lope a straightaway without veering left or right. He should lope across the pasture on a loose rein, with no signs of running off. Also, I do not teach a 2-year-old to do any hard, fast stops or turn arounds.

NECK REINING

Guiding by neck reining is taught to horses through a series of transitional stages during the colt's 2-year-old and 3-year-old year. I use a combination of direct rein (two hands) and indirect rein (one hand). By the time I put the finishing touches on a 3-year-old's training program, I can guide him by neck reining with one hand alone.

A direct rein puts direct pressure between the horse's mouth and one of the rider's hands. It is often referred to as "plow" reining. With the use of a hand on each rein, I gently pull the horse in the direction I want to go when I take the slack out of one rein and give slack with the other. For example, to turn to the right, I take the slack out of the right rein with my right hand and release any pressure on the left rein with my left hand. That gentle pull tilts the horse's nose to the right and we turn in that direction.

Indirect rein means the horse is guided by the pressure on his neck instead of his mouth. For example, in that turn to the right, while I directly pulled on the horse's mouth with my right hand, I would lay the left rein across his neck at the same time. Eventually as training progresses during a horse's 3-year-old year, I use more neck pressure than mouth pressure. Through repetition, the horse learns to

A direct rein puts direct pressure between the horse's mouth and the rider's hands.

respond more to the indirect rein pressure on his neck and less to the direct pressure on his mouth.

In the early stages of training a 2-year-old, his first experiences with two-handed direct, rein pressure are during the first saddlings in the round pen when I use a halter and lead rope as head gear. Shortly thereafter, I switch to a hackamore or 0-ring snaffle which require two hands as well because they both work on direct rein pressure. You can accomplish little if you don't use two hands with a snaffle or hackamore. I ride the colt in a snaffle or hackamore for the rest of the 2-year-old basic training program and for the first couple of months during his review as a 3-year-old.

Around March of a colt's 3-year-old year, I start using a seven inch shank snaffle (shank bit with a jointed mouthpiece) with a loose chin strap. By this time he is solid with his basics, having been ridden approximately six months. Throughout that time, I have used indirect rein pressure

All exercises are done at a walk and trot before they are attempted at a lope. Here, Bob extends the trot of 2-year-old to warm up muscles prior to a work out.

along with direct rein pressure.

Now, as I slip into the beginning stages of more complicated maneuver work, I use the shank snaffle and two hands. When I feel the colt is comfortable with that arrangement, I use one hand from time to time. Whenever we have a problem, I immediately go back to using two hands until the problem is fixed. I don't require the colt to comprehend one-handed neck reining at this point. It is too early to force him to do that.

Gradually, I use a little more one-handed reining and a little less two-handed reining. By fall, I use a grazing bit with a seven inch shank and I correctly adjust the curb chain (see Chapter 15 "Equipment and Bits"). With the added pressure of the adjusted curb chain, the horse becomes sharper on the neck reining naturally. I haven't scared him with the idea all at once. Throughout a nine month period, he has come to know and feel the difference between rein pressure, 0-ring snaffle, shank snaffle, loose curb chain, grazing bit and correctly adjusted curb chain. He makes the transition to one-handed neck reining easily.

Once the colt learns to trot in a circle with his nose tipped to the inside, he handles it at a lope easily.

SUPPLING

I believe in getting a colt's body supple from the beginning. I use exercises to soften his body parts. Simple suppling exercises are appropriate for 2-year-olds and more advanced exercises are appropriate for 3-year-olds. The advanced exercises are described in Chapter 9 "Advanced Suppling Exercises and Correct Body Alignment."

Mainly, I want to make sure the 2-year-old's body moves straight and that is accomplished by learning to follow his nose. He should give his head nicely in either direction. Wherever I put his nose, his body should follow. When loping, I don't let him lean to the right or left with his body. I don't correct him harshly at this stage, just bump his rib cage with the calf of my leg until he aligns his body. You can tell whether or not a horse is moving straight by looking at your reins. The horse shouldn't be leaning on one or the other. If he is, he is moving crookedly.

At this level, I don't do any advanced suppling exercises, such as poll flexion and hip displacement. These maneuvers are reserved for the 3-year-old program.

Flexing polls and moving hips on a 2-year-old would be premature. Throw too much at a young horse and he'll become apprehensive. It would be intimidating for a youngster who is just learning the basics of guiding and how to handle a rider's weight.

The only body parts I supple on a 2-year-old, green colt are nose, neck and rib. I want those parts to give softly to my hands and legs.

NOSE AND NECK EXERCISES

When the colt graduates to a hackamore or 0-ring snaffle bit, he makes the transition easily. The halter, hackamore or snaffle bit all operate on direct rein contact. The colt understands that when I tug lightly on the left rein, he should move to the left and when I tug lightly on the right

By the time the colt has finished the 2-year-old training program, he should be able to perform perfectly round circles.

rein, he should move to the right (see "Breaking" section in Chapter 6, "The 2-Year-Old: Preparation and Breaking").

Suppling the colt's nose and neck using a hackamore or snaffle bit is similar to the exercises we did in the halter and lead rope. All we have done is change the equipment.

Asking a horse for his head is one of the first things I do when I warm up a horse before working it. If he gives it to me without any resistance in both directions, I know my guidance system is probably in fairly good order.

RIB EXERCISES

As I walk, and later trot, circles with the young colt, I work on rib exercises. Until I can manipulate the horse's ribs, I won't have control of his body. Walking small circles tells me what the horse's ribs are doing. Horses can move their ribs around just like people can. The best way to know if a horse's ribs are up or down, in or out is to develop a feel for it.

The way to do that is tip the horse's nose to the left and walk a circle. Don't forget to give the horse slack in the right rein. Using your inside or left leg, press against his ribs where the stirrup hangs. When the horse relaxes, drops his head and walks in a circle with a little bow in the reins, then he has lifted his rib, in other words, moved it over, and softened his middle body. As we circle, I want the horse's body to be in a slight arc from his nose to his hip.

If, as you tip the horse's nose to the left and ask him to follow it, he freezes or backs up instead, he has jammed or pushed his rib to the left also and locked you out. You have to bump his left rib cage continually until he gets tired of you banging on his side and eventually softens it. When he does, the rib moves over. When the rib is out of the way, it's easy for the horse to turn and follow his nose to the left.

Often, a horse drifts out of a circle because he is over-bent. He is moving too far away from my inside leg pressure. For example, in a left circle, a horse may drift outward or pull to the right too far. He is over-bending around my left leg. I release some of the pressure on my left leg, take my right leg and push his right rib cage back or over to the middle of the circle.

CIRCLING

Teaching the elements of the circle to a 2-year-old is done first at the walk and the trot. Once a horse understands the basic suppling exercises, which are giving his nose and neck to the right and left easily and moving away from leg pressure against his ribs, he has the foundation for a circle. Only after the horse is solid circling at the walk and trot do I attempt it at a lope.

I want a 2-year-old to lope a circle with its neck straight out in front of him. I am not interested in him flexing his poll, just putting his head out in front of himself naturally and comfortably.

I don't want the horse really bent around my leg; but I do want his nose slightly tilted to the inside. I want the nose soft. By that I mean, if I take the nose and tip it to the inside,

THE 2-YEAR-OLD: BASIC TRAINING

I want the horse to give it to me easily. I don't want the horse to pull at all. A horse has to give its nose slightly to the inside to lope a circle correctly.

Cues for lead departures that were introduced when I first loped the colt are reinforced at this point. He begins to understand that when I tip his nose to the inside, move his inside rib over and lay my outside leg against his flank, he is to take the appropriate lead. Actually, I put his body in position to take the lead I want. As time goes by, he becomes sharper whenever I give him the cue for a lead (see Chapter 6, "The 2-Year-Old: Preparation and Breaking").

Circles are crucial to a 2-year-old's basic training program. I practice loping daily. By the time the horse has completed his 2-year-old program, he should be solid in his circles. He should walk, trot and lope circles on a loose rein. In fact, loping perfect circles is required of all my horses, whether they are two years old or 10.

BACKING UP

I introduce backing up to my 2-year-olds during the initial stages of breaking them to saddle. There is no set time, anywhere from the first day to the first two weeks into breaking. When to start backing up is more of a feeling. You feel when the time is right. In some instances, young colts back up easily the first day, but that is rare. Usually, successful attempts at backing up a horse don't come until a week to 10 days after the first saddling. Then the colt is used to someone on his back, guiding and giving his head easily from right to left. He has learned to give to the pressure on his nose. He knows the routine of being ridden and his mind is attentive to you. Backing up is much easier at that time.

When you teach a young horse to take that first step backwards, never pull on him or let him pull on you. If you do, his mouth may go numb, he may back a few steps, freeze up on you and quit. Nothing happens except his head comes up and his mouth opens.

Instead, don't put any pressure on the horse's mouth. Squeeze him up into the bridle and take the slack out of the reins. Capture the horse's face so he can't go forward. Gently bump a rein or lift up on it. If the colt takes a hold of your hands by grabbing the bit and pulling, don't jerk him, just hold your hands firmly. Then tap the horse lightly on the shoulder with the side of your foot until he stops pulling your hands. Pulling or jerking the face makes a young horse lock up even more. When you lift up on the rein and tap the horse's body, the only escape he has is reverse. If the horse still doesn't move, use your legs to bump his hips and ribs until they soften. As soon as they do, the horse is going to give and back up. He learns to escape the pressure by backing away from it.

If the young horse still doesn't get the idea to back up, walk him into a corner and repeat the above procedure. The added element of a wall in front of him may make him understand that what you want is not forward movement, but backward movement.

The moment the horse takes a step backwards, release

any pressure you have on him. Don't let the colt back up very far the first few times. Always have it be your idea to stop. If you back a colt until he quits on you, he'll quit a few steps earlier each time. Before you know it, he'll decide he doesn't want to back up at all. Instead, back him one or two steps and then stop him and walk him forward before you ask him to back again. Always make it your idea to quit backing. If you do, he'll back farther, faster and more willingly as he waits for you to tell him when to quit. After a week or so, he should back as far as you ask him to willingly.

When the horse takes a few steps backwards, stop and walk forward. This is important. Never back up, stop, then back up and stop again. It's like winding a watch. You can wind it until you break the stem. A horse balks if he is backed continually without any relief. When you back a horse, his muscles tighten up and cramp, especially when the horse is

The last week or two before Bob turns a 2-year-old out to pasture, he changes leads to see how the youngster handles them.

young and has not backed up much. By walking the horse forward, the muscles loosen and relax. Then you can back him. A horse always backs up better if you walk him forward before you ask him to back. Again, never ask a horse to back so far that he quits backing willingly. Always quit before the horse does.

Also, never ask a young horse to back faster than he wants to in the early stages of training. Let him back up at his own pace. It's much too soon to expect speed in a back up at this point.

FINISHING UP

The last week or two before I turn a 2-year-old out to pasture I change leads on him a couple of times each way to see how he handles the maneuvers. I ask for a lead change in a straight line, usually out in the field where no fences force us to stop or turn (see Chapter 10 "Circles and Lead Changes").

The method I use is simple and not one necessarily meant to teach the horse to change leads. I merely want to see how the horse handles a change in weight distribution. That tells me if he is a natural lead changer or not.

At the lope, I step in the outside stirrup and turn the horse's nose in the opposite direction. For example, if the horse is loping in the right lead, I step in the right stirrup, actually stand and put my weight in it, and gently tip the horse's nose to the left. Then I wait for the horse to change leads on his own. I don't use leg cues at this time. I change the horse's balance point and send him in another direction to see how he handles it. Does he change leads to compensate for the change in balance and weight? Or does he stay in the same lead and maintain the unbalanced movement? Most horses change leads to keep themselves in balance. Otherwise, they feel as if they are going to fall down. A 2-year-old that is uncoordinated at this time and doesn't change leads well isn't necessarily doomed as a reining prospect. As horses grow and mature, they develop more motor skills. The casual lead changes simply give me a hint as to what I might expect out of that horse as a 3-year-old.

And finally, I like to take 2-year-olds on trail rides through the woods and have them cross creeks and step over logs. In short, they should show the qualities of a dependable riding animal.

As far as length of riding time goes, during the first month, I ride the 2-year-olds on the average of 30 minutes a day. That is about as much concentration and effort as a young horse can handle without tiring or becoming bored. Riding a young horse until he is tired or bored damages him mentally and physically.

When I am satisfied with the progress that a 2-year-old has achieved in the initial breaking phase, I put him out to pasture until his 3-year-old year. However, he isn't completely forgotten. He is still brought up to the barn every 60 days for veterinary care and farriery work. The ground work has been laid; the preparation complete. His career as a future reining horse is off to a good start.

"NEVER RUN A HORSE OUT OF AIR."

8

The 3-Year-Old: Conditioning and Guidelines for a Training Program

Training a reining horse to be a finished 3-year-old ready for competition is an art. It takes a good horseman to do it consistently. It demands a lot of thinking, planning and a good program. You need a capable equine athlete, with a great mind and the best legs possible. Then, you, as the rider, must have common sense.

PREPARATION

I begin serious work with the coming 3-year-olds immediately after I return from the NRHA Futurity, which is the first week in December. They are still 2-year-olds at this time; but they technically turn 3 on January 1, the universal birthday of all horses.

The first month should be devoted to veterinary care and farriery work and a good, solid conditioning program.

All horses are wormed and inoculated as they have been every 60 days since birth.

They are shod with regular keg shoes on the front feet and one inch slide plates on the rear (see Chapter 14 "Tips on Shoeing Reining Horses"). The only time I would use a different shoe than a one inch plate is if the horse is timid stopping or weak conformationally in the loins. I don't go to a bigger plate. Instead, I use a one inch trailer with a one and a quarter to a one and one half inch toe. More toe weight encourages a horse to stride deeper with the first step into the stop.

REVIEW AND CONDITIONING

Most of the coming 3-year-olds have had about six months to rest after their initial training. They are brought up out of the pasture and put through a refresher course to

(previous pages) *After a refresher course in the basics and a good conditioning program, this 3-year-old is fit and ready for a year of intense work.*

A review of the basics includes getting the colt to give his nose (right), *to move away from leg pressure* (below) *and to remember the meaning of "whoa"* (bottom).

remind them of their earlier lessons.

During that first 30 day period, there is absolutely no intense training done on the young reining prospects. They are worked much the same as they were during the initial breaking process. We start out in the round pen once more, but as soon the horses are relaxed, we go to the slide track. The basics are repeated. We work on guiding, getting them to give their noses softly to the right and left. Stopping and the meaning of "whoa" is reinforced. We perform some simple suppling exercises, such as bending and flexing body parts. I want them to remember how to keep their bodies straight between the bridle reins.

The first month is strictly a refresher course and a legging up process. A colt that has been out on pasture for months is soft. He is not up to any physical exertion. If you start riding him hard immediately and try to teach him things, you can damage him physically, mentally or both. The horse will be sore and stressed. You'll create problems that will never be corrected throughout the training program. You'll cause a good horse to go bad or to be only half as good as he could have been.

Interval Training

I use a form of interval training for conditioning. I don't get involved in the in-depth techniques of interval training, but I do use some of its principles.

The first week I start out with two, four minute miles each day. At a lope or slow gallop, a horse can cover a mile in about four minutes. It's helpful to measure the distance with a vehicle's odometer. I use my slide track as a measurement. Three complete laps around my slide track is one mile.

Anytime I bring a horse out of the stall, I warm him up with walking and trotting for 15, 20 minutes, whatever it takes to loosen stiff muscles and get the horse into the right frame of mind for working. Then we lope the mile. Afterwards, we walk for 10 minutes which allows the horse to fill up with air. His pulse and respiration return to normal. Then I lope another four minute mile in the other direction. What I am doing is building the horse's leg muscles and lung capacity.

I add two to three minutes to the mile each week. In 30 days, the horse is loping about 10 minutes each way with a 10 minute walk in between. He is now fit and ready for more extensive work.

Also, since I've schooled lightly on the basics during the weeks of conditioning, by this time, the horse should remember the minimum basic maneuvers and have a good foundation for the rest of the year. After this initial conditioning period and basic refresher course, the young horse is prepared for more advanced maneuvers. Chapters 9 through 13 detail the reining horse's formal education.

Air Theory

Throughout my entire training program, one of the rules I follow religiously is never run a horse out of air. I am a fanatic on air. I think conditioning is mostly air. You can have legs tight, muscles hard and bellies tucked up, but if horses don't have lungs full of air, they can't perform to the maximum. If a horse is blowing hard and you continue to school him, you are going to hurt him.

I've never known a horse that bowed a tendon, popped a splint, pulled a ligament or had a major injury that was not out of air at the time it happened. I don't care what kind of storm I am in with a horse, when he starts breathing hard, I stop. I either drop the reins and walk or throw a leg over the saddle horn and relax for 10 minutes.

If you don't stop, you may be lucky once or twice and not hurt him, but sooner or later you will. You may think you're lucky, but then in a couple of months you'll discover that the horse is a quitter. He is looking for a way out of a bad situation. The truth is, he may not be a quitter. Maybe he is a good horse that is sick of the way he is being ridden.

If you want a horse to like his job, to be happy under saddle, to want to guide, stop and turn around, then back off if he runs out of air.

There have been many times when I've run into problems with a horse. It wouldn't cooperate a bit. I stopped, wandered around for 10 or 15 minutes and let him air up. When I started again, I couldn't find the problem. Everything was fine.

There is a physiological basis for the air theory. Air oxygenates blood, which in turn feeds the muscles. Starved muscles do not have the ability to perform since they lose their strength. When a horse is in that situation, his bones are put into positions they normally wouldn't be in because they are no longer supported by the strength of the muscles. The ligaments take over the work of support. Tendons are stretched because the body is in an abnormal position and

Interval training builds wind power and strong muscles, tendons and ligaments. The conditioning process includes hard gallops combined with periods of rest.

Allowing a tired horse to rest and fill up with air after hard exercise prevents him from being damaged mentally and physically.

in a fatigued mode.

There are two types of respiration in horses: respiration with air (aerobic) and without it (anaerobic). A horse's muscles can function in an air-deficient state for only so long. You need to know when your horse reaches that point. From then on a horse is physically incapable of performing difficult maneuvers. When he is out of air and his muscles, tendons and ligaments are spent, you hurt him if you continue to ride.

Each horse's point of no return is different. It's up to you to watch for the signs. If he is breathing hard and his sides are heaving, let him rest.

Never run a horse out of air.

GUIDELINES FOR A TRAINING PROGRAM

There are five major movements in reining a horse: circles, lead changes, stops, back ups and turn arounds. I group them into three categories because of the relationship they have to one another. My training techniques revolve within these categories and, with respect to the organization of this book, each category has its own chapter.

Circles and lead changes are handled in Chapter 10. They are together because, in a reining pattern, lead changes are accomplished through circling.

Stops and back ups are in one category because they are associated with the development of the horse's mouth. In Chapter 11, I explain how to use the back up in developing a stop. In a reining pattern, back ups are done immediately following stops.

Rollbacks and turn arounds or spins are related to one another in that a rollback is one half of a turn around. A rollback is a 180 degree turn and a turn around is 360 degrees. They are discussed in Chapter 12.

The following ideas are guidelines I have developed over the course of my training career. I have found that they help me organize my program from day to day, week to week and year to year.

I follow a fairly consistent daily and weekly regimen in my training program.

A typical day consists of warm-up and suppling exercises in the beginning of the training session. I follow that with lots of circles. While circling, I work on guiding and lead changes. I practice speed control in circles and on straight-aways. I lope angles and D-shaped circles. I stop and sit or walk around and let my horses completely fill up with air. When they catch their breath and are breathing normally again, I work on stops, rollbacks and turn arounds. Some days I don't practice turn arounds and other days I don't practice stops. I may do one or the other. Some days I do a little of each. It varies from day to day depending upon what I think each horse needs (see illustration 8 A).

My weekly work-out schedule follows a distinct pattern. Throughout the week, I begin slowly, build to a peak in training, then return to a relaxed session (see illustration 8 B).

On Mondays, my horses have had two days off. The only time I ride them on the weekends is if we are at a horse show

8 A — DAILY ROUTINE

1. Warm up and suppling exerises
2. Circles, work on guiding
3. Circles, work on lead change positioning daily, actual lead changes periodically throughout the week
4. Speed control, in circles and straightaways
5. Stop, relax, let horse catch breath and air up
6. Stops and rollbacks
7. Turn Arounds

8 B — WEEKLY SCHEDULE

Sunday	rest
Monday	extensive warm-up, suppling exercises, light maneuver work-out
Tuesday	suppling exercises, more in-depth maneuver work-out
Wednesday	suppling exercises, building to peak level of maneuver work-out
Thursday	suppling exercises, peak level of maneuver work-out
Friday	suppling exercises, light work-out
Saturday	rest

or if they missed one day during the week. On Monday, I go through an extensive warm-up period. I return to the basic suppling and softening exercises, even on my older, experienced horses.

On Tuesdays, I blend in more in-depth training maneuvers. I build from Tuesday to Thursday. I ask a little more on Tuesday than I did on Monday; a little more on Wednesday than I did on Tuesday and a little more on Thursday than I did on Wednesday.

On Fridays, I return to a work-out similar to Mondays. I go back to basics and finish the week with a quiet day. My horses go into the weekend in a relaxed frame of mind.

With the basic training and suppling exercises, horses develop a solid foundation for each of the reining maneuvers. I work everything together, not spins one month and stops the next. All of it is blended throughout the year. I do the same thing everyday, only more of it as the year goes by.

Throughout the year, as I speed up my program, I find that I spend 50 percent of my time suppling my horse's body (see Chapter 9, "Advanced Suppling Exercises and Correct Body Alignment"). As horses do more advanced maneuvers, they have a tendency to stiffen some of their body parts. That's when I quit what I am doing and return to the suppling exercises.

I stop, turn around and circle my horses everyday. I don't change leads everyday, however. When I do change leads, it is in a pasture or on a slide track where space and time are not factors. I don't want to be rushed by fences. I want to hold the horse's shoulders up, move his hip over and then sit and wait until his body is in a correct position and he is in a relaxed frame of mind. I don't want to hurry and change because the fence is coming up (see Chapter 10 "Circles and Lead Changes").

I spend a good portion of the year keeping horses' attitudes right, more accepting of the maneuvers, more relaxed and confident. I do this by handling them quietly and consistently. No scare tactics or rushed commands. I give them the opportunity to understand what I want and the time to perform it. Patience and common sense win out. In the end, I have a quiet, willing performance horse.

To recap the beginning stages of my training program, by the time my horses are ready to start intense training, they've had approximately six months of the basics. Three to four of those months were spent in initial breaking as 2-year-olds and the rest of the time in conditioning and repeating their earlier education as 3-year-olds.

By April or May, I introduce speed control on its most basic level (see Chapter 13 "Speed Control"). I don't run the horses hard. Rather, I increase speed gradually to teach them the difference in speeding up and slowing down. I don't start really running or galloping the horses hard till mid-summer. I continue to sharpen them on the maneuvers and work riding on a loose rein.

By late summer or early fall, the horses are performing at a high degree of difficulty with more speed involved. The same basic program that I started with in January extends

throughout the year. The exception is that the maneuvers get more complicated and faster.

At the end of the program around November and December, all the moving parts of my finished horses move, are soft, supple and performing in high gear.

If at any time in the program, a horse gets scared or is tight, I go directly back to the basics and suppling exercises. I get the horse relaxed again. The name of the reining horse game is softness and suppleness. Without that, nothing can be accomplished.

By late summer or early fall of the 3-year-old training program, reining horse prospects are performing in high gear. This bay can spin a blur at the slightest command.

9

Advanced Suppling Exercises and Correct Body Alignment

From the beginning and throughout my training program, I make sure the horse's body is completely supple and aligned correctly. A day doesn't go by that I don't soften and supple each horse before I work it. The reasons are simple. Not only do I loosen up a stiff body, but I warm up cold muscles at the same time. I give the horse a chance to do his work comfortably.

The horse's body must be supple to perform the basic reining maneuvers: circle, stop, spin, roll back, change leads, and back up. Speed control (the ability to adjust speed at a gallop) is also judged in reining patterns and it's not possible unless a horse is softly in hand in the bridle.

When a horse has a supple body, I should be able to control his every movement with my finger tips and legs. There are several objectives in suppling. I want to be able to tip the horse's nose in either direction when I apply light rein pressure. The neck should move from left to right easily as it follows the horse's nose. When I squeeze both my legs on the horse's barrel, he should move forward and if I hold my reins steady, the horse should hit the end of the bridle, stop and give his chin softly to the pressure. He should break or flex in the poll, not the neck, as his chin gives to the bit pressure. I should be able to lay my leg on his rib cage and lift his rib up; in other words, push it over and have his body bend slightly around my leg. Also, with my legs, I want to be able to push his hips to the left and right. Every moving part of his body should be at my command.

I introduce all suppling exercises at a walk. Only when the horse understands them thoroughly at that gait, do I repeat the exercises at a trot. Doing them at the lope is much easier when the horse understands them at the walk and

trot. However, most of the suppling exercises that are described in this chapter are walking maneuvers only. They soften body parts so that advanced work at the trot and lope can be performed. When I ask for the exercises, I use the same hand and leg coordination at the trot and lope that I use at the walk.

Anytime you are supplling at a trot or lope and it isn't working because the horse is fighting you, you are pushing him too fast. Back off. Nine times out of 10, he'll become supple again when you put him back into a walk and start over.

There are degrees of suppling and what I do to the horse depends upon his age. The suppling exercises I use on a 2-year-old coincide with the basics the horse learns when he is first broke. I want him to give me his head and neck in either direction and I want him to move off my leg when I apply pressure to his rib cage. The exercises I ask a 3-year-old or older horse are definitely more advanced. I expect him

(previous pages) *A supple body is the prerequisite to any advanced maneuvers.*

(below) *When a horse flexes at the poll properly, he tips his nose downward and keeps his face perpendicular to the ground.*

to break in the poll and move his hips wherever I put them.

SUPPLING EXERCISES

I don't attempt to soften a horse's poll and hip until he is quite well broke. He should have been ridden for about five months at that time. That includes the three months of basic training done as a 2-year-old and the first couple of months of his 3-year-old year, which was devoted to preparation and conditioning (See Chapter 8, "The 3-Year-Old: Conditioning and Guidelines for a Training Program"). He should have a good foundation of walk, trot, lope, stop, turn around and back up and be soft in his nose, neck and rib before I try anything more advanced. This is approximately February or March, early spring, of his 3-year-old year. I still use an 0-ring snaffle or hackamore at this stage of training.

Poll Exercises

One of the objectives in suppling is to develop a flexible poll. The horse's poll is the juncture between his skull and his spine. It attaches his head to his neck and is located between his ears. It is a flexible joint. The horse can raise or lower his head and move it from side to side. We, as riders, want to have control of the horse's head and its movement, because when we do, we have control of the horse.

By flexing or breaking at the poll, I mean bending at that joint. The horse tips his nose and chin toward his chest. A term I use is "capturing the horse's face." For proper flexion, the head should be perpendicular to the ground. I never want the nose and chin to be so far behind perpendicular that the chin almost touches the horse's chest. In this case, the horse is over-bent. Other terms often used are "behind the bridle" or "behind the bit." Actually, the horse is evading the pressure of the bit, trying to get away from the pain of his mouth or nose being pulled too much.

I should mention a point of conformation here (see Chapter 4 "Selecting the Reining Prospect"). For a horse to properly flex at the poll, he must have a clean throatlatch. In other words, there must be enough room or clearance between the horse's neck muscles and the underside of his jaw to allow the horse to breath. A horse's trachea is located in this area and if it is pinched off because the horse doesn't have enough of a throatlatch to bend easily, a horse can't take in enough air to breathe.

Never force flexion at the poll by pulling back on the bridle to capture the horse's face. Instead, squeeze your legs on the horse's barrel. The horse understands that this is the signal to move forward. Hold a rein steady in each hand. Don't let your reins be extremely loose, just have a bow in the lines. When the horse is propelled forward by pressure on his rib cage from your legs, he literally is driven forward into the bridle. This is what is meant by "driving the horse up into the bridle." It is the basis for teaching a horse to drive with his hindquarters. It teaches the horse to move his legs more underneath his body. The slack disappears from the reins because the horse has moved forward into it. In effect, the horse runs into a wall. He can't go forward because the bridle

A good poll exercise is walking forward, then backing up with the horse in the bridle. Drive the horse up into the bridle while moving forward. Stop, release the horse's head. Then lift slack and ask the horse to back up.

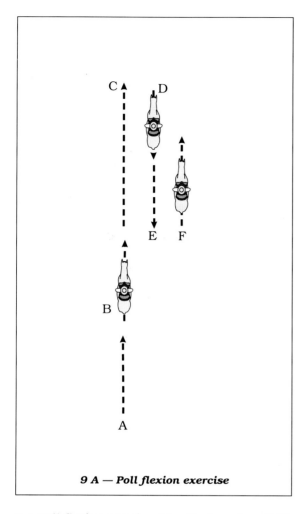

9 A — Poll flexion exercise

(9 A) *Poll flexion exercise. Flex the horse's poll (A). Walk forward (B). Stop and release the horse's head and relax (C). Lift the slack out of the reins and back u p (D). Stop and release the horse's head and relax (E). Flex the horse's poll and walk forward (F).*

doesn't let him; yet you are pushing him forward with your legs. The only way to handle the pressure on his nose and mouth is to give to it. He does so by tipping his nose and softening his chin. He has to break or flex in the poll to do this.

Remember when the horse hits the end of the slack, don't pull on the reins, but balance, or steady, his face with your hands until it is perpendicular to the ground. With light, little bumps, ask him to drop his chin or soften his jaw. The light, little bumps are not a hard pull on the reins. They are light tugs. Tug or bump the reins lightly. I use my little fingers in an alternating or see-saw fashion. That encourages the horse to drop or soften his jaw. If a horse's jaw is rigid and unyielding, it transmits throughout his entire body. What you are aiming for is a soft and supple body, not a tight, rigid one. A horse that gives you his jaw willingly is giving you a signal that he is willing to cooperate with other parts of his body as well.

Walk around driving the horse into the bridle with your legs. Bump the reins with your fingers to remind him where you want his head. When he backs off the bridle, in other words, gives to your rein pressure and puts his head back into the perpendicular position, stop bumping and give him his head. That means release your hold on his head. Say "whoa," stop and let him relax. Don't expect too much too quickly. Give the horse a chance to understand what it is you want.

Another suppling exercise involves moving forward and then backing up. Ask the horse to break at the poll, as you did before, and walk forward without moving your hands. Say "whoa." When he stops without pulling on your hands, release his head and give him slack in the reins. Relax. This is the basis for a stop. Later on in training, it is the forerunner for the sliding stop done at speed. As in all maneuvers, the horse has to learn to walk before he can run.

Then lift the slack, without pulling, and ask him to back. Hold your hands in a fixed position and squeeze with your legs. The horse is getting a mixed signal here that he must figure out. While it seems to him that you are asking him to go forward, you are not allowing him with your fixed hands and taut reins. If the horse gets confused and refuses to back, tap him with your legs on his ribs, elbows or shoulders. You want to shake him out of his frozen stance. His only escape is to take a step backwards. When he does, release your hold and let him relax. Always release the reins and pick up a new mouth. That means the pressure on the horse's mouth or nose (in the case of a hackamore) is removed before more is applied when the reins are lifted again. Leaning on the reins or holding too tight doesn't accomplish anything. It teaches the horse to resist the pull.

Then drive him back up into the bridle and make him break at the poll before he takes the first step forward. A word of caution here. Never force a horse to break in the poll while moving in reverse. Always make a horse break in the poll with forward motion. If you pull on a horse's mouth while backing up, eventually you get a dead-feeling, slow back up. It also encourages the horse to open his mouth (see illustration 9 A).

This exercise helps the horse to become soft in the bridle and is the first step in teaching the horse how to stop. When you can walk a horse forward, say "whoa" and he breaks over in the poll, he has the basics of the stop.

This exercise is important and I do it a lot. But to perform this exercise and work only on softening the poll is not enough. The body must be supple too.

Rib Exercises

I use several exercises to supple a horse's rib cage. Some work on the ribs alone and others in combination with the hips (see below).

As I did with the 2-year-old, I soften a horse's ribs by walking circles, bending the horse's body around my inside leg. I tip the horse's nose to the inside of the circle. Again, when I take the slack out of the rein to tip the nose to the inside, I loosen slack on the outside rein so the horse has a chance to turn his head slightly. I bump my inside leg against his ribs if I feel the horse is sticking his rib into the circle. If he is drifting out of the circle, then I use my outside leg to push his rib cage back into the circle. His ribs move back and forth at the direction of my legs. This is basically the same circling exercise I did to the horse at age two.

I also supple ribs while walking forward. I ask the horse to walk forward and push him up into the bridle with the same hand and leg coordination I used in earlier exercises. My hands are steady and my legs control the horse's body. I lay my right leg on his right rib moving it over and continue walking forward but at an angle to the left. In dressage, this is called "two-tracking." Since he is moving at a angle, the horse literally makes two different sets of tracks with his legs as he is moving forward. I say "whoa," release his head and

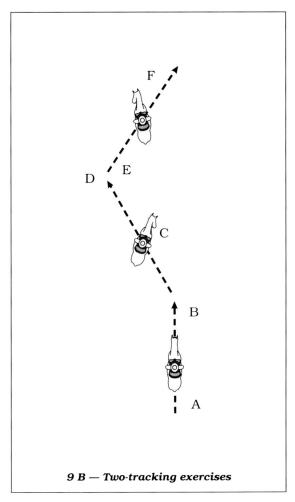

9 B — Two-tracking exercises

(9 B above) *Two-tracking exercise. Flex the horse's poll and walk forward (A). Lay right leg on horse's rib cage and move it over at a walk (B). The horse should be walking at an angle to the left (C). Stop, release the horse's head and relax (D). Flex the horse's poll, lay left leg on horse's rib cage and move it over at a walk (E). Horse should be walking at an angle to the right (F).*

(left) *Soften the horse's ribs by walking circles, bending the horse's body around your inside leg.*

relax. Then I jump him up in the bridle again, only this time I lay my left leg on his left rib and we walk forward at an angle to the right (see illustration 9 B).

Hip Exercises

When the horse fully understands suppling his body from the ribs forward, I introduce hip exercises. In order to work on the hip, however, I must have the rest of the body soft and pliable in my hands. Therefore, the hip exercises are in conjunction with moving other parts of the horse's body as well.

I use the same two-tracking exercise pattern, however; I put the horse's body in an arc position while we are moving forward. I walk the horse forward asking it to break in the poll. My hands hold the horse's head steady and straight. I move the right rib by bumping it with my right calf. The horse responds by bending around my right or inside leg. I move the left hip over to the right by taking my left calf, placing it behind the girth slightly and pushing the hip to the right. The horse's body is in an arc position while we are walking to the left. I say "whoa," stop and release the horse's head.

Next, I reverse the procedure. I put the horse in the bridle once more, but this time I want to move in an arc to the right. I hold his head steady, while I move his left rib to the right with my left calf. I place my right calf behind the girth and push the right hip to the left. His body is now in a left arc moving to the right.

below left) *To move the horse's hip to the left, move the left rib over with your left leg, place your right leg behind girth and push the hip to the left.*

(below right) *To move the horse's hip to the right, hold the horse's head steady. Move the right rib over with your right leg. Take your left leg behind the girth and push the hip over to the right.*

Using the same hand and leg coordination I described above, I perform the same exercise while backing up. The hips lead in this exercise. I put the horse into the arc position and go forward. Stop, release, then pick him up again and this time ask him to back up pushing his rib to the left and the hip to the right. We back up with the horse leading with his hip to the right. Stop, release. Then push him up into the bridle again and walk forward in an arc position to the right. Stop, release. Then put him into the bridle again and back up, only this time to the left. I move the rib to the right and the hip to the left. In effect, I am freeing up the horse's entire body.

In this useful exercise I accomplish two things. I break the horse over in the poll, softening it, but also I move the horse's body around, softening it as well.

Shoulder Exercises

I don't do suppling exercises for the shoulders. For a horse to perform maneuvers correctly, his shoulders should stay in the middle. By that I mean, a horse has two shoulder blades and they should be equal or level to one another when the horse is performing. A horse that drops a shoulder, in other words, one shoulder blade is lower than the other, always leans in the direction of the dropped shoulder. It only makes sense that if a horse leans, he can't move straight. Think of a car with a flat tire. The car pulls in the direction of the flat. It is the same with horses.

Horses most often drop their shoulders when moving in a circle. The more the shoulder drops, the more the horse leans into the circle and the tighter and smaller it gets. Even in a straight line, a horse that drops a shoulder is not moving straight between the bridle reins. He'll lean one direction or the other. His body is crooked and he won't be able to stop, turn or do anything correctly.

Therefore, I try not to supple shoulders and get them too loose. There are times, say in a turn around maneuver, when the shoulder may lead a little (see Chapter 12 "Rollbacks and Turn Arounds"). However, I never allow it to get too erratic or out of line.

Bend-Counterbend Exercise

I do use the bend-counterbend exercise in finish work on a turn around, especially if the horse's shoulder is up too high or he is not stepping cleanly enough with his inside front leg. Turn around problems usually show up around late summer or early fall as I ask for more speed in the maneuver. This exercise really gets a horse to stepping around correctly.

For this exercise, tip the horse's nose to the right walking a circle to the right. Keep pressure on the right rein and loosen pressure on the left rein. Lay your inside or right leg into the horse's right rib cage and your left leg behind the girth to push the hip to the right. The horse should be moving in an arc to the right.

Now release some of the pressure that your left leg applied to the horse's hip. Using a good amount of pressure, (right) **For a counterbend to the right, the horse is bent in a left arc while moving in a circle to the right.**

(bottom right) **A view of a counterbend to the right from behind.**

bump with your right leg to make the horse actually move off in a circle to the left. What was your inside leg, the right leg, now becomes the outside leg since the horse has changed from a right circle to a left one. Everything about the horse's body remains the same, his nose is tipped to the right, his neck is slightly bent to the right, his body is in a right arc. But the horse is circling to the left, with his body in a right arc. His left shoulder is leading the maneuver. It is a difficult

(left) ***Another example of a counter bend to the right, viewed from the side.***

(bottom left) ***A view of a counterbend to the right from the front.***

maneuver to explain (see photo). Bend-counterbend is a highly advanced suppling exercise. Obviously, I don't attempt it until other more basic suppling concepts are understood and easy for the horse.

BODY ALIGNMENT

Body alignment refers to the alignment of the spine, from the poll, neck, shoulders, ribs and hips (see illustration 9 C).

It is directly tied to suppling exercises. The only way to align the horse's body is through the suppling and softening of the body parts.

Every horse, until he is soft, supple and schooled correctly, leans to one direction more than the other. He either has his body stuck out to the left or to the right. If the front of the horse's body leans to the left, the back part of his body leans to the right. That is the way a horse must balance himself if his body is not aligned straight. Horses are four-legged animals and if they lean their front ends and their back ends in the same direction, they lose balance and fall down. It is simple mechanics (see illustration 9 D).

Stopping, turning, circling, changing leads and backing up are keyed to body alignment. If your horse's body is aligned properly, it is easy to teach the maneuvers.

Usually the ribs and hips cause the greatest alignment problems. For example, if the front end leans to the left, the hind end automatically leans to the right. Most horses are a bit crooked like that when in a straight line. That's why I start out at a walk, soften the horse in the poll and if he wants to throw his shoulder, or front end, to the left and hip, or hindquarters, to the right, I school exactly the opposite, moving the rib to the right and hip to the left, trying to keep the shoulders in the middle. As in the exercises above, I control his ribs and hips with my legs. I keep his shoulders in the middle by making sure his nose and neck are pointing

This horse's body is aligned from his poll through to his hips.

straight ahead. However, if I have to, I tap the offending shoulder with my foot to put it back in line.

I don't move the shoulders as much as I do the ribs, however. I like to keep the shoulders in the middle as much as possible. While I am fixing and softening an alignment problem, I do get the shoulder off center to some degree, away from the direction the horse is leaning. But once I get the horse suppled and balanced, where he is not leaning to the right or left, I put the shoulder back in the center, which means the shoulder blades are level. I use my hands and legs as I mentioned above to correct any shoulder problems.

In order for a horse to be correct in every maneuver, his shoulders must be straight in the middle. As I said, I don't move shoulders around as much as I do ribs and hips. I found that if you get too radical in bending and moving the shoulders, the horse is erratic going from one maneuver to the next. By suppling the nose, neck and ribs to control the front end, you have more correct maneuvers. Shoulders do move with the ribs, but I don't supple or move them directly on a regular basis as I do the other body parts.

Putting a horse into a circle tells you immediately what his body alignment and guidance systems are like. I am a fanatic about being able to guide a horse in perfectly round circles with my hand directly above his neck (see Chapter 10 "Circles and Lead Changes"). If my hand is six to eight inches left or right of the mane, then the horse is pushing or leaning one direction or another. He is not riding between the bridle reins; nor is he in correct body position. Riding between the bridle reins means exactly what it says. A well-balanced, softly guided animal does not lean on either rein. If I hold my rein hand straight out in front of me and the horse's neck is closer to one side than the other, I know the horse's alignment is off and, therefore, his guidance system will be off. I won't be able to control where he goes as well.

Guiding is what riding a reining horse is all about. If at any time, my horse's guiding does not seem quite as good as it did a few days or a week ago, I know I have alignment problems. All other training stops. I work on nothing but re-aligning the horse's spine and guiding until they are corrected. Alignment problems are handled through suppling exercises.

For example, when I lope a circle, I want the chin soft, the rib over and the hip just a hair to the inside. Just a little, not much. If you let the horse drop the shoulder and rib to the inside of the circle, the horse leans on the inside rein. He won't be able to stride deeply underneath himself and that may cause him to fall out of lead behind. Again, it's all mechanics. If the rib is too low to the inside of the circle, that pushes the hip to the outside and the horse falls out of lead.

To fix a cross-firing problem, I supple and align the horse's body to get the horse between the bridle reins once again. I soften the rib by bumping it with my inside leg. Whenever I do this, I always take the slack out of the reins and push the horse up into the bridle. Don't spur, just bump the rib with your inside leg and take your outside leg back a little and push the hip over.

(9 C below) *A diagram of a properly aligned body from poll, neck, shoulders, ribs and hips.*

(9 D bottom) *Until soft and supple, a horse's body may lean to the right or left. If the front end leans to the left, the hindquarters lean to the right.*

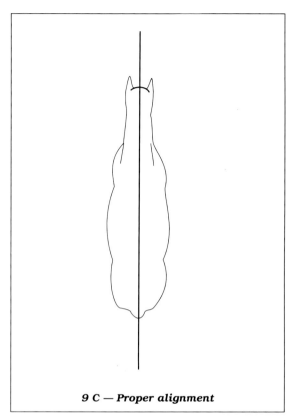

9 C — Proper alignment

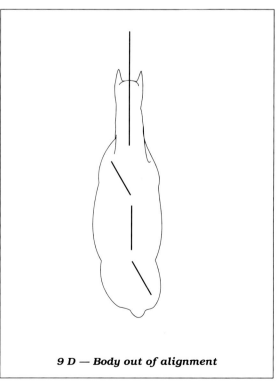

9 D — Body out of alignment

Riding a horse in a circle tells you immediately how a horse's body is aligned. If you can keep your reins in the middle of the horse's neck and he does not lean on either one, his body is aligned properly.

The same alignment principle applies to the stop. If a horse is leaning on one rein, he cannot get into the ground perfectly straight. He'll stop crooked and possibly drag a hind leg instead of holding it in the ground. To me, stopping is a by-product of correct alignment. If you get the poll, neck, shoulder, rib and hip supple and your horse lopes in a straight line, then when you lift the slack out of the reins, he has to stop straight.

When people bring me their reining horses with stopping problems, I don't have to ride them to know the cause. Most of them can't lope a straight line without leaning.

You cannot soften and supple a body in one day. It may takes days, even weeks. And depending upon how bad it is, how old he is and how long he has been that way, it could take months to get that alignment correct.

There are no easy fixes if you want a good horse. You can take any horse and put him through a quick 30 day training session. You can scare him into doing things, jar this around, jar that around and get a temporary fix. You can make somebody think you have done a good job. But if someone else rides him, in a week he will be the same burro he was before you started with him.

If you want to get a horse trained right and enjoy him for many years, do it slowly. You've got to soften, supple and align the horse's entire body. I've had horses that were quite easy to get aligned and others that were tough. I've had great reining horses that all of their lives had one little place that I had to soften everyday. If I didn't, it would get stiff and after a few weeks, I would have the old problem back.

I've also had horses whose stiff parts were helped tremendously with equine chiropractic work. Horses do get joints and other body structures out of alignment. If they do, it hurts to move. They try to protect that part by getting more out of alignment. Sometimes, the only thing that corrects the problem is physical manipulation.

The most common stiffness in horses is leaning their front ends to the left and their hips to the right. Eight out of ten have this problem. They have to be suppled in every area regardless of the degree of their stiffness.

Some horses are born naturally soft and others naturally stiff. The stiffer they are, the slower and harder it is to supple them. I've had horses that were quite stiff, but when they were supple, soft and all working parts were in alignment, they were great. Stiff horses are usually tough, hard knockers. They may be a little thicker mentally, too, but once you get through to them, they are real warriors. Often, these horses are more suited for trainers or professionals.

Horses that are more naturally soft and easy to supple are usually kinder mentally. They are horses you can prepare for an amateur rider to take home and maintain themselves with only an occasional tune up.

Training reining horses is not just teaching maneuvers. I spend the first six to seven months suppling, softening and aligning every movable part. When you have total control of a horse's body, it is effortless to soften a stiff part and get it back into alignment.

If a horse's spine is not aligned, he cannot stop straight.

*"THE PERFECT CIRCLE
IS PERFECTLY ROUND."*

10

Circles and
Lead Changes

CIRCLES

Circles are the foundation of the reining horse. This is a familiar statement, but one with a lot of truth to it. It is directly related to the fact that all other reining maneuvers are built upon a solid basis of correct body alignment for the horse. Correct body alignment, or the lack of it, is obvious the minute you ride a horse in a circle. I'll explain why.

All aspects of riding are tied to guiding, which is the ability to put a horse wherever you want it. If your horse is not guiding well in one direction or the other, he'll also have trouble in his turn arounds, lead changes and rollbacks in that direction.

When I lope a horse, I want to lope a straight line with my hand fixed right in the middle of the horse's mane. A horse is moving straight when his body stays between the bridle reins, not pulling to one side or the other.

The same with a circle. I want to lope a circle and not have the horse lean in or out of it. My hand should be right in the middle of the horse's mane. My horse is in correct body alignment when I can have him lope a large, fast circle, then a small, slow one, leave the circle and still continue loping in a straight line with my rein hand never straying from the middle of the horse's mane.

Anytime a horse feels heavy in the face, as if he is pulling or lugging, and has a rib or shoulder stuck out at a lope, he pulls in the direction he is stuck out. If you are loping and your horse has a hip or rib stuck out to the left, he'll pull to the left. He'll also have left lead change problems, left turn around problems and left rollback problems. If a horse's left shoulder or rib is stuck to the left, he will have his right hip stuck out to the right an equal amount.

A horse's body works like a swivel. When the front end is stuck out one direction, the back end is stuck out an equal amount the other direction in order to keep the horse balanced. If the front end and the back end were stuck out in the same direction, the horse would fall down. He couldn't stand up that way.

A horse's spine runs from the top of his head to the tip of his tail bone. A horse whose spine isn't straight because he has a body part stuck out in one direction or another is going to have problems guiding. He is going to pull one direction or the other. One turn around is better than the other. One lead change is going to be better than the other. He'll stop crooked.

Only a properly aligned body can handle maneuvers correctly. Moving in a straight line, a horse's body is in correct alignment when his spine is straight from his head to his tail. When circling, a horse's spine is in an arc position, the same degree as the circumference of the circle. In a large circle, the horse's body is bent only slightly. In a small circle, the horse's body is bent tightly around the rider's inside leg.

There is an old saying that every horse has a favorite side, the same as people are right or left-handed. This lopsidedness is directly related to body alignment. I must agree that 98 percent of the horses I have trained have had a direction they preferred. I have had a couple of horses, though, that never had a weak side. However, that is only a couple out of hundreds. Allowing a horse to learn that one side is his favorite creates a habit that gets worse as training proceeds.

I don't believe in encouraging a bad side. I go back to the suppling exercises (see Chapter 9, "Advanced Supplying Exercises and Correct Body Alignment") at the first sign of stiffness. I work two thirds on the bad side to one third on the good side. I never work only on the bad side and leave the good side alone. That's the fastest way I know to have the good side become the bad side and the bad side become the good side.

When I discover which side my horse favors, I start on a two-thirds, one third balancing program right away. In a few months, the horse is balanced on both sides.

The perfect circle is perfectly round. Many amateurs or beginning riders have trouble with round circles and make them lopsided instead. There is no secret to describing a perfect zero in the dirt. Circles are not hard to do if you do them a lot. They can be difficult if they are not part of your regular routine. Learning to ride round circles comes with many hours of practice. There is no better way to learn how to ride a perfectly round circle.

When I was a young man, I used to have a circle path out in the pasture. I would put my horses on that path, give them lots of rein and let them follow that 60 foot circle. I did this before I understood body alignment. I really didn't know what I was doing at the time, but that path helped me teach my horses alignment. All I knew was that it improved their circles. What they were doing was getting their spines in correct alignment themselves without me doing any adjust-

(previous pages) *A perfect circle is perfectly round.*

(below) *A horse is moving straight when his body stays between the bridle reins.*

Bob teaches round circles through suppling exercises in which he uses his hands and legs to control every part of the horse's body.

ing, which I couldn't do at the time anyway because I didn't have a clue as to what to do.

Perfectly round circles are taught through suppling exercises, the same ones I use to soften body parts. The object is to have the horse move in a circle without leaning on one rein or the other. I accomplish this by using my hands and legs to control every part of the horse's body, something

I can't do unless the horse's body is supple.

For example, in a circle to the right, I tip the horse's nose to the right slightly by taking the slack out of the right rein and asking for the horse's nose. I loosen the slack in the left rein so the horse can easily give his head to the right without being in a bind.

I put my right calf into the horse's right side moving his rib over. Only when the horse moves his rib out of the way can he bend around my leg. I take my left leg and put it on the horse's left hip encouraging it to move to the inside of the circle. From nose to tail, the horse is bent in an arc to the right.

Over a period of time, cues become more refined. Once the horse learns to keep his rib and hip over while circling, I do not have to keep my legs on him the entire time. He learns to bend his spine into the circle after months of practice.

In a circle, tip the horse's nose to the inside and lay your inside leg into his rib cage.

Circles become lopsided when the horse's body is not in correct alignment. To fix an alignment problem, I readjust the horse's spine. First, I take the slack out of the reins and balance the horse's face between them. I bump the nose, asking the horse to bring it in. Then I release it. I never hang on a horse's mouth, although at times, I maintain light, direct contact. I take hold of the horse's face, put it wherever I want it over and over again until he leaves it there and is comfortable and happy with it there.

Next, I work on his body position. If the horse is leaning to the left because his belly is stuck to the left, I bang the left side of his belly like a drum with the calf of my left leg. I bump it until it moves over. When it does, I stop bumping and sit quietly.

In a circle, when my horse drifts to the outside, I bump his rib cage with my outside leg. When he lugs to the inside, I bump with the inside leg. The bumping encourages the horse's rib on that side to move over, which re-aligns his spine and, consequently, his movement.

I don't spur for this manuever. Sharp, jabbing, repeated spurring scares a horse. I simply bump with my calf continually to move the body part over. Spurring too hard and too much makes a horse scared and want to leave the circle or push the offending body part harder and lean worse.

If a horse is resistant or slow to learn this exercise, I flex his poll at the lope and squeeze him into the bridle with my legs for direct contact and control. Then I carefully use my spurs as an aid only. For example, if the horse if drifting to the outside as we are circling to the right, I reach back with my left leg and lay a spur on the left hip that is stuck out of the circle. I push hard, not jab, and move the left hip down into the circle. I put the calf of my right leg on the right rib, push and move that rib over.

Only, when I have total control of every moving part of the horse's body, do I teach lead changes.

LEAD CHANGES

I don't actually begin my lead change program until around the fifth or sixth month of training, depending upon the horse's capabilities. By that time, a horse is reasonably supple in his body and attentive to my commands. By about the ninth month, most horses are fairly solid with lead changes. As with all the maneuvers, I don't work on lead changes a lot at any one particular time. It is rare for me to change leads more than once each way. There are a lot of days when I don't change leads at all. However, if I don't, I position the horse for lead changes anyway without actually changing him. It's important that I can position his body even if I don't change leads. By positioning his body, I mean, tipping his nose to the inside of the circle and moving his inside rib over.

A rider gets into trouble by teaching his horse to associate a change of direction and a lead change as one maneuver. They must be taught as two separate maneuvers. When a horse leaves the circle he is in, whether at an angle or on a straightaway, he must not lean or push out of the circle or

If the horse drifts to the outside of the circle, bump him with your outside leg to bring him back into the circle.

(10 A right) *An elliptical circle to the right.*

(10 B below) *A D-shaped circle to the right.*

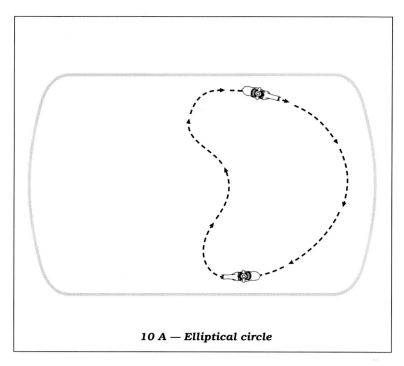

10 A — Elliptical circle

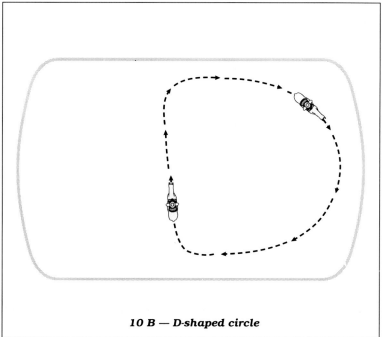

10 B — D-shaped circle

against the outside bridle rein in anticipation of a direction change. When he does, he throws his shoulders in the direction of the new circle and develops bad habits that are hard to break.

Before I start changing leads, I teach the horse to leave a circle and lope at an angle out across the pen, as if he were going to change leads. Instead, I bring him back to the circle the same direction we are going. This somewhat elliptical circle is the forerunner of riding a D-shaped circle. When I am confident the horse can handle this elliptical circle exercise, I graduate to loping D-shaped circles (see illustrations 10 A & B).

Teaching a horse to correctly negotiate a D-shaped circle is a large part of my lead change program. In such a circle, the flat part of the D goes across the center of the arena. Initially, I school the horse with suppling exercises as we go down the straight line of the D, not the round part of the circle. I tip his nose to the outside of the circle and lift his shoulder. I do so by taking the outside rein and putting it against the horse's neck. I also use my outside leg against his rib cage pushing it to the inside. Doing both has the effect of lifting the shoulder. This sets a horse up for a lead change whether you do one or not. If I wanted to change leads at this point, all I would have to do is release my inside leg and put my outside leg against the horse and we would change leads. However, for this exercise, what I want to do is limber the horse's body before we hit the end of the D or straight line. Then I tip his nose back into the circle. When I can bend and flex the horse's body through the D-shaped part of the circle and the horse returns to the circle quietly and relaxed, I am ready to teach the horse lead changes.

However, first I do some exercises which prevent the horse from anticipating what I am asking him to do. I lope several kinds of circles to keep the horse paying attention to me. There is no set number of circles that I do for this exercise. Sometimes I lope two or three round circles, two or three elliptical circles, then two or three D-shaped circles, followed by two more round circles and one D-shaped circle. It depends upon whether or not the horse is resisting me, pushing against the bridle reins and not wanting to straighten out across the center. Later on in the program, if a horse has a problem anticipating lead changes, I do a lot of this as well as counter cantering.

Counter cantering is another way to really use the D-shaped circle to prevent or correct anticipation problems. Because it is complicated and a horse must be totally supple, it is one of the finish maneuvers I do in preparing for the show ring. The exercise helps the horse to relax across the middle instead of worrying about changing leads. In a counter canter, the horse moves on the wrong lead for the direction of the circle. For example, in a circle to the left, the horse remains on the right lead. To accomplish this, when we lope down the middle or the flat part of the D, I tip the horse's nose to the left and take my left leg and push the rib over to the right. I keep the horse in the right lead while we circle to the left.

After I have completed the circle, I come back to the center and lope the flat or D part again. Only this time, I tip the horse's nose back to the right and put my right leg on his right rib, move it over and go back into the right circle. I have just loped a left circle and a right circle both in the right lead. By tipping the nose the other way and moving the rib, I've put the horse in perfect position to change leads both directions. This exercise relaxes a horse across the center of the pen while positioning him for a lead change.

However, early on in training for lead changes, I don't ask the horse to change leads immediately. First, I go back to the walk. A tremendous amount of my basic training is

Before teaching lead changes, Bob supples the horse down the straight line of the D-shaped circle by tipping the horse's nose to the outside of the circle and lifting his shoulder. This sets up the horse for the lead change.

Lead change sequence going from a right lead to a left lead (far right). The horse is moving on the right lead (middle). He switches in mid-air to a left lead (right).

done at the walk. There are days when I get on a horse and walk for an hour suppling, stopping, backing up, moving the hip from right to left in reverse, moving the nose from right to left in reverse, pushing the horse up into the bridle and walking forward.

Training is a continual suppling process. It's like taking two steps backwards, then one giant step forward, followed by another two steps backwards. I constantly supple the horse's body, reminding him that I have total control and that nothing I ask him to do is beyond his capabilities or understanding.

At the walk, I teach my horse that I can hold his shoulder perfectly in the middle and move his hip to the left, then to the right (see hip displacement exercises described in Chapter 9, "Advanced Suppling Exercises and Correct Body Alignment"). It is important that my horse is solid in this maneuver at a walk before I ask for it at a lope.

For an actual lead change, I lope several circles casually. I don't get in a hurry. If the horse should make a mistake, I don't scare him by punishing with a jerk or a jab.

For example, in changing from a right lead to a left lead, I lope the horse in a right circle and leave the circle at an angle as we have done before. Then I take the left rein and hold it snugly. There is light pressure on the left rein so that it is taut. There is no pressure on the right rein. By doing so, the horse's left shoulder remains lifted and doesn't fall. In other words, there is no chance that it will drop down into the circle. Both of the horse's shoulders are level at this point. I gently reach back and push the right hip with the calf of my right leg and release any pressure on the left leg. This produces a hind-foot first lead change to the left lead.

A horse should change leads with his hind legs first. One that changes front feet first throws his shoulders into the lead change. Once you allow that habit to form, it only gets

worse. The horse drops his shoulder deeper and deeper into the circle and eventually starts dragging a hind lead. In other words, the horse changes leads in front and not behind. This is a severe penalty in reining horse classes, not to mention being terribly uncomfortable for the rider to sit.

If I position the horse's body correctly and he thoroughly understands riding out of the circle at an angle, softening his poll, moving his body away from my leg pressure and steadying his shoulders, lead changes happen quite easily.

However, a horse that has been the object of a lot of forced or spurred lead changes is much harder to correct than one that has been started with a good, quiet program. Anticipating lead changes is one of the worst problems to handle. The horse is insecure and scared of what happens next. It's hard to show a horse that is bad coming across the middle of the pen, not only for a non-pro, but a professional as well.

Anticipating a lead change and crossfiring (when the horse is on one lead with front leg and on the other with the hind leg) are two of the most common lead change problems. For solutions, I go back to the basics of my lead change program and perform the same exercises, such as loping D-shaped circles and counter-cantering.

Anticipation is caused from too many lead changes without correct body positioning. D-shaped circles and counter-cantering as explained earlier usually eliminate that problem. The horse learns to relax in his circles and wait for a command from the rider, not predict his next maneuver.

Crossfiring or not changing leads behind is the result of a horse changing leads with his shoulder first and being stiff in the hip. That's why I always hold the shoulders up and never let a shoulder move into the lead change first. I keep the horse's shoulders in the middle or level with one another.

The horse's hip should be the first thing to move into a lead change, in other words, a hind leg first lead change.

As in all things with performance in horses, this is form to function. A horse can function only as his form allows. If a horse's front end is leaning left (shoulder is leaning), his hind end has to lean right (hip is on the right lead behind). If a horse moves into a lead change shoulder first, his hind end goes to the right. Whatever direction the shoulder goes, the hindquarters go the opposite direction. If the shoulder leads into a lead change, the horse has a slim chance of changing leads behind since he needs his hip on the inside of the circle, not the outside. This is why the shoulder has to remain in the center and the hip has to make the first move into the lead change. If you let a horse change leads shoulder first, even a good-leaded horse starts dragging leads behind.

Lead changes are not something I drill into a horse. Asking a horse to change leads repeatedly makes him dread it. He worries about the next lead change and anticipates it. I usually change leads once in each direction, then quit.

If I want to change leads more than twice, I leave the

A horse that takes deep strides underneath himself usually finds it easy to change leads.

arena or slide track and head for a big pasture where I can lope a long way on a straight line without obstructions. Fences would force me to change directions. I ask the horse for a lead change on a straight line with no change in direction involved whatsoever. Changing leads on a straight line out in the pasture is really no different from changing leads down the straight line of the D-shaped circle. For example, if you are in a right lead and want to change to the left, take the slack out of the left rein and tip the horse's nose slightly to the left. Move the left rib over to the right and get it out of the way for a left lead change by putting your left leg on the rib cage and pushing. Since the horse was on the right lead, his right hip was leading causing his hind leg to move forward first. When you want to change leads to the left, lay your right leg against the horse's right hip behind the cinch and push at the same time releasing any pressure you had on the left leg. Simply, take the left leg off the rib cage.

If the horse doesn't change for 20 strides, I just sit there and wait. The big pasture gives me plenty of room to maneuver. I don't allow the horse to think that changing leads is a big deal and one that I am forcing him to do immediately.

Horses that change leads naturally are born that way. I can tell whether or not a horse is a natural at it by watching him out in the pasture at play. Every time a natural lead changer changes directions, he does so easily with his front and rear legs in synchronization. More than likely, when you ride that horse, all you have to do is teach him to keep his shoulders in the middle and to move his hips at your command.

If you don't have an opportunity to watch the horse out in pasture, you'll have to test him under saddle. Put him into a lope and change directions slightly, maybe five degrees. See how he handles the change of direction in a straight line.

I can usually tell if a horse is a natural at changing leads by the way a horse lopes. I gallop him and feel his legs move underneath me. If I can feel his hip coming up under me and hitting me in the seat of the pants, he can change leads.

If it feels like his hind legs are strung out behind him, they are not coming directly up under his body. Such a horse probably can't change leads easily. He'll have to throw his shoulders into the lead to catch himself and end up dragging a hind lead. A good lead changer takes deep strides with his hind legs.

You can teach a poor lead changer to get the job done, but it takes a lot of solid, basic work. You have to teach such a horse to lope correctly first by getting him to drive with his hindquarters. For that you go back to the basics of putting a horse in the bridle. You would squeeze him with your legs propelling him forward into the bit which is held stationary by your fixed hands on the reins. The horse learns to gather himself and move collectedly.

A poor loper and lead changer is wrong somewhere in his trapezoid (see Chapter 4, "Selecting the Reining Prospect"). He is built mechanically wrong somewhere to make him so uncoordinated.

11

Stops and Back Ups

A good back up is an important tool in teaching a horse to stop. I use the back up as a suppling exercise. I want the horse to be able to bend and move all of his working parts in reverse.

BACK UP

Before I teach the horse to stop, I teach him how to back up properly. Second to guiding and circles, back ups are the most important part of my program. I want my horses to guide in reverse as well as they guide going forward.

When I ride forward, I push a horse up into the bridle by squeezing both legs. I make him give me his face and soften in the chin and poll.   However, I never pull on a horse in reverse. I ask a horse to back up by lifting the reins and taking the slack out of them. When he hits the end of the slack and has no where to go, he takes a step back. I don't want to get to the point where the chin strap tightens as I take the slack out of the reins. Pulling on a horse causes it to back up slowly and heavily. What I aim for is a light, responsive back up where the horse begins to back as soon as he feels the slack tighten, not the grip of the chin strap.

A horse's natural instinct is to push against pressure. He must be taught to move away from pressure in backing up the same way he is taught in other aspects of training.

A horse gets heavy in the face (pulls on your hands) in reverse if he sticks out a hip or a rib. If you feel the rib starting to poke out to the left, the horse is going to get heavy on the left rein. Bump the left rib with the calf of your leg, move it over and soften it. If he moves his hip to the right, he'll be heavy on the right side of his face and on the right rein.

(previous pages) *A powerful stop is the trademark of a top reining horse.*

(above) *Ask a horse to back up by lifting the reins and taking the slack out of them. As the horse hits the end of the slack and has no where else to go, he takes a step back.*

Bump the right hip and knock it over to soften it and bring it back into line.

I ask my horses to back with my hands, but I guide the movement of their hips with my legs. For example, if I want to back to the right and the horse is putting his hip to the left, I push the hip to the right with my left leg. If the horse moves his hip to the right and I want to go to the left, I push it to the left with my right leg. I push the hip in the direction I want it to go.

If you guide your horse in reverse with your hands, you may inadvertently pull on him. But if you lift your hands straight up or back, take the slack out of the reins and use your legs to guide him, you're ready to correct your horse if he veers in one direction or another.

I use backing a horse and guiding him in reverse as a suppling exercise. I seldom back a horse straight because I'm usually guiding him somewhere. By letting a horse back up on his own, nine times out of 10, the horse backs up with a hip stuck out one direction and a shoulder out the other direction. The horse learns to back up crooked. I want my horses to learn to back up perfectly from the beginning so I don't give them a chance to learn to do it any other way than my way. Whatever direction I put them, forward, backward or sideways, I want it to be at my command.

To guide a horse in reverse, I push the hip and rib to the right and guide him to the right or I push the hip and rib to the left and guide him to the left.

If I have a horse that is not backing lightly, I may spend 30 minutes working on a back up. You can do a lot of damage if you do it incorrectly. You can make a horse freeze up and he won't move at all. Be careful how you do this exercise.

For a good back up exercise, get out in the middle of the arena or a pasture and walk the horse forward 20 feet. Say "whoa." Stop and drop the reins. Always drop the reins after you stop a horse. Then pick up a "new mouth," a phrase which means you take pressure off the mouth before you apply new pressure in asking the horse to do something. If you stop a horse and instantly ask him to back, you have too much of a hold of him. Release a horse after you stop him, pick up a new mouth and take the slack out of the reins. Ask him to back and wait for him to start. At this time, if he leans a little bit to one direction or the other, push the offending part over with the calf of your leg. If the horse still does not listen, kiss or cluck to him. To my horses, that kissing noise is a signal to hurry up. I use it throughout my training program. Whenever they hear it, they speed up what ever they are doing.

If he still doesn't listen, I take the side of my foot and bump him on the shoulders, alternately touching first the right and then the left. I hold the reins taut, but don't pull on them. I sit there and irritate the horse, slapping him on the shoulders with my feet. Finally, the only escape he has is to back off the bridle. As soon as he does, I let him back a few steps. I say "whoa," stop him and give him his head. Then I push him up into the bridle, soften him at the poll and walk him 20 feet forward again. I may tip his nose to the right and then to the left, suppling his neck as we walk. I repeat "whoa," let him stop and give him his head. I finish by taking the slack out of the reins slowly and asking him to back once more.

My horses learn that when they are standing still and feel the slack coming out of the reins, it is a signal to back up. Taking the slack out of the reins is the heaviest pull they are going to get. All my horses back up when I remove the slack and they start to stop from the slack as well. They learn to pay attention when I move my hands slowly. When needed, I enforce it with a kissing sound followed by slapping my legs on their shoulders.

Only after a horse is broke and solid in backing up do I ask him to do it with speed. With a finished horse, I never have to take hold of his face when I back him. The entire back up is accomplished when I take up the slack in the reins. When I lift my hand a couple of inches, there is still a bow in the reins, but we are moving backwards. If I take the slack out of the chin strap and pull on him, he would slow down immediately and quit backing up. He isn't used to being pulled on. The feeling would be new to him. A good, show-stopping, fast back up is one that a horse does from slack and on his own. You will never see a horse that is being pulled on back fast and correctly.

I don't ask my horses to back up quickly everyday, which would make them lose the desire to back fast. However, I do want them to do it with cadence. Listen to the horse's footfalls. They should sound like a marching soldier, very rhythmic, much like "one, two, one, two, one, two." A horse that is stiff anywhere will have it show up in the sound of his back up. It will be "one, two, one....two.. one, two, one, two....one...two." The sound is inconsistent. Cadence is the key. A cadenced back up means a horse's body is soft and supple.

I make the horse move all his working body parts in reverse. Since I never let him lug on the bridle, the horse becomes soft and responsive going backwards. I've seen lots of horses that could turn a blur in both directions and stop big, but when they backed, they did it sluggishly. To me a horse that isn't supple in reverse is only three quarters broke. The other fourth isn't broke.

You should work on softness, give and suppleness in reverse as much as you do going forward. Horses have split brains, a right half and a left half. Each side functions separately and you must teach each separately. If you turn a horse to the left and never turn him to the right, he won't know how to turn to the right. You have to teach him to turn in both directions. It's the same with backing up. A horse can be soft and supple going forward; but if you never supple him in reverse, he won't be soft in reverse. You have to soften and supple the horse to the right, left, forward and backward to totally capture all the horse's working parts.

A good back up on a loose rein is the ultimate test of whether or not a horse has a light, responsive mouth. Any horse that backs up slowly or reluctantly does not have a fully developed mouth. I can tell more about a horse in his

(below) *Ask a horse to back up with your hands, but guide the movement of his hips with your legs. Here, Bob guides the horse to the right in reverse by pushing the hip in that direction.*

(bottom) *Bob guides the horse to the left in reverse by pushing the hip to the left.*

(right) *A fast back up is accomplished with a light, responsive mouth.*

(below) *The horse learns to back up the second you lift the slack of the reins.*

back up than any other maneuver.

For instance, if you want to know where your horse's weak point is or where he is stiff or what part of his body is causing you problems, sit squarely in the middle of the saddle, put your rein hand directly in the middle of the horse's mane, don't use any leg pressure and ask him to back up.

If he backs perfectly straight, the horse is supple throughout his body and he should have a nice mouth as well.

If, however, he backs up with his hip off to the left, then he is stiff there. The same with other parts of his body. If he roots his nose in the air when you ask him to back, he is stiff in the poll. No horse can be stiff in any part of his body and still back up with brilliance.

If my horses are backing nicely, they are stopping nicely. I can really polish a stop from a good back up. But if they aren't backing just right, their sliding stops are off as well. For a high quality back up and stop, you need a light mouth on a horse. The horse's mouth is a tattletale. It is one of the most important lines of communication between you and your horse. Resistance there means trouble elsewhere.

STOP

When talking about a stop, one of the first things that comes to mind is lightness of mouth. A mouth is light only if the working parts behind it are soft. A stiff poll or neck makes the horse feel heavy in the mouth. If the hips, ribs or shoulders are stuck out or locked up anywhere, you'll find resistance in the mouth. Any stiff part of a horse's body is felt in the mouth.

A good mouth is light and responsive because it has not been jerked and snatched into submission by uneducated hands. A good mouth is the result of long, slow, careful suppling exercises that soften a horse's body. A horse that is comfortable in what he is doing is willing to work. Willing horses have light mouths.

There are horses that stop in well-manicured ground only. When those horses have to stop in bad or deep ground, they can't. They don't have any depth in their mouths. The kind of depth I am talking about has to do with softness of poll, neck, shoulders, ribs and hips. When all of these things are soft and pliable, then you have depth in the mouth and tools to work with.

Also, a horse has to have a good trapezoid to stop well (see Chapter 4, "Selecting the Reining Horse"). He has to have the kind of conformation that makes it easy to stop correctly. If he doesn't have the necessary physical equipment, it hurts to stop the way reining horses are required in competition.

I start teaching a horse to stop with several supling exercises done at a walk (see Chapter 9, "Advanced Supling Exercises and Correct Body Alignment). First, at a standstill, I bend or flex the horse's poll by taking the slack out of the reins and tipping his nose downward. I want his face

Use poll flexion exercises in teaching the horse to stop. Ask the horse to break in the poll and move forward for 30 feet. Say "whoa." When the horse stops squarely without pulling on your hands, he is ready to learn sliding stops.

In this sliding stop sequence, the horse locks up his hindquarters, yet remains loose in the front end.

perpendicular to the ground. I squeeze my legs and ask him to walk forward bridled this way for approximately 30 feet. Then I ask for a stop by saying "whoa." When the horse stops squarely every time without pulling on my hands, he is ready for the next step.

Again, at a standstill, I take the slack out of the reins, make the horse break at the poll and give his chin. But, before I ask him to walk forward this time, I move his left hip over to the left with my right leg. I keep his head and neck straight in the middle. We walk forward and I say "whoa." I do the same with the right hip. Then I repeat the exercise with the right and left shoulders.

I move the shoulders with the reins. If you want to move the shoulder to the left, you move it with the right rein. Move the shoulder to the right with the left rein. Remember in guiding a horse, you move his ribs and hips with your legs and his shoulder, neck and face with the your hands on the reins.

When the horse is steady and relaxed at this maneuver, I take it one step farther. I pick up the slack in the reins, push the horse up into the bridle, move the left hip over to the left and back up. I do the same with the right hip. What we are doing is going forward and backward with the horse's body in an arc to the right and left.

To have a good foundation for a stop, you must be able to move any part of the horse's body anywhere. If you stop the horse at a lope before these things are accomplished, you'll only succeed in teaching him bad habits. Your horse will learn to lock up his shoulders and be heavy in the mouth.

When I am confident that my horse understands his lessons at a walk, I trot him. I trot him both bridled up and on a loose rein. I move his shoulders, ribs and hips, each time asking him to stop squarely when I whisper "whoa." In order for the horse to stop squarely, I release everything first before I ask for a stop. As I am moving the neck, shoulders, hips and ribs around in these exercises, I have control of the horse as I move his body parts. I have to release my hold on these parts so they can straighten out enough to stop. A few strides before I say "whoa" I release everything and let the horse's drive line or spine straighten out.

When I do stop the horse at a lope, I take the slack out of the reins in a definite rhythm. The faster I go, the slower I take the slack out of the reins.

This is a misunderstood area in stopping. It's human nature to think that the faster you are going, the faster you should say "whoa" and pick up on the reins. This is wrong. Instead, when you stop the horse, take the same amount of time to pick up the slack of the reins as it takes for the horse to complete one full stride. You should be in rhythm with the horse's galloping.

As you say "whoa" slowly, take the slack out of the reins slowly. It is impossible to take the slack out of the reins slowly if your voice says "whoa" quickly. Your hand moves at exactly the same speed as your voice.

Taking the slack out of the reins slowly enables your

(above) *A example of an early phase of a sliding stop showing the horse committing his hindquarters to the ground by locking up his hind legs.*

(below) *"Fencing" a horse puts the finishing touches on a stop. Run the horse up to a gate or a barrier and ask for a stop. Fencing teaches a young horse to keep his hindquarters underneath himself.*

(bottom) *If a horse stops poorly, wait until he is completely stopped and correct that part of his body that was stiff and made him stop crooked.*

To stop correctly, a horse has to remain elevated in his front end while taking deep strides with his hindquarters. When he stops, this horse buries his hindquarters while his front legs remain in motion.

This view of a sliding stop from the rear shows how a horse breaks in the loins to come to a hard stop.

horse to commit himself to stopping in a relaxed manner. Snatching the horse and taking the slack out of the reins fast forces the horse to go to the ground quickly, scared and incorrectly.

The approach to any maneuver is the key factor in its success. No maneuver will be any better or any prettier than the first step into it. When you ask your horse for a stop, concentrate on saying "whoa" slowly.

I put the finishing touches to stopping by "fencing" the horse. You fence a horse by running him up to a gate, wall or some other barrier and asking for a stop. At each end of my slide track, I have a 20 foot gate. The gates are positioned 265 feet apart and placed perpendicular to the track.

I do most of my fencing at a slow lope. I don't do much of it at speed, especially with young horses. Between the gates, I put the horse into a nice, easy gallop. When we get about 60 to 70 feet from the gate, I increase speed a little. I like a horse to build speed before I ask him to stop.

When we get 30 feet away, I say "whoa" and lift the slack out of the reins gently. If he stops softly and correctly, I just sit there.

If he stops crooked or poorly somehow, I wait until he is completely halted. I correct the part of his body that was stiff and which made him stop crooked. If it was his left hip, I put it in line by taking my left leg and pushing it back. If the horse's left hip was stuck out in the stop, his right shoulder would have been also. Because of the swivel action of a horse's body, it would have to be. If the front part of the horse's body was stuck out one way, the hind end would be stuck out in the other direction. Therefore, I make sure the right shoulder is lined up. I exaggerate the correction so the horse understands what I want from him; but I don't punish. I quietly correct his body position and soften the offending area by using my hands and legs to put the part that is stuck out back in line. Then I sit there two or three minutes and let the horse think about it. Afterwards, I turn him around

or roll him back over his hocks and lope to a stop at the other gate (see Chapter 12 "Rollbacks and Turn Arounds").

The approach or run down is one of the most important parts to a stop. You can feel if a horse is not galloping straight. Put your rein hand in the middle of his mane. If he pulls to the right or left, he is not in a position to stop straight.

If the horse is pulling to the left, I take the slack out of the left rein and push his left shoulder over to the right with my leg. I continue galloping down the track with his left side held over to the right in an exaggerated fashion. Remember, we are not running fast. This is a slow, controlled lope. It is impossible to teach a horse to stop correctly by running him hard to a stop. I say "whoa" and have him stop in that position. I hold him in that position at the end of the stop for a few minutes. Then I gallop him back the other direction.

What I am trying to do is teach the horse to run in a perfectly straight line. With his spine straight, the horse won't lean or push in either direction.

A horse cannot stop pretty with all of its weight on its forehand. In order to stop correctly, the horse has to be elevated in its front end taking deep strides with the hind-quarters.

A horse that runs with his head down too low and most of his weight on his forehand is probably strung out behind. He jams his front end into the ground, not putting on the brakes behind first.

In order for a horse to stick his hindquarters into the ground and hold them there as they do in the reining horse's famous sliding stop, the poll must be soft. In other words, the rider must be able to flex the horse's poll. If his poll is soft, the horse's spine is elevated. When the back comes up, the hips naturally go down and make it easy for the horse to hold his rear legs stationary while his front legs continue to pedal.

The length of a sliding stop is related to two things. First, the more speed you have built up before you ask the horse to stop, the more momentum you will have and the farther you will slide. Speed gives you momentum and consequently more distance in a stop.

Secondly, whether or not the horse's body is stiff or supple also controls the length of the slide. Horses with stiff bodies slide half or three quarters as far as horses with relaxed, supple bodies. Stiff working body parts that are stuck out cause stiffness that goes through the mouth. In other words, if a horse's mouth is not responsive, neither will his body be. The horse pulls on you and you on him. Pulling makes the horse's front end quit moving and shortens the stride. Instead of a soft, supple stop, you'll get a heavy, jerky stop.

After I fence the horse to school him on the basics of stopping, I go out to the slide track and do two to three laps around the track to get stopping off his mind. When I do ask him to stop again, I do it slowly. I don't want the horse to anticipate his stops. He'll beat me to the punch and start hopping on his front end. Galloping free and easy out on the track helps eliminate some of this.

(opposite) *This sliding stop sequence from a front view shows the pedaling action of a horse's front legs.*

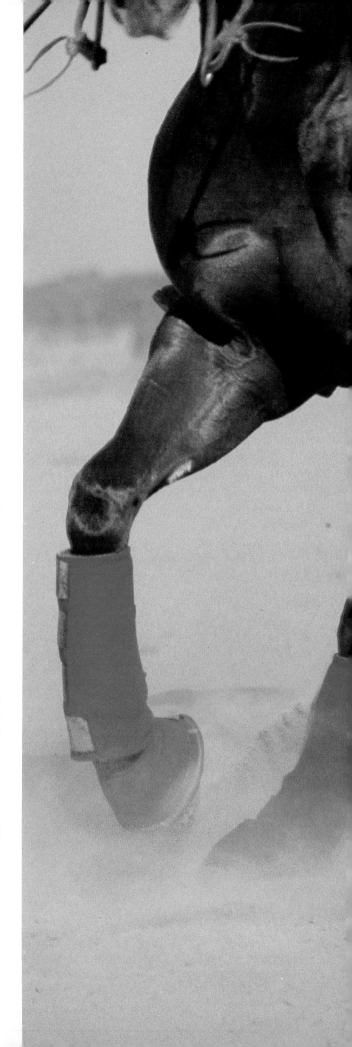

12

Rollbacks and Turn Arounds

As maneuvers, rollbacks and turn arounds are related. A rollback is half a turn around, a 180 degree turn on the hocks, and a turn around is a 360 degree turn on the hocks. However, after a rollback, the rider leaves at a lope. In a turn around, the rider hesitates before he continues loping (see illustration 12 A).

Like everything else in reining, suppleness is a prerequisite for both maneuvers. Before you can teach a horse to turn around, you must have him giving his nose in both directions and have control of his rib cage and shoulders (see Chapter 9, "Advanced Suppling Exercises and Correct Body Alignment").

I don't introduce either maneuver until my horse is stopping and backing up well. He doesn't have to stop long and hard, maybe slide two or three feet. But, he must be secure in it. A horse has to be able to stop and back up before you can expect him to rollback and he has to be able to rollback before you can expect him to turn around in a spin.

ROLLBACKS

A rollback is a stationary turn on the haunches. In a rollback, a horse locks up his hindquarters, one hind leg acts as a pivot leg and the other legs turn around it.

I introduce rollbacks by having my horse follow his nose when I pull it around to the left or right. Wherever his nose goes, the horse should follow. It is a simple concept and one horses easily understand. However, if a horse gets stuck in one spot and won't move his legs, I encourage him by bumping his ribs with my outside leg to get his body to chase after his nose.

As with all the maneuvers, I teach rollbacks from a walk

(previous page) **In a turn around, the inside pivot leg remains relatively stationary throughout the maneuver.**

(12 A right) **A rollback is a 180 degree turn on the hocks. A turn around or spin is a 360 turn on the hocks.**

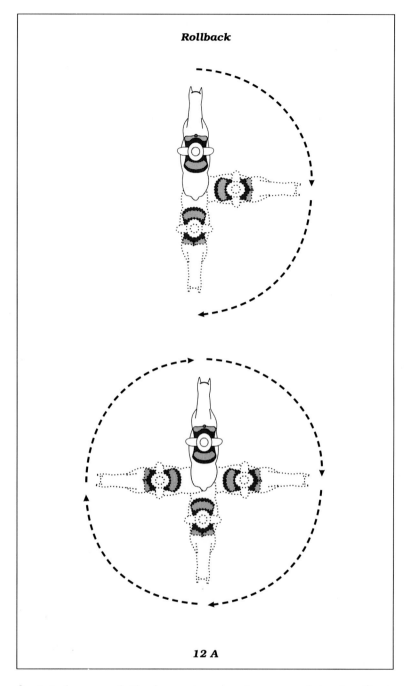

Rollback

12 A

first. I always ask the horse to come to a complete stop first. He must be able to get both hind legs underneath to perform the maneuver and he can't do that unless he is stopped.

Sometimes, when I am teaching a horse to rollback from a walk, I back him up one step and then rollback. By backing up one step, it puts the horse in the ground a little deeper and makes him come around cleaner with his front legs. It helps put some snap in the turn.

When I want to rollback, say to the right, I hold my outside or left rein snug, but not tight, and I use my inside or right rein to tip the horse's nose slightly to the right in the direction of the rollback. I give only enough slack with my left to allow the horse to tip his nose to the inside of the rollback. The reason for the somewhat snug left rein is that I don't want the horse to be able to overbend his body in the turn. I want his body to swing around as straight as possible in this maneuver, not bend around my inside or right leg. If the outside or left rein were too loose, the horse would be able to bend his head and neck too far and get out of position for the 180 degree turn. I want the horse to tip his nose, not bend his body excessively.

When the nose is pulled to the right, the horse's inside or right hind leg remains stationary as the pivot leg, while the other three legs step around it in the turn. Done properly, the inside or right front leg should lead first into the rollback, followed by the left front and hind legs. I encourage this through hand and leg coordination. With my hands operating as I said above, I bump my right leg into the horse's rib cage to move the right side of his rib cage over to the left. That way I get the rib out of the way so the right shoulder and front leg can lead the way into the rollback. Then, my left leg bumps the horse's left side or flank to get him to move to the right in the rollback.

When we have completed the 180 degree turn to the right, I release all pressure on the horse's head and sides and we walk off straight. When I quit turning his head and bumping his sides, the horse stops his turning motion and walks off.

I meander all over the slide track continually changing directions with the horse. I walk in a straight line, pull the horse's nose to the left, turn around and then walk off in a straight line again. I repeat the procedure pulling the horse's nose to the right, turning around and walking off. Done enough times, this exercise makes the horse become extremely light in the bridle. In time, the mere suggestion of a stop gets the horse to plant his hind legs in the ground, wait for the signal to turn, then follow his nose in the direction of the turn moving the other three feet around his planted hind foot (see illustration 12 B).

After the horse has mastered the rolling back procedure from the walk, I do it at a trot and lope. The cues are the same.

When we practice this maneuver at a trot, the horse trots off after the rollback and the same when we are loping. The horse learns to leave the rollback in the gait we started.

If the right hind leg is stationary and the right front leg leads into the rollback, the horse should come out on the right lead. In an actual reining pattern, the horse comes out on the proper lead for the next maneuver if he executes this type of rollback after a stop. Rollbacks come after sliding stops in NRHA reining patterns. Since all rollbacks are performed in the direction of the outside wall of the arena, the horse is on the correct lead to go down the wall or fence for the next sliding stop.

It is the momentum of the horse's speed during trotting and loping that produces much of the snap seen in the typical rollback. When a horse stops after trotting and especially loping, he still has some forward motion inertia. I time my cues to use that inertia or energy in the rollback. Instead of allowing the forward momentum to move us

Introduce rollbacks by having the horse follow his nose when you pull it around to the right or left.

In this rollback sequence, the horse rolls back to the right. A. Hold the outside or left rein snug, but not tight. Use inside or right hand to tip the horse's nose to the right.

B. The horse begins his turn to the inside with his inside front leg. The inside hind leg becomes the pivot leg.

C. As the horse continues to turn to the inside, the rider holds the horse's body relatively straight.

D. As the horse begins to turn, bump with your outside leg to encourage him to move around.

E. A good view of the horse's body, with shoulders in the middle, nose tipped to the inside and rider's hand and leg coordination.

F. As the horse completes the right rollback, he comes out on the right lead.

forward, I turn the horse in the other direction. It looks as if the horse is almost running in place; but, in effect, he has stopped, and is simply turning the other direction and continuing his gait.

The first few weeks I introduce rollbacks, I don't use them as rollbacks, but as suppling and correction exercises, especially for fixing crooked stops.

For a horse that leans to the right when I stop him, I take his nose, roll him back to the left and lope down to the other end of the track. I take his nose and immediately rollback to the left again. I do this two or three times until he stops perfectly square. When he does, I sit there for two or three minutes. The horse thinks he is going to rollback to the left. I do the opposite and rollback to the right. This is more of a mental exercise designed to keep the horse alert to my commands. It prevents him from anticipating which direc-

(12 B) **Rollback exercise. A. Walk in a straight line B. Pull the horse's nose to the right, turn around and walk off in a straight line again. C and D. Perform right rollbacks. E. Perform a left rollback and walk off in a straight line. F and G. Perform left rollbacks here as well. Maneuver all over the slide track repeating the procedure.**

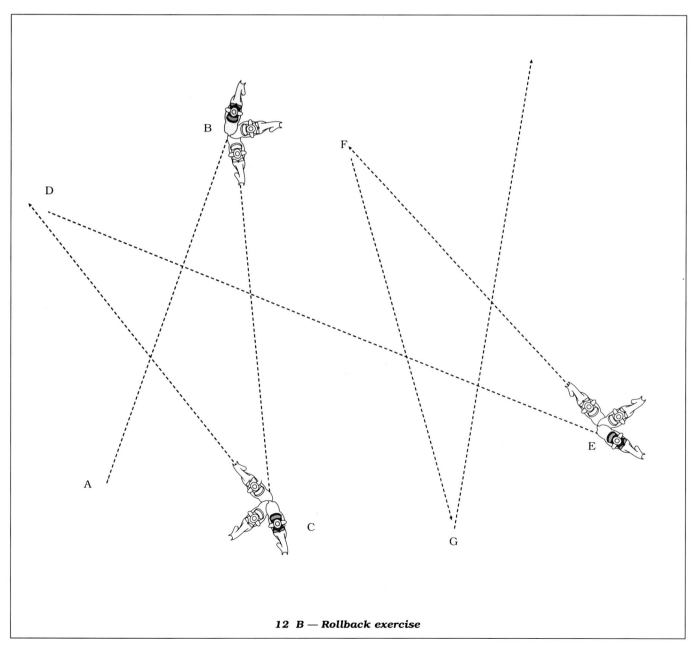

12 B — Rollback exercise

tion I ask him to go.

I mix up this exercise to keep a horse sharp and paying attention to me. Sometimes, I stop, back him up first, then rollback. The horse waits for my various cues and stays light in the bridle that way.

One word of caution here. In the early stages, be careful not to stop and rollback immediately over and over again. After a while, instead of listening to your commands, the horse anticipates what you want him to do. He turns into a circus horse. Every time you stop him, he rolls back on his own and takes off in the other direction.

To avoid this, I often stop and sit there a short while, then take the horse's nose and rollback slowly. Also, I don't ask the horse to rollback until he reaches the end of his stop.

It is important to teach a horse to leave a rollback at a lope. Under the NRHA judging system, the rider receives a half point penalty for trotting out of a rollback two steps and a two point penalty for trotting beyond two steps.

I don't want the horse to lunge out of a rollback. He should leave it cleanly at a quiet lope.

On the fencing track, I run a horse up to the gate and stop him. I sit there and make him stand straight and square. When I am ready to go the other direction, I quietly roll him over his hocks and expect him to lope out of there, not trot.

In the early stages of teaching rollbacks, I find that when a horse bends his body to follow his nose, his shoulders are late. In other words, the shoulders follow behind the movement, instead of with it.

As the horse becomes more broke and more attentive to my rein hand, I want his body to be straight instead of bending into a rollback. Even though his nose should be slightly tipped to the inside, I want his neck and body between the bridle reins.

If the horse's body is bent, as in the shape of a "C," the shoulder is late making it is easy for the horse to come out of the rollback at a trot. Also, in this case, the outside leg leads and the horse comes out on the wrong lead.

While it is not a penalty in a reining pattern to come out of a rollback on the wrong lead, it is not as impressive as doing it correctly in the first place. Also in a pattern, you would have to change leads anyway before you get to the top of the curve for the next run down to a stop. In this case, reining patterns require you to be on the proper lead for the run down to a stop.

When the shoulder is straight between the bridle reins or even leading slightly, the inside leg leads. If this is the case, the horse comes out of the rollback cleaner, gets into a lope easier and is on the correct lead.

In rollbacks, I use my legs as needed to straighten the horse's rib cage and shoulders. Legs enforce hands. I ask a horse to stop and turn with my hands, but use my legs to keep his body correct.

When I ask a horse to rollback to the left and he throws his rib cage to the left, I use the calf of my left leg to bump that rib over.

In rollbacks or turn arounds, the horse's shoulders should be in the middle (top) *and his inside front leg leads* (bottom).

If the horse is over bending and bowing his rib to the outside, which is to the right in a left rollback, I use my outside leg to move the rib over.

Remember that if a horse is bowing his rib to the inside (or bending his body), his shoulder is going to come around too quickly. You have to bump the rib which should slow the shoulder down.

If the horse bows his rib cage to the outside, the shoulder is going to be too late. In this case, you need to push the outside rib back into the center of the turn.

TURN AROUNDS

After the horse has mastered rollbacks, he is ready for a complete turn around or spin.

The first step in a turn around is basically a rollback. I introduce the maneuver in a circling exercise. For a turn around to the left, I walk in a small, six or seven foot circle to the left, tipping the horse's nose to the left or inside. I take the calf of my inside, or left leg, and bump the rib cage over.

(12 C) *Turn around exercise. Walk a six or seven foot circle to the left, turn around one or two times, then walk off (A). Walk another six or seven foot circle to the right, turn around one or two times, then walk off (B). Repeat all over the slide track (C).*

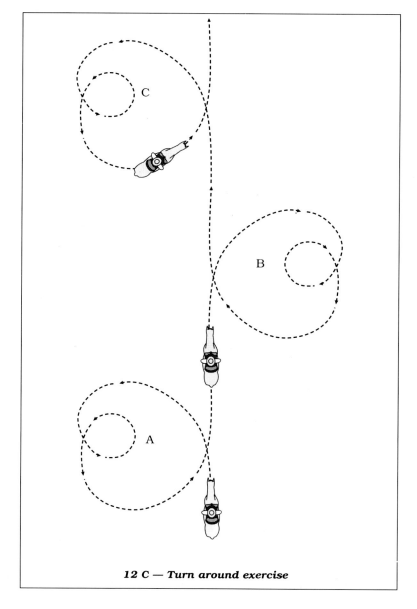

12 C — Turn around exercise

I keep walking until I feel his nose soften and his rib move off my leg. When they do, I stop, tip his nose more by shortening the inside rein, release my inside leg off the horse's side, use my outside leg to push the horse over and turn the horse around. Then I walk out of it. I may turn him around one and one half to two times before I walk off. The first thing I want the horse to learn is to tip his nose softly, hold his rib over and step around (see illustration 12 C).

From the beginning, I want the horse to step with cadence, which means each stride he takes is exactly the same length as the next one.

On a turn around, the inside front leg should take the first step. If the rib on the inside is stuck out, the inside front leg can't move as well. Moving the rib over by bumping it with my leg frees the leg to move.

Once the horse starts turning around freely and using his inside front leg well, I take my outside leg, reach up and tap him on the elbow or shoulder. What I am doing is moving the outside shoulder down to center so the horse can turn flat. It also encourages the outside leg to extend and speed up.

Moving a horse's shoulder "to center" means that both shoulder blades are level. One is not higher than the other.

Using the term "flat" in describing a turn around can be confusing. What it simply means is that a horse's body is reasonably level from his poll through to the hindquarters. His spine is as straight as it can be to perform the maneuver. The horse's head is not up in the air, his back is not hollowed out and his hindquarters are not stuck out behind.

Everything about the horse's body has to be in correct position for a cadenced turn around. If it isn't, the inside and outside legs take two different lengths of stride. The spin is not going to be smooth and flat.

The mechanics of the way a horse's body works influence everything he does in reining or other performance events. What one part of a horse's body does affects how another part reacts. For example, in a turn around, if the rib is stuck out, it throws the hip to the outside and the horse spins on his outside hind foot instead of his inside hind foot. When the rib is pushed over or out of the way, the inside hip is underneath the horse which causes him to use his inside hind leg as a pivot leg.

Let's dissect the mechanics of a turn around. First, the inside rib must be pushed over so the inside front leg can reach out and step. If the horse leans to the inside with his rib and shoulder (sticks them out), then the inside front leg is blocked and can't move and extend. It moves a little, but takes short, quick steps. By moving the rib over, it frees the inside leg to take long, fluid steps.

It is worth noting that young horses sometimes have problems with executing turn arounds in the beginning. They are not familiar with lateral movement. It takes a while for their muscles to stretch so they can take large, long strides. As weeks go by, a young horse gets freer in his lateral movement and turn arounds come more easily. Keep your horse's physical limits in mind as you train.

Turn Around sequence. A. For a turn around to the left, the left hind leg remains stationary and the left front leg leads into the turn.

B. The three other legs move around the inside pivot foot.

C. The horse's momentum swings him around to the left.

D. The left hind foot still remains stationary as the right front leg begins to cross in front of the left front leg.

E. The horse continues to cross over until

F. the horse must balance himself with his two front legs crossed. To be balanced and not fall, the horse has to catch himself with his inside front leg on the next stride.

A good example of a "flat" spin. The horse is level from poll to croup as he spins around his hind legs.

Secondly, in the mechanics of a turn around, while the rib controls the movement of the inside front leg, the shoulder controls the movement of the outside front leg. A shoulder that is too high forces the outside front leg to swing high and come down in short, choppy strides. Bringing the shoulder down to center, or making it level with the other shoulder blade, flattens the flight path of the outside leg from high to low and helps the leg to extend. If the shoulder is up, the leg moves high. If the shoulder is down, the leg moves laterally and low.

When everything is correct, the rib is slightly up and the shoulders are in the middle, then both front legs can take steps of the same length.

I step a horse forward into a turn around, not pull him back into it. Stepping forward into a turn around encourages the horse's head and neck to remain low, which is where I want them. This is also a function of body mechanics. When a horse moves forward, his back naturally comes up and his head goes down. Pulling a horse back into a turn around makes his head and neck come up and his back hollow. His front legs scramble in front of him as he tries to keep his balance. The turn around looks trashy when the horse is out of position. Therefore, I encourage the horse to begin any turn around by taking one step forward before he gets into the turn around. I never expect a horse to turn around after I have asked him to back up.

A horse has to be soft in his poll and chin to turn around properly. There is no getting around it. Any resistance or rigidity in his neck brings his head up and he automatically sucks backward. You've got the same problem you would if you pulled him back into the turn around instead of walking him forward.

When a horse is comfortable with the walking circle exercise, I vary the routine. I walk several circles to the right, stop, turn him to the right, stop again and sit there. Then I walk circles to the left, stop, turn him to the left, stop again and sit there. I introduce stopping after a turn around by dropping my hand and not walking off immediately. There are only two times when I say "whoa" to a horse. One is when I ask for a sliding stop and the other is when I want the horse to shut down after a turn around (see illustration 12 D).

After several of these circles, the horse becomes familiar with the routine. Then I change it. Next, I walk a much larger circle to the right, stop and turn to the right. After turning around, I walk off in the direction of the turn, stop and turn to the left. This is an extremely useful exercise to teach a horse proper body positioning for a turn around. What I am doing is teaching the horse to position himself for a turn around one way and then immediately get into position to turn around the other way (see illustration 12 E).

CORRECTING PROBLEMS WITH TURN AROUNDS

Certain problems do arise in teaching turn arounds. About six weeks into a turn around program, I often find that horses get a little over bent in their necks and their shoulders get out of whack. Everything is just a little too loose. At this point, I want to bring the shoulder back to center. I walk a circle to the left, tip the horse's nose to the left and stop. Instead of turning to the left as usual, I turn to the right, actually making him lead into the turn around with the right shoulder. This gets the shoulder back underneath the horse.

I don't overdo this, just enough to get the shoulder straight again. When I do this exercise, I take the slack out of the reins and hold the horse's face. I don't pull on the reins, only balance the horse between the bridle reins. If I did this exercise with the horse's head thrown away, he'd get too low in front and start leaning with his shoulders. I lift the shoulders slightly. That makes the horse extend with his front legs.

You can also have a problem with the horse extending his legs out too far in front. This is a common dilemma and one that can't be fixed on a loose rein either. I take the slack out of the reins and squeeze the horse up into the bridle. By containing his face and elevating his front end, I keep the shoulders in the middle. As we turn around, I bump each

Turn around sequence. An example of a flat or level spin performed at speed by a well-trained 3-year-old.

shoulder with my legs in an alternating fashion. That makes him pull his front legs back underneath himself. I do this for a few days and then turn the horse's face loose again. At this point, a horse usually drops his head and flattens out into a nice, cadenced spin.

Never turn a horse around faster than he can turn and maintain cadence. Speed will come if you teach him to turn slowly and correctly first.

On a finished horse that I am ready to show, I may allow the shoulder to lead a little into a turn around as long as the rib is still is good position, not bowed out too far the other direction. That way the horse stays on the pivot foot, but the spin becomes quicker and fancier naturally. However, it is not something I do everyday. If you let a horse lead with his inside shoulder all the time, he will get deeper and deeper into the spin with his shoulder. In about three weeks, you'll be in trouble and not know what happened.

The biggest problem with spins riders have in the show pen is trying to turn too hard too fast.

After a horse becomes solid in the basics of the turn around, he usually becomes faster and snappier on his own. And it is at this time that I feel I can bump a horse with my outside leg to speed him up. If the outside shoulder is a little high, I bump it there or in the elbow to put it back in place, and that usually speeds up the maneuver. If the shoulder is where I want it and the horse is just too slow, I reach behind the cinch and bump his ribs or flank to quicken him. I will use a spur if necessary to get his attention. I also use a kissing noise to tell my horses that I want them to hurry up. It's a noise they are familiar with; one they have heard throughout their training. It means go faster.

A pretty spin is built slowly. Most NRHA patterns have four spins in both directions. I take the first three steps to get into the turn around quietly. After I pass the first quarter of the spin, I start building speed. By the time I have made one complete revolution, I am at peak speed for the turn around and finish the other three revolutions at that speed. Such turn arounds mark exceptionally high in reining competition.

By the time my horse is finished and ready to show, I can dispense with the inside leg bumping up the rib cage unless

the horse needs tuning and softening. I use my outside leg only to start the horse moving around. From then on, my horse runs away from the rein against his neck. I lay my outside leg on the horse's barrel and outside rein on his neck at the same time and wait. I don't crowd or force the horse into the first step. I let the horse take one, two, maybe three steps slowly and quietly into the turn around. I never blurt into a fast turn around.

If you force a horse to turn fast before he can do it correctly, he learns to dread it. A horse that learns correctly likes to turn around and speeds up on his own.

For the longevity of your horse's career, don't spin him a thousand miles an hour all the time. After a while, it turns into a scary maneuver for him. Work on correctness and precision. Speed comes with confidence.

(12 D below left) *Turn around exercise. A. Walk several large circles to the right, stop and turn around to the right, stop and stand there B. Then walk several circles to the left, stop and turn around to the left, stop and stand there. Walk out of the circle*

(12 E below right) *Turn around Exercise. A. Vary the circling routine, walk a much larger circle to the right, stop and turn to the right. B. After turning around, walk off to the right, stop and turn to the left (C).*

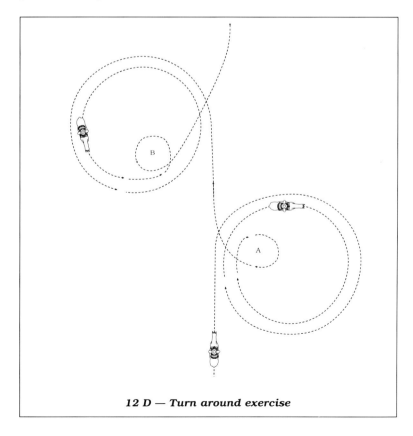

12 D — Turn around exercise

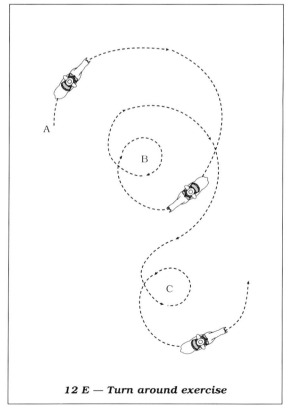

12 E — Turn around exercise

13

Speed
Control

Speed control means you control the speed, literally. If your horse takes hold of the bit and runs through the bridle, you are out of control, going nowhere fast. Teaching a horse quietness and discipline at speed is crucial in a reining pattern or in any performance event which requires accelerated speeds.

If you lope a horse slowly all the time and the only time you gallop him is in the show pen when you circle or run down to a sliding stop, running becomes an excitable maneuver. It is scary to the horse since he isn't familiar with and confident in going at a high rate of speed.

The key to a reining horse is galloping correctly. His training is 50 percent mental and 50 percent physical. A reining horse that doesn't gallop quietly will cause you slight problems in every area of training and probably a major problem in one or two areas.

Many riders are afraid to run their horses. They think running makes horses hard to handle. They can be a handful if they have been stuck with a spur or slapped with a rein. Riders must learn to build speed slowly in a non-threatening way. No horse is going to run quietly unless he has been run enough to learn to run relaxed.

I don't concentrate on galloping and speed control in the early stages of training. I first get the horse broke and guiding well. About mid-summer, after I have the horse stopping and turning around with confidence, I add controlled galloping to the program.

Speed control revolves around cues and body language. A horse can read your body language like a blind man reads braille. They feel everything about you, including your moods. That is why it is important to be a consistent rider.

(previous pages) *Horses have to be taught to run quietly.*

Speed control revolves around cues and body language. To encourage a horse to go faster, "chase" him. (above) *In chasing, the rider leans forward from the waist and runs his hand up the horse's neck. To slow down a horse, sit down and drop your hand in front of the saddle horn* (right).

If you do things differently every time you ask a horse to do something, he can't read you. He'll get confused and sometimes angry. Horses relate to consistency.

My older, more experienced horses know what I am going to do before I ask for it. When I stop them, I never have to take all the slack out of the reins. They are already stopping. Or when I ask for a spin, I merely suggest it with a rein and they turn. They've learned to read the subtle cues of my body language before a rein touches them.

When you walk into the show pen, have yourself in a

good frame of mind and as relaxed as possible. Most riders get wound up before a class; their adrenalin flows. I doubt there are many exceptions. Concentrate on keeping yourself as close to normal as possible because a horse responds to the way you do things and the way you feel. The pace your horse takes and your entire pattern are a reflection of your mental state and body language.

My cues for speed control are simple. I "chase" the horse to speed up and sit down in the saddle to slow down.

The term "chasing" means to lean forward from the waist

The horse learns to hit a pleasure lope, the second the rider sits down in the saddle. A distinct speed differential earns points in the show ring.

and run your hand up on the horse's neck. Whenever you lean forward, your buttocks lift out of the saddle. You put more weight over the horse's center of gravity and it allows the horse to run faster. Lean forward, but quietly. Don't do anything to scare the horse, such as spur him. Running your hand up the horse's neck encourages him to hustle. In effect, you are saying "Go ahead, it's okay."

How far you lean forward and how far you run your hand up the horse's neck, whether it is an inch or a foot, is up to you. It's the rider's preference. It makes no difference how far you lean or where your hand is. What makes a difference is that you chase quietly and consistently. Don't do anything radical that would scare the horse, such as spurring or slapping the reins on either side of the horse's body. You'd startle the horse and a horse that runs scared is not going to run controlled. You have to teach a reining horse to run quietly, relaxed and controlled. Chasing quietly has to do with the atmosphere you are creating while the horse is running.

Also, leaning forward and running your hand up the horse's neck are cues, and like all cues, should be done consistently so the horse understands what it is you are asking him to do. If you run your hand mid-way up the horse's neck and hold it approximately six inches above the mane, then that is where you should put it every time you chase. If you lean slightly forward by rocking on your seat bones only, or if you lean far forward so that your head and neck are practically parallel to the horse's neck, then do that each time. Whatever you do to indicate to the horse that you want him to move faster, do it identically every time you ride.

To ask a horse to slow down, sit down lightly in the saddle and drop your rein hand down on the horse's neck at the withers. The combination of weight in the saddle and the lack of forward rein movement alerts the horse to come back in hand and slow down.

Also, at a gallop, tighten your body a little. When you want to drop down to a slow lope, relax and let your body go almost limp. In time, your horse quickly associates leaning forward with going fast and sitting down with slowing down.

A good exercise is to lope three or four large, fast circles, then sit down and lope three or four small circles. Lean forward again and lope one big fast one and then sit down for a slow one. The horse learns to go into a slow lope at any time you ask, not just after several large circles. I make the horse run a little faster than he wants to run. When I feel that he wants to slow down on his own, then I sit down, drop my hand and let him slow down. I do this consistently until he understands that when I lean forward and move my hand forward, he should speed up, and the second I relax, quit hustling him and drop my hand, he should slow down. Once a horse is solid on the cues, I mix up the circles. I lope one big, fast circle and four small, slow ones or two slow ones and three fast ones.

Most horses are rather fresh at the beginning of a training session. Lope several circles to get the edge off of them before you begin serious work.

Make sure your horse is reliable with speed control in a circle before you introduce it on a straight line. My slide track is 850 feet long and 250 feet wide, but any rectangular-shaped track will do for this exercise.

Put your horse into a slow lope and lope to one end of the slide track. Make the curve in a slow lope and continue down to the other end of the track. After you come out of that curve, about 100 feet into the straight line down the track, start building your speed by leaning forward and chasing your horse. By the time you are half way down the track, you should be running at a good clip. Run all the way down to the end of the track and round the curve. When you hit the center of that short end, sit down, drop your hand and ask your horse for a slow lope (see illustration 13A).

Teaching speed control in a straight line has its disadvantages. You can inadvertently teach your horse to get dumpy in his front end while stopping. Don't ever ask a horse to slow down on the run down to a sliding stop. Properly, your horse should be gaining speed all the way to the stop. When a horse gains speed, his front end is elevated and it is easier for him to bury his hindquarters for an impressive stop.

Wait until you get to the curve to drop your hand and sit down. While it is striking to see a horse run hard, have his rider pitch the slack in the reins and have the horse hit a pleasure lope, it can interfere with the manner in which the horse stops. By slowing down on curves instead, you won't have that problem.

While you want to encourage a horse to shut down his speed from a gallop to a slow lope, you never want to rush from a slow lope to a dead run. Always build your speed, blending slow strides into fast ones fluidly. In reining patterns, all maneuvers are weighted equally. It is just as important to have good circles with tremendous speed variations as it is to have big stops and fancy turn arounds.

Remember to increase speed slowly. For example, in a pattern that asks for a slow, small circle followed by a fast, large one, build speed from the middle of the circle or dead center in the arena to the first quarter of the new circle. You have several strides from the center of the arena to the top of the new circle to increase speed. After you pass the first quarter of the circle, you should be going at top speed for that horse.

You are going to run across every type of mentality in horses, from high strung and nervous to extremely laid back and lazy. They all have to be handled differently when it comes to galloping. Tailor your speed control program to suit your horse's disposition.

One of my futurity horses that later graduated to an open horse, Two T Pachuco Wimpy, is a good example of a lazy horse. Chuck, as we call him, is a good horse, but he doesn't like to run. It was easy to teach him everything except run. Showing him what speed control meant was a breeze since, from the start, he was more than happy to slow down in a matter of one stride. When I'd ask him to run, he'd stick his head in the air, worry about what he was doing and try to slow down every stride. To overcome his fear of running, I made him run one big, quick lap around my slide track everyday. It took a month but he finally dropped his head, quit fretting and accepted running as a maneuver. To this day, I still have to make him run, but at least he does it relaxed. He had to learn to run relaxed and the only way he could learn was to do it.

The first few times you run a lazy or laid back horse, he may become scared. Run four or five big circles with him. Usually, by the third or fourth circle, he starts to come back in hand. He figures out the program, lowers his head and relaxes. The minute you sit down and ask for a slow lope, he will give it to you. Lazy horses pick up speed control quickly. After the second or third day, they've generally got it down pat. Going slow is part of their personality to begin with.

Nervous or gassy horses, on the other hand, need different schooling. They don't need any excuses to run. That's fine as long as they learn to run relaxed.

A gassy horse continues to want to run even after you've galloped four or five large, fast circles. Keep riding those fast circles until you feel him lower his head and begin to relax. The second he does, take hold of the reins and softly pull him down to a slow lope. Lope a couple of small circles, then take the slack out of the reins and gently pull him down to a trot. Trot a couple of small circles, stop him and sit there. Do this every day once in each direction. In a week or two, the horse learns that when you sit down and take the slack out of the reins, he should slow down on his own, without being pulled down. He should start looking forward to it. After a while, you can leave a bow in the reins and as soon as you sit down and drop your hand on his neck, he'll switch gears and slow down.

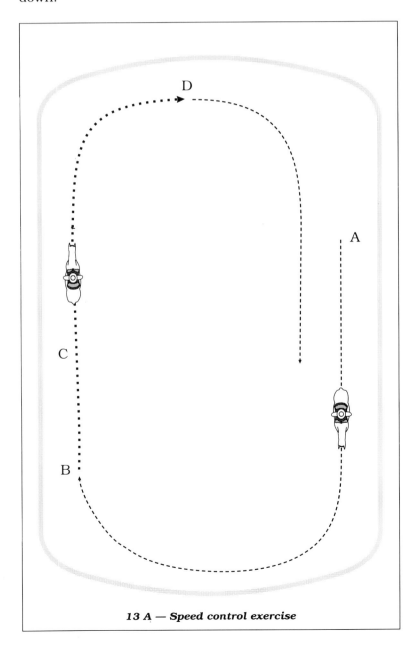

13 A — Speed control exercise

(13 A) *Speed control exercise. Put horse into a slow lope and lope to one end of the slide track. Round the curve (A). Build speed about 100 feet into the straightaway (B). By the time you are half-way down the track, be at top speed (C). Round the curve. When you hit the center of the short end, sit down, drop your hand and ask the horse to slow down (D).*

If running is part of a horse's daily program, it won't scare him, make him mad or anxious. He accepts it as another thing he does in life to please you.

There are some horses that don't want to slow down. This type of horse wants to run every time you take hold of him. We usually refer to them as "hot" horses. They are nervous, excitable horses and lose it when they run. They won't make reining horses or dependable performance horses. A good prospect for reining wants to lope slowly naturally. He doesn't want to run off with you every time you sit in the saddle. Don't bother with "hot" horses. You can teach hot horses speed control to some degree, but the first time they are under pressure, such as in a competition, they are going to blow. You can make a reining horse of sorts out of a hot horse, but not a quality reining horse. They are a waste of time. Go find a horse with a good attitude and a quiet frame of mind.

Speed control has been one of my best tools for correct-

(13 B) *Lead change problem exercise. Chase horse in several, large, fast circles until you feel horse wanting to slow down (A). Come across the middle and change leads (B). After lead change, sit down, drop hand and ask horse to slow down (C).*

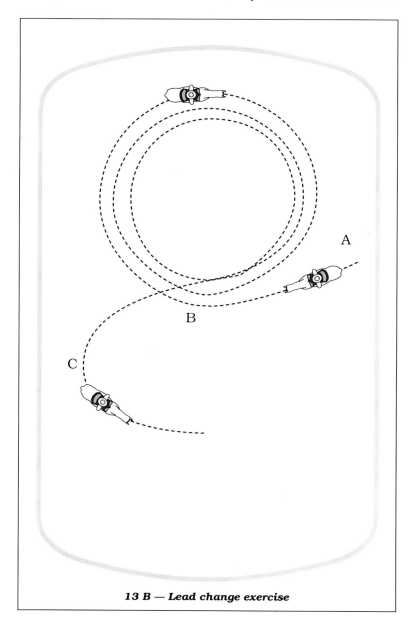

13 B — Lead change exercise

ing problems in other areas of training. For example, many horses have lead change problems. They may be bad-leaded to begin with or scared of changing leads. Others riders may have spurred them or changed leads too often.

With such a horse, I don't attempt any lead changes until I get him solid in speed control in his circles first. I chase the horse in two or three large, fast circles until I feel him wanting to slow down. A horse that is galloping hard has his hind legs out behind him. It is harder for him to change leads that way. I wait until the horse tells me he wants to quit. Then I come across the center of the pen and change leads. When I feel we are securely in the new lead, I sit down, drop my hand and ask the horse to slow. What this does is make a horse become relaxed with lead changes. He thinks of changing leads and slowing down as one maneuver. A horse that is thinking of slowing down strides deeper underneath himself. That makes it easier for him to change leads (see illustration 13 B).

I don't slow down before the lead change because I don't want to change the rhythm or flow of my circles until after the change is completed. Also, there is a chance that the horse might drop his shoulder as he slows before the lead change.

If the pattern calls for another large, fast circle after a lead change, I have to hustle most of my horses because they associate changing leads with slowing down. However, I don't mind that. Since many horses feel they have to speed up to change leads, if you get this program firmly fixed in their minds, you can "replace stampede and change leads" with "slow down and change leads."

I usually don't change leads more than once a day. I don't want a horse to begin anticipating. After two or three weeks, I have a quiet lead changer where once I had a nervous wreck.

A good speed control program is something I use extensively to maintain older, more experienced horses. My open and non-pro horses don't need schooling everyday; but they are galloped to keep them legged up. When I tune my horses a week before a show, I usually school them on all maneuvers to make sure they are sharp. A couple of the days during that week, I gallop them and use speed control in circles and on straightaways. If they aren't galloping correctly, none of the other maneuvers will work. This is also a good program for keeping horses quiet, yet sharp on the maneuvers. I keep them craving the desire to go slow. This is the key to making older, finished horses last indefinitely. A horse that is ridden intelligently at home and not shown excessively on the road should be able to last a long time.

Speed control is one of the most important parts of my finish program and carries on throughout the rest of the horse's show career. The biggest stops and the fanciest turns won't win anything if you can't control them. Because they are so physical, horses with a tremendous amount of athletic ability would scare themselves in an all out effort. Galloping keeps them relaxed and contained. It keeps them mentally right.

*"THE MOST IMPORTANT FACTOR IN SHOEING A
PERFORMANCE HORSE IS TO HAVE HIM LAND
LEVEL ON THE GROUND."*

14

Tips On
Shoeing the
Reining Horse

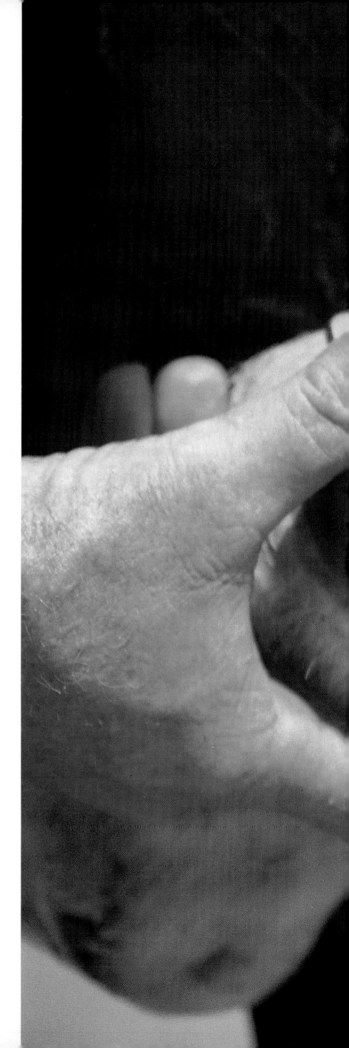

No matter what kind of performance horse it is, reining, cutting, roping, pleasure or whatever, a horse must move in balance with his body. It is the horse shoer's job to trim and shoe for proper balance.

My farrier for many years, Rich McDonald, does not do any corrective shoeing on my reining horses. He simply trims them flat and level, according to each horse's leg conformation.

He trims the feet as short as possible to ensure that the horse moves naturally. Horses with toes that are too long or heels that are too high do not stride naturally or prettily. Eventually, excessively long feet cause problems. You can compare it to a human being. If a person wore shoes one size larger than normal for even one day, he would feel a lot more stress and strain on his legs than if he wore shoes that fit properly.

The most important factor in shoeing a performance horse is to have him land level on the ground. You can notice this by watching the horse move at a walk. View him from the front and side. Does the inside or outside of the shoe hit the ground first? Or does he put the entire foot down level?

If his walk is level, he will probably trot and lope that way too. If he doesn't land perfectly level, his timing will be off and only get worse as he speeds up. All foot and leg problems intensify as the horse moves faster.

A reining horse must be able to stop squarely in his tracks and turn sharply in rollbacks and spins. If he is not shod level or balanced, he would fall out of his tracks trying to catch himself. The shoe could be throwing him off in his performance.

There is no standard angle at which to shoe a reining

136

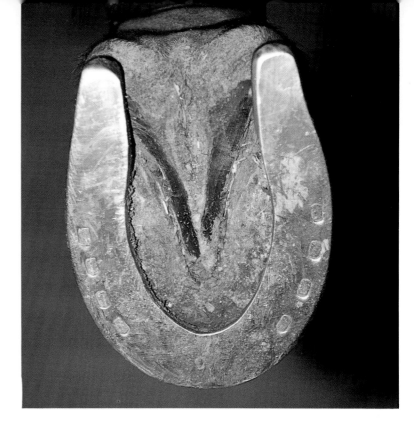

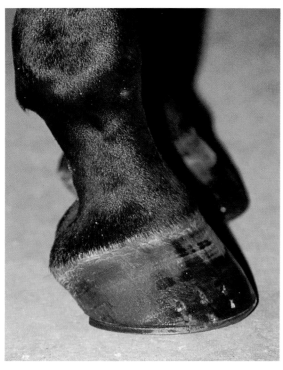

(previous pages) *Horses' feet should be in balance with their conformation. A protractor is an instrument that helps farriers to balance horses' feet.*

(top) *Slide plates are hand-made shoes specifically for reining horses.*

(above) *This horse's feet have been trimmed to match her pastern angles.*

horse, or any horse for that matter. The angle of the horse's hoof should match the angle of his pastern. Generally, most horses are comfortable at 55 degrees in their front feet and a little steeper, say 52 degrees behind. Horses' hind pasterns are normally at a higher angle.

I have all my horses, even the 2-year-olds, shod with keg shoes in front and one inch wide shoes behind and never change them. There is an adjustment period every time you change the width of the shoe. My horses get used to wearing one size shoes and I don't lose any training time.

The standard keg shoe size is 3/4 inch wide. Keg shoes are manufactured or factory-made. They are not hand-crafted by a blacksmith. Because of its shorter width, the standard shoe bites a little more into the dirt than an inch slide plate. Slide plates are usually hand-made shoes specifically for reining horses. A narrower shoe drags on the ground more so than a wider shoe. Also, a wider shoe makes the horse a little lighter in the bridle because he can stop and slide easier. The less he pushes in the rear, the lighter he feels in the bridle. Ninety percent of my slide plates are one inch wide, one quarter of an inch thick and tapered or beveled at the toe.

Normally, every horse I ride wears inch plates. I rarely use shoes wider than an inch and then only in extraordinary cases where the horse needs a heavier shoe to stay in the ground. The only time I go to more than an inch plate is when a horse is conformationally incorrect.

Some people shoe their reining horses with extra wide plates, 1 1/4 to 1 1/2 inches. Some slide plates go the extreme and practically cover the entire bottom of the hoof.

I don't like shoes wider than an inch because, in many instances, horses don't have enough cup or concavity to their soles to hold the ground when they move fast. An extra wide shoe makes horses slip and slide in the dirt and lose their balance. They scramble for security rather than gallop with confident strides.

Shoes that cover the entire sole are good for sliding only. The horse cannot grip the ground and this is dangerous in fast circles. A lot of scramblers drag a hind lead in their circles because they can't get a good hold of the ground.

Although extra wide slide plates do make a horse slide far because of their sled-like action, they prohibit a horse from being able to hold his slide in the ground. Many times, one leg or the other slides out to the side. The horse can't control his slippery feet.

Also, putting heavy shoes on a horse destroys his good movement. Heavy shoes work well for gaited horses in making them lift their feet. However, we prefer Western performance horses to have light, natural, low to the ground action. We don't want high knee and hock action. We want the horse's legs to barely skim the earth, often called "daisy clipping." A pretty mover is an efficient mover. He wastes less time and energy in the air and uses more of it on the ground.

I use trailers on my horses' hind shoes. Trailers are extensions of the shoe beyond the normal shoe limits. However, mine extend no farther than the bulb of the heel. Trailers help horses in their sliding stops. Horses' toes don't rise as they slide across the ground. Trailers help guide the flight of the foot. The trailer balances the foot and keeps it on the ground longer.

I do use trailers on a lot of my horses for the above reasons. However, I especially use them on horses that are "cow-hocked" and "sickle-hocked." "Cow-hocked" is a term used to describe horses that toe out behind. Instead of sliding in a straight line, horses which toe out behind spread their hind feet apart as they slide along the surface of the ground. "Sickle-hocked" horses also have trouble with their stops. Their hind legs are in the shape of a sickle and the horses stand too far underneath themselves. The cannon bones on their hind legs are set at an angle to the hock, instead of coming straight down from it. Horses that need trailers are usually incorrectly made somewhere from the hock to the hoof.

I don't put trailers on 2-year-olds. Sliding too far too soon might scare a young horse and he would give up trying to stop before he began. As he progresses in his training and is confident of his stopping ability, I add more trailer and a tapered toe. By tapering the side that comes in contact with the dirt, the shoe doesn't drag across the surface of the ground with its sharp edge.

Some horses are natural stoppers that find it easy to lock up behind and slide 40 feet. Natural stoppers have three things in common: they are conformationally correct, (see Chapter 4 "Selecting the Reining Prospect"), they have good mouths and a big desire to please.

I shoe regularly every five weeks. That seems to be the average amount of time to re-shoe a performance horse. Horses' hoofs grow approximately one quarter inch a month. By the time a horse needs to be re-shod, his feet may have grown three eighths of an inch, which is enough of a difference to change the horse's angles and way of going.

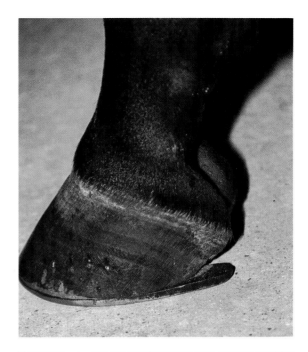

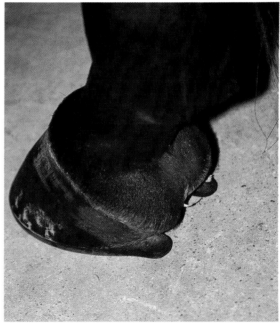

Two views of a trailer. (top picture) Looking down and (above picture) from the side. Trailers are extensions of the hind shoe that help horses stabilize their sliding stops.

15

Equipment
and Bits

Tack and equipment are the tools of a horse trainer's trade. He needs them to get his job done. There is no substitute for good fitting equipment, but even good equipment is useless unless it is cared for and adjusted properly.

SADDLES

Saddles and bridles are the primary pieces of equipment. Since I spend many hours in the saddle, I am particular about the kind of saddle I have. I ride one that is designed to fit me. However, I can't tell anybody what kind of saddle is best for them. We are all made differently and require a different type of saddle.

What interests me in a saddle is how effective I am in it. It must allow me to use my legs and body to ride my horse. This is more important than how comfortable the saddle is.

In a reining horse saddle, I want the same closeness to a horse that I would have in an English-type saddle. There are few Western saddles designed to let you feel your legs on the horse's sides. Most Western saddles have a lot of bulk between you and the horse. This is definitely a disadvantage for the intricate maneuvers a reiner has to perform at top speed.

My saddle has an in-skirt rigging which eliminates much of the bulk of the D-rings and thick latigo straps that the typical Western saddle has.

Also, the fenders are cupped out where my leg sits. I can brace against the fenders, much like the knee rolls of a hunter/jumper saddle. This helps me maintain a good body position during the accelerated spins of a turn around.

I like to sit in the middle of my saddle, not on the cantle. The shape of my saddle seat puts me in the middle. The

(previous pages) *Bob Loomis' spurs have 10 point rowels. There is enough rowel to get a horse to move off of it. However, the rowels are dull and don't scare a horse.*

The Bob Loomis reining saddle has an in-skirt rigging (upper left) *which eliminates a lot of the saddle bulk, medium height swells* (upper right) *which don't push the rider on the cantle and cupped-out fenders* (above) *which act as knee rolls or leg supports.*

swells are not so high that they push me back on the cantle. My legs hang straight down underneath me and because of the lack of bulk, I can put them directly on the horse's sides. This lets me use leg aids to their maximum. Since a lot of what I do on a horse is communicated through my legs, I need ready access to the horse's sides.

There are other characteristics that I like in a saddle. I prefer short saddle horns that give enough clearance for my rein hand to move.

Also, there is no substitute for quality leather and workmanship. I like the feel of well-made saddles. When I sit in a saddle, I want to mold into it and you only get that feeling from good leather. A good saddle has had a lot of ground work done in the seat. That means the seat has been carved and the leather molded onto the saddle tree by craftsmen.

BITS AND BITTING

Bits and bitting can be two of the most confusing aspects of horsemanship. The science of bitting is beyond the scope of this book. However, I will explain what works for my purposes in teaching and riding reining horses.

Bits work on certain pressure points on the horse's mouth and face; the bars of the mouth (areas of lower jaw devoid of teeth), the tongue, the roof of the mouth and the chin. Whatever bit you use and the way you adjust it influences one or more of these areas. However, no influence is as great as your hands on the reins. They have the strongest effect on the bit in your horse's mouth.

The three bits I use throughout most of my training program are an O-ring snaffle, a jointed mouthpiece on a seven inch shank and a loose-jawed, half inch low port on a seven inch shank.

Most of my bits are made by master bit-maker Greg

Darnall. Twenty years ago, I had a favorite shank with a jointed mouthpiece, often referred to as a Western snaffle. The combination of the mouthpiece and seven inch shank did well on almost every horse I trained. I had Darnall copy the bit and make me another one. It worked so well, he put other mouthpieces on it.

We found that the magic was in the shank, which is now called the "Loomis" shank. The length from the mouthpiece to the top of the bit and from the mouthpiece to the bottom of the bit is the key. The curve of the shank and the leverage the bit exerts suits most horses. They respond to it well. If the shanks are well-balanced, as Darnall's are, any mouthpiece works.

Before Darnall made my bits, I used a Crockett-Renaulde aluminum shank, copper mouthpiece with a low port. It was especially useful on any light-mouthed horses. I still use it today on horses that need an extra-light feel to the bit.

I got my first Crockett-Renaulde years ago when I was showing a fractious mare at the Denver Stock Show. While in Denver, I loved to go to Roy Barnes tack store. I'd go through his stock room in the back and look at the stuff he had piled up that was 50 years old. He couldn't sell it, but he hated to throw it away. I found a box of about 100 of these old bits. I bought one. It worked so well on everything I had, I called him and bought the whole box. All my friends wanted one too. For many years, it was a standard bit in the reining horse industry.

I start all 2-year-olds in a halter and then shift to a bosal when the animal gives its nose nicely to my hands. From there I usually go to a soft core, rawhide bosal or hackamore, no metal core wrapped in leather. The hackamore is big and thick, with a large diameter, around three quarters of an inch to an inch. Good hackamores are expensive. They are made of latigo leather, which is soft. Inexpensive hackamores can have metal cores or are made of rawhide, which is stiff. A soft hackamore actually has a lot more feel to it than a stiff one. A horseman knowledgeable about hackamores can really get a feel for the amount of pressure that is on the horse's nose or jaw with a good hackamore over a poor one. Hard core and rawhide hackamores sore a horse's jaw and nose easily.

The hackamore is similar in feel to the pull of the halter so it is a nice piece of transition head gear. The colt graduates to an O-ring snaffle as soon as he shows progress in the hackamore. In the early stages of breaking, I do shift back and forth between the hackamore and the snaffle before I decide which one the horse likes best. Eventually, though, all colts graduate to the O-ring snaffle. I may use that bit for six months, especially throughout all the basic training. My goal is to get a horse confident in it and performing all the maneuvers solidly before I go to a shank bit.

I won't put a shank bit on a horse that is pushing on me or one that I have to pull. Putting a shank bit on a young horse too soon slows down a training program. It does

(below) **Good hackamore bosals have a soft-core and are made of latigo leather.**

(bottom) **Snaffle bits are the traditional head gear for training young horses.**

143

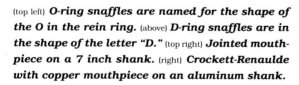

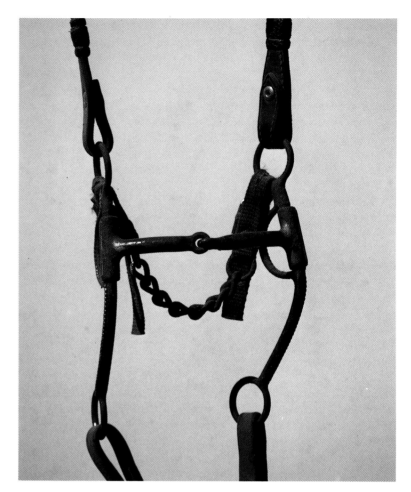

(top left) **O-ring snaffles are named for the shape of the O in the rein ring.** (above) **D-ring snaffles are in the shape of the letter "D."** (top right) **Jointed mouthpiece on a 7 inch shank.** (right) **Crockett-Renaulde with copper mouthpiece on an aluminum shank.**

(opposite top) **One half inch low port on a 7 inch shank.** (opposite bottom) **Three eighths inch low port on a 7 inch shank.**

nothing but teach a horse to pull against the rider's hand. I want my horse to be able to guide well and stop before I put him in a shank bit with a jointed mouthpiece and a chin strap.

When I do switch to the jointed mouthpiece shank bit, I am in no hurry to take the horse out of this bit either. I won't change the bit again until he is solid in all his maneuvers with this bit as well. I usually keep the horse in this bit until a couple of months prior to the NRHA Futurity. Then I switch to a loose-jawed one half inch low port with a seven inch shank. I like the loose-jaw mouthpiece that is hinged to the shank because it is similar to the bit I had on the horse. He adapts to it quickly and I lose less training time.

In bitting a horse, you need to be aware of the contour of his mouth. Open it and look inside before you decide what type of bit to use. If the horse has a large tongue, he will probably be a little heavy and pushy. Usually, a big tongue has thick, scaly skin and is less sensitive to the pressure placed upon it by the bit. Using a mullen mouthpiece (one with a slight curve to it) or a straight bar is generally not effective and could possibly cut such a tongue. There usually isn't much feel in a thick tongue. The best way to get more feel in a horse like this is to use a bit with a high port. The high port gives the horse some tongue relief. In other words, the tongue has a place to go.

Other horses, especially finely bred ones, have thin tongues covered with thin skin. They are especially sensitive to bit pressure. You can put a mullen mouth or straight bar in such a horse's mouth and you won't bother the tongue. It is so thin, it fits down in the cavity of the jaw. However, this horse's bars are usually thin-skinned as well and sometimes too much bit pressure from a solid bar bit bruises them. Sometimes, shank snaffles (bits with jointed mouthpieces) are best for these horses.

However, when I introduce my horses to a solid bar mouthpiece after I have used the jointed one, I always wrap the mouthpiece where it lays on the bars. I cut a four inch long strip of latex rubber (adhesive) tape and wrap it three times over the steel. Latex rubber can be found in any drugstore. It makes the mouthpiece much thicker and gives the mouth protection. I have found that a horse is much lighter on this than on steel.

I want to keep the bars as soft and tender as they were. Bruising bars makes a horse apprehensive and worried about his face. If you go one step farther and actually sore the bars, you will lose feeling, possibly permanently. I may take the wrapping off before I show the horse, but it won't hurt to leave it on. It depends upon the horse.

I like low port mouthpieces because the tongue has a little room with them. Such bits distribute the pressure about 50 percent between the tongue and bars and 50 percent to the chin. This is ideal unless you have a horse with an excessively thick tongue.

Roof or palate pressure is for older, experienced bridle horses, not young futurity prospects. Bits, with extremely high ports such as spade bits with spoons, half breeds or

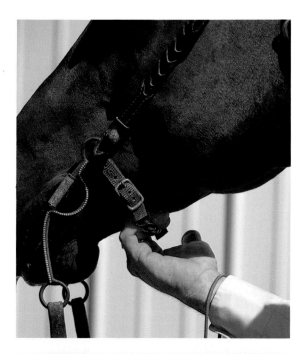

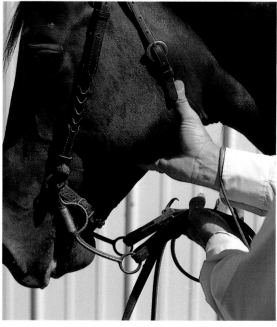

(top) *The chin strap should lay flat against the horse's jaw.* (above) *Adjust the chin strap so that the bit takes hold after the back three quarters of the swing.*

cathedrals, should only be in the hands of knowledgeable bridle horse riders. Few people know how to use roof pressure correctly.

THE BRIDLE — HEADSTALL, CHIN OR CURB STRAP AND CAVESSON

The type of chin or curb strap you use and its adjustment make a big difference in the way the bit action works on the horse. I use a half inch chain chin strap throughout my training program. I make sure it lays flat against the horse's chin, not twisted. When the horse comes into contact with the metal, it encourages him to back off the bit, not lean into it.

Leather chin straps were made for bits that use roof or palate pressure. If you use a leather chin strap on a bit that utilizes bar or tongue pressure, you may very well teach the horse to be heavy in the bridle. You are giving him something to lug and push against.

How you adjust the chin strap makes all the difference in the way a bit feels to a horse. If it is tight, it grabs the horse's chin before the full action of the bit takes place. The full action of the bit occurs when you take the slack out of the reins.

I like the chin strap to be adjusted where the bit takes hold after the back three quarters of the swing of the shank. In other words, as the shank sweeps back when the reins are pulled, I want the chin strap to take effect after the bit has acted on the horse's mouth.

When I say "whoa" and take the slack out of the reins slowly, that is when my horses go to the ground. Before I completely take that slack out, my horses are already in the ground and locked up. Actually, all I have to do then is balance them on the bridle, which means I take the slack out of the reins, but I don't pull on the horse's mouth.

If the chin strap is too tight, your bit will not have enough swing, it bites down too quickly on the chin.

If you have a chin strap so loose that the shank of the bit is as far back as it can go when the reins are pulled, the chin strap won't have a chance to work. The horse will start pulling on you.

You want the chin strap to engage just as the bit gets to the end of the swing of the shank. You get the full advantage of the swing before the strap takes effect.

When you change the holes of the headstall or chin strap, you change the entire balance of the bridle and bit action. Two months before the futurity, I figure out which bit each horse is comfortable in and never change from that point on. The bridle is adjusted perfectly for that horse and is used by no other horse.

Changing your chin strap or headstall one hole up or down is a dramatic change in the bite of the bridle. If you go one hole up with the headstall, it lays the bit up higher in the mouth and makes your chin strap tighter.

If you let the headstall down a hole, it is going to drop the bit lower in the horse's mouth and make your chin strap loose. If I drop the headstall down a hole, I tighten the chin strap one notch. If I raise the headstall, I let the chin strap out a notch.

Traditionally, wrinkles in the corners of the mouth have been used as guides as to how high to adjust a headstall. I don't follow the wrinkle theory. I like to rest the bit where it touches the upper corners of the lips and no farther. A horse develops a good feel in his mouth when he learns to pick up a bit and hold it. This is where the term "packing a bridle" comes from. He can't learn to pick up the bit and hold it with his tongue if the bit is too snug in his mouth.

Never pull the bridle out of a horse's mouth and rake it over his teeth when you slip the headstall off. You could make the horse lose his desire to pick the bit up again. I am never in such a hurry that I won't wait until the horse lets go of the bit on his own. If he won't spit it out in a reasonable length of time, I take hold of the bit gently and work it out of his mouth slowly.

A horse that learns to pick up his bit and hold it never gaps his mouth. A horse that gaps his mouth either has the bit flopping around too loose or the bit is adjusted too tightly.

I like to use cavessons on my horses. When I do put a shank bit on a young horse, I wait for a couple of weeks until the horse is comfortable with the new bit before I add the cavesson. I use it below the mouthpiece like a dropped noseband. I adjust it so that I can put two fingers between it and the horse's nose. That way a horse can open his mouth a half inch to an inch before he comes into contact with it. It is a correction device and reminds him to keep his mouth shut.

If the dropped noseband is on too tight, the horse can't open his mouth at all. When you do eventually take it off, the horse opens his mouth worse than ever and you've succeeded in creating a bad habit.

Cavessons or dropped nosebands prevent a horse from learning to flap his lower lip as a nervous habit. They encourage quiet mouths.

Cavessons prevent horses from opening their mouths too wide.

MARTINGALES

I use running martingales with O-ring snaffles during the early stages of training. I adjust the rings of the martingale to come up to the withers. Adjusted any lower and the martingale produces a pulley effect on the horse's mouth. I want the martingale to aid in keeping the horse from raising his head too high. I don't want it so tight it forces the horse's head down and causes him to be behind the bit.

During my finish work, I sometimes have a horse that wants to elevate his head, neck and front end too much and break through the bridle. I use a twisted wire snaffle and a running martingale adjusted half way up the shoulders. This is tight, but I use it only for a couple of days. I supple the horse in this and school him on the maneuvers. It softens the horse and teaches him not to brace against the bridle. He backs off rather quickly. Once he gives to the bridle, I take off the twisted wire and martingale. If I leave them on past that point, he would start jamming his front end into the ground when he stops. Then I have fixed one problem but

(top) *An example of a properly fitted snaffle bit, cavesson and martingale.*

(above) *An example of a running martingale adjusted so the rings come up to the withers.*

created a worse one. It usually takes about three days to fix such a problem. After that, it has an adverse effect.

SPURS

Spurs are aids, not tools of torture. I use a 10 point rowel spur that is fairly dull. I don't do the kind of spurring that sticks a horse. In my program, I lay the spur against the horse and push to make my point. Ten point spurs are good for pushing. With a 10 point spur, you have enough rowel to get the horse to move off of it, but it doesn't scare the horse as would spurs with long, pointed spikes.

PROTECTIVE LEG GEAR

Protective leg gear is important for the comfort of the reining horse. Splint boots, bell boots, skid boots and knee guards are required equipment for any reining horse enthusiast.

When a young horse is learning to use his feet, especially the fast-paced turnarounds and sliding stops, he steps on his feet or burns his fetlocks on the ground. Any injury to his feet wastes precious training time while you are waiting for the feet to heal.

Splint boots protect the splint bone, their namesake, as well as the entire cannon bone area from the knee down to and sometimes including the fetlock or ankle. There are different types of splint boots. Some just cover the cannon bone and others extend to the fetlocks or ankles.

I put splint boots on as religiously as I do a saddle and bridle. I don't care what stage of training the horse is in or how seasoned the horse is, I use splint boots when I tack him up. I use lightweight bell boots in conjunction with splint boots. Bell boots protect the horse's coronary band. However, heavy bell boots make the horse pick up his legs higher and that interferes with the horse's pretty movement.

In the course of learning how to put one foot over the other to turnaround, some horses hit the front of their knees with the accessory carpal bone on the back of their opposite knee. That bone rakes across the front of the knee and causes it to swell. I use knee guards on those horses that need it. If I see a little swelling on the horse's knee, I reach for the guards immediately. Horses usually hit their knees when they have their front feet out too far in front of them. When they learn to bring their feet back underneath themselves and step over with rhythm and cadence, they stop hitting their knees.

Good knee guards are hard to find. Most Western tack stores don't carry them or even know what they are. I have found high quality rubber knee guards at supply stores or catalogues that sell equipment for Standardbred racehorses. They need them in the regular course of their training. Tack supply businesses that cater to trainers involved with trotters and pacers carry them.

After a horse learns to use his front legs, he usually doesn't need bell boots or knee guards. However, I never do without splint boots.

In the early stages of training a young horse to stop, I may not need skid boots, but I always use them when I ask a horse to stop at speed. Skid boots protect the fetlocks of the hind legs from burning off hide as they contact the ground during sliding stops. I don't like the skid boots with hard rubber caps on them. They may last longer, but they also rub sores on the horse's fetlocks. I use skid boots made of good leather or synthetic materials.

No matter what piece of equipment you have, if you let it get dirty and stiff, it will cause you problems. Keep equipment clean and pliable. Use saddle soap and oil to preserve any leather goods.

Protective leg gear includes (top) *knee guards,* (above) *skid boots and* (left) *splint and bell boots.*

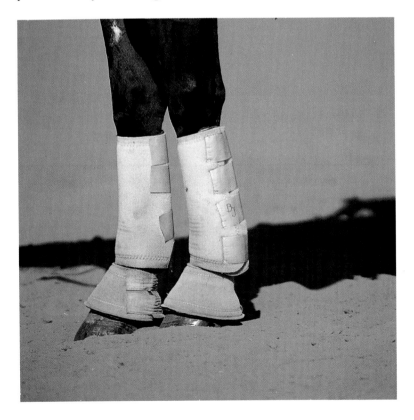

16

Mental Preparation for the Show Ring

One of the most important prerequisites for show ring competition is mental preparation. You can spend a whole year or more teaching your horse the mechanics of the maneuvers and if you both don't have it together mentally before you go into the arena, you've wasted your time and your horse's talents.

If you've come to the horse show with your horse peaked and ready to perform, just before you enter the class is not the time to run, stop, turn hard and burn him up. That is the quickest way to blow your horse's mind. Instead, back off, go back to basics. Make your horse listen to your commands; keep his maneuvers correct. Don't ask him for all he has to give at this point. More classes are lost in the warm-up pen than anywhere else. Riders rattle their horses' brains and fatigue their muscles. The horses have nothing left when it's their turn to show.

Have your horse sharp the day before you show him, but back off at the in-gate. When you're waiting for your number to come up, relax, gallop him quietly, soften and supple him. Let the horse down mentally before you walk into the pen.

Besides understanding your horse's mental state, one of the main aspects of mental preparation is to know your own disposition. If you are a tightly wound person, you need to relax and if you are a laid back person, you need to find a way to get motivated.

I tend to get wound up before I show. There are several things I do to help myself. One is that I don't have anything with sugar or caffeine in it the day of the show. Those stimulants make me walk faster, talk faster and think faster. They pump me up too much. I show better if I stay away from sugar and caffeine.

(previous pages) *In the early morning fog, this competitor mentally prepares for his class.*

(above) *One of Bob's show ring stars, Ready To Star, won the Pre-Futurity, Select Futurity and the Texas Classic. Ready To Star was also sixth in the NRHA Futurity. The stallion is by Boss Nowata Star and out of Ready Sugar Bars.*

I don't like to have any last minute problems before I show. Careful planning and organization is the key. I make sure that my horse is ready early, my equipment is clean and adjusted properly, my number is on and my chaps are at hand.

I make sure everything is ready 30 minutes before the class. That way I can get to the show pen in a casual manner. There I ride my horse quietly until it is my turn. This is crucial to my mental attitude. I don't like last minute rushing.

Although this is the best program for me, it may not be for you. If you have a laid back character, you may need something to stimulate you and get your adrenalin flowing. However, I would say that an organized program works for most people.

One of the worst things you can do to yourself is get upset before you show. Fighting with your horse before a class can be disastrous, as can arguing with someone. Stressful situations in your life don't help either.

You have to make a mental dump of everything on your mind and in your life right before you enter the arena. Train yourself to forget everything else. Nothing should be on your mind but the pattern you are about to run. That is why you are there and what you have worked so hard to accomplish. Don't blow it now.

One thing I do not like to do is spend time with negative people. I definitely will not hire a negative person to work for me. I wouldn't dream of hauling to a horse show with someone that was negative.

Negative thinking is a disease. Like cancer, it spreads everywhere. It spills over to your horse, your performance, your business and your family. Surrounding yourself with negative thinking and negative people hinders you drastically as a showman.

I am positive about everything. I know in my own experience that life is great and it is getting better everyday. That is the philosophy I live by.

I really believe in surrounding myself, my business, my whole life with optimistic thinking and confident people. I recommend reading books on the power of positive thinking. The books have made me even more secure and stronger in that line of thought.

Henry Ford once said, "If you think you can or you can't, you are correct." This is one of the most factual statements I've ever heard.

If you are a negative person, your performance will be as such, not only your performance in the arena, but your performance in life as well.

Horses are sensitive creatures. They can sense your mood and pick up on your vibrations. Often, your state of mind affects theirs. If you are upset or think something is going to go wrong, then it probably will.

A bad attitude defeats you even before you get into the pen. It causes you to distrust your horse and your whole training program. You find yourself picking at your horse. He reacts to your doubt and anxiety and becomes mentally stressed by the time you two enter the pen.

One of the best runs I've ever had in the arena I took on a gamble. It stands as a clear example of trust, but it was a calculated risk. I had a little mare named Betsy Bar Cody. I trained her all year as one of my futurity horses. I noticed, as the year went by, that she rode best the first 10 or 15 minutes of the work-out. She was bright-eyed. willing and performed perfectly in the early stages of our ride. She could do a lot of stuff in that 10 minute time period. But after she warmed up, she got cranky and pinned her ears back. Most horses don't listen well when they are fresh. You have to take the edge off them first. This mare was just the opposite. This told me that she probably didn't have much bottom or heart, as they say.

I showed her in the NRHA Futurity and she placed seventh, but she was crabby about it. A couple of months later, I entered her in a $10,000 added futurity in Denver. I thought about how bright-eyed and bushy-tailed she was in the first 10 minutes of riding, so I changed my usual game plan to suit her. The day of the finals was cold and blustery. It was 30 degrees and the wind was howling out of the Rocky Mountains. Right next to the Denver Coliseum is a 12 foot chain link fence which borders the interstate highway. I told the boy who was working for me to tack her up and tie her to the fence for 30 minutes. Two horses before our turn, he was to bring her to me in the arena. Her eyes were big and shiny; her ears stood straight up. I got on her, turned her once each way and then stepped into the pen. She was magnificent. It was the best run I ever had on that mare. We won the futurity.

It is nerve-wracking to take a fresh horse into a $10,000 added finals, but I trusted my judgment. I didn't let any negative thoughts bother my plan and there could have been several considering the conditions. But I knew my horse. I figured out what was best for her. I didn't second guess my instincts and I maintained a positive attitude.

What I am getting at with this illustration is that if you have trained your horse for a year and know what works for him, trust your knowledge of this horse and your training program. Trust that you will do a good job.

Another side to this story is that you should show your horse as fresh as you can without jeopardizing your chances with a fractious horse. Fatigued horses look tired in the arena. They lose some of the brilliance they had in the warm up pen. Fresh horses always present a more pleasing appearance to the judge than do horses that had the starch ridden out of them.

I don't care how good or bad the other exhibitors' runs have been or how the judges are marking or what they are looking for, I don't change my ride on a particular horse. I show my horse the way I trained him at home and to the best of his abilities. When you change your run to suit judges or when you try to outdo somebody else's run, you beat yourself. When you deviate from the performance you planned, you make a tactical error that will probably cost you the class.

Top Torino Cody was a finalist in the NRHA Futurity and Derby. He is a gelded son of Topsail Cody.

17

Judging Reining

Competition is the lifeblood of any performance horse organization, such as the National Reining Horse Association. Without the incentives and rewards of high-level contests, associations lack motivation and drive. They need a reason for being. Good, old-fashioned, "my horse is better than your horse" stirs the blood of any horseman, but only if the contest is fairly executed and honestly judged.

The NRHA provides both for riders interested in reining horses. According to the purpose of the association as stated in the NRHA Handbook:

"The National Reining Horse Association is a non-profit organization dedicated to the promotion of the Reining Horse. The Association was formed in 1966 to encourage the showing of Reining Horses by providing worthwhile purses for which they can compete, by developing a standard method under which all reining contests can be conducted, and by acting as a forum for their breeders and trainers."

This chapter is an edited version of the NRHA Handbook and Judge's Guide. It is printed with the permission of the association. It is not meant to take the place of either of those booklets. Please refer to the current NRHA Handbook and Judge's Guide for up-to-date information on judging and scoring reining patterns. Rules change from year to year. However, the following paragraphs should help you get started in understanding NRHA's unique judging system.

The American Quarter Horse Association recognized the NRHA's judging system in 1986 and recommends, but does not require, that their judges use it in AQHA approved shows. Please contact the AQHA for an updated rulebook if you plan to compete in an AQHA show.

The NRHA's and AQHA's addresses are in the Appendix.

The purpose of a reining horse and the intent behind reining horse competition is the heart and soul of the sport.

To quote the handbooks of both the NRHA and the AQHA:

"To rein a horse is not only to guide him but also to control his every movement. The best reined horse should be willingly guided or controlled with little or no apparent resistance and dictated to completely. Any movement on his own must be considered a lack of control. All deviations from the exact written pattern must be considered a lack of/ or temporary loss of control and therefore a fault that must be marked down according to severity of deviation. Credit should be given for smoothness, finesse, attitude, quickness and authority of performing various maneuvers, while using controlled speed."

Throughout the remainder of this chapter, all material in quotes is taken directly from the NRHA's Handbook or Judge's Guide.

REQUIRED MANEUVERS

There are eight maneuvers required of a reining horse in any pattern. Each pattern has its own series of maneuver combinations that the rider and horse must execute exactly. There are anywhere from nine to 13 different combinations of maneuvers. Remembering the pattern and performing it sequentially are the responsibilities of each competitor.

Stops

The rider asks the horse to come to a halt after a controlled gallop. The horse brings the "hind feet and hocks under himself in a locked position and slides on rear shoes." The preferred stop is one where the horse drops or lowers his hindquarters and brings his rear legs underneath him while his front legs continue forward motion in a pedaling fashion.

Spins (turn around)

"Spins are a series of 360 degree turns, executed over a stationary (inside) hind leg." The pivot leg should remain fixed throughout the spin. "Horses should demonstrate a similar cadence in speed in the right and left spins."

Rollbacks

"Rollbacks are 180 degree turns over the hindquarters." They are performed immediately following stops. The horse should not step ahead or back up prior to rolling back.

Circles

Circles are round paths sharing a common center and performed at a lope in a specific location. "There must be a clearly defined difference in the speed and size of the small, slow and large, fast circles." Each circle to the right should match the circle to the left in size and speed.

Back Ups

"The horse moves in reverse motion in a straight line a required distance."

Hesitate

"In a hesitate, the horse is required to remain motionless and relaxed." Hesitates are called for in certain areas of the patterns to show that the horse can stand quietly after being asked to move at speed. They demonstrate the horse's obedience.

Lead Changes

The horse changes leading legs from one side of the body to the other. In other words, if the horse is moving at a lope in the right lead, he must change to the left lead. Lead changes must be performed at specific locations in the pattern.

Run Downs

Run downs are runs performed in a straight line down the center or side of the arena according to the pattern. They are the approach to a stop and must be performed "at approximately the same speed as demonstrated in the large, fast circles."

SCORING

In judging a reining pattern, judges are asked to evaluate maneuvers individually. Each maneuver is then "scored in 1/2 point increments from a low of -1 1/2 to a high of +1 1/2. The total of the scores determines the exhibitor's final cumulative score.

The scoring scale is as follows:
- 1 1/2   Extremely poor
- 1   Very Poor
- 1/2   Poor
  0   Average
+ 1/2   Good
+ 1   Very good
+ 1 1/2   Excellent

After the pattern has been run, a judge may elect to use a mark "between -1 and +1 as a further evaluation of the horse's overall performance." That score is then added to the maneuver scores for a total composite score.

Scoring is determined on a 60-80 basis, with 70 considered an average performance.

Judges use official score sheets to record their individual assessments of each maneuver (see Appendix). The sheet has boxes in which the individual maneuver scores are written. Judges have stewards or scribes who are responsible for writing in the verbal scores given to them by the judges. Above the maneuver boxes are penalty boxes in which penalty scores are written. If the horse incurred a penalty on a particular maneuver, then the scribe records that in the appropriate box. The penalties scores are subtracted from the maneuver scores to determine the final score.

Judges can deduct anywhere from 1/2 point to five points depending upon the severity of the penalty.

The penalties are as follows:

5 points
a. freezing up in spins or rollbacks;
b. spurring in front of cinch;
c. use of free hand to instill fear;
d. touching saddle with free hand;
e. fall to the ground by horse or rider.

4 points
a. no change of lead for a complete circle.

3 points
a. delayed change of lead from start to 3/4 of a circle;
b. failure to change lead when a change is specified immediately prior to a run to the end of the pen.

2 points
a. break of gait. (not used when break in gait occurs in the first 1/4 of a circle of a canter departure);
b. delayed change of lead from start to 1/2 of the circle;
c. starting circle at a jog or exiting rollbacks at a jog beyond two strides but less than 1/2 circle or 1/2 the length of the arena;
d. failure to go beyond markers;
e. failure to change lead immediately prior to a run to the end of the pen if lead is picked up prior to stop.

1 point
a. delayed change of lead from start to 1/4 of the circle;
b. for over or under spinning up to 1/4 of a turn;
c. failure to change lead immediately prior to a run to the end of the pen if lead is picked up within two strides.

1/2 point
a. delayed change of lead by one stride;
b. starting circle at a jog or exiting rollbacks at a jog up to two strides;
c. for over or under spinning up to 1/8 of a turn.

The following situations result in a score of 60:
a. use of more than index or first finger between reins;
b. use of two hands or changing hands;
c. use of finger between romal reins. Free hand must be at least 16" from rein hand and not used to alter the tension or length of the reins from the bridle to the reining hand;
d. failure to complete pattern as written;
e. performing the maneuvers other than in specified order;
f. the inclusion of maneuvers not specified;
g. equipment failure that delays completion of pattern;
h. balking or refusal of command where pattern is delayed;
i. running away or refusal to guide where it becomes impossible to discern whether the entry is on pattern;
j. jogging in excess of 1/2 circle or 1/2 length of the arena while starting a circle, circling or exiting a rollback;
k. overspins of more than 1/4 turn.

The following situations result in no score:

a. willful abuse of animal in show arena;
b. use of illegal equipment, including wire on bits, bosals or curb chains;
c. use of illegal bits, bosals or curb chains;
d. use of tack collars, tie downs or nosebands;
e. use of electric shockers, whips or bats;
f. use of any attachment which alters the movement of or circulation to the tail;
g. failure to provide horse and equipment to the appropriate judge for inspection;
h. disrespect or misconduct by the exhibitor.

EQUIPMENT

a. bits, must be free of mechanical devices;
b. rope or leather bosals free of wire, iron or mechanical devices.
c. curb chains, must be at least 1/2" in width, free of barbs, wire or twists and lay flat against horse's jaw.

Topsail Cody marked the highest scores in NRHA history when he won the 1980 NRHA Futurity. The judges awarded him two 78's and 78 1/2.

159

18

Pattern Strategy

Showing reining horses is like being a draftsman and a pool player. You have to know how to draw your pattern and execute it exactly and you have to know where your next move is going to be.

There are many variables to think about in any reining competition. Pattern strategy is both mental and physical. There are several things you can do to help yourself get through the class.

The number one rule is to never run your pattern to suit a particular judge. Often, before a class you hear people ask, "What does this judge like? Does he like a hard run or a soft run? Is he partial to marking big stops or are fast spins his favorite?"

When you try to please a certain judge, you are bound to make mistakes. Your horse will be confused as to what you are trying to do. Every horse responds to the show ring differently. If you show your horse to the best of his ability that day, you will mark the highest you are capable. If you deviate from that and listen to everybody talk in the bleachers, you won't mark as well as if you had stayed with your original game plan.

In reinings with one or more preliminary go-rounds, don't burn up your horse in the eliminations. You may have nothing left for the finals. You do have to do enough to make the finals, however. Show your horse to the best of his ability, but back off a little. Don't put extreme pressure on him. Go for correctness instead of blazing speed. You may have your best runs doing that. In the finals, use your horse to his maximum, but no more. If you try to surpass your horse's talents, you will end up with nothing. Never crowd a horse beyond his capabilities, mentally or physically.

(previous pages) **_Knowing the pattern, remembering it and then executing it according to your horse's best abilities are all part of being a good showman._**

Ideally, a good showman is a rider who marks a respectable score in the first go-round, the same or a bit better in the second and has his best run in the finals. If you mark the same score all the way through, then you are a consistent showman. If your first go-round is your best, you may be a poor showman. However, you may be a good showman, but your horse is a cheater or you scared it into not performing well.

Be aware of where the markers are. Each pattern has pylons or cones that designate the boundaries of the pattern and where maneuvers are to take place. I always study the arena to find dead center, around which the entire pattern should be run. The center marker is dead center of the arena lengthwise. To determine the center of the width of the arena, I look for the middle of the in-gate. I then draw an imaginary + in the center of the arena where the two lines cross. That is where I stop, spin, change leads or whatever is called in the pattern to be performed in the center.

You can win a lot of reinings by simply running a correct pattern, following it exactly according to the rule book specifications. Make your circles perfectly round. Run large, fast circles definitely large and fast. Do the same for small, slow circles. Your runs down the fence should be straight as an arrow. Your rollbacks should be performed at 180 degrees or half a circle. Lope out of your rollbacks and back into the same tracks you made getting to the stop.

If there is a stop and a back up in your pattern, be conscious of your horse's ability to back up. If he is a horse that backs crooked or poorly, don't go too far past center or you will have a long distance to back up. But if your horse backs fancy, go farther past center and show him off.

All of the patterns ask you to hesitate somewhere in the run. "Hesitate" means stop for approximately three seconds.

Patterns that ask you to run down the wall or fence require that you stay 20 feet off the wall. Running too close to the wall can get you in a lot of trouble. A horse that runs too close to the wall tends to lean into it with his shoulders and rib cage. When a horse leans, he can't run in a straight line and probably won't stop well either. He'll be crooked.

Also, since all rollbacks are towards the wall, you may not have enough room to maneuver. Worse yet, you may run over one of the judges, who are always positioned along the wall. They won't be impressed with your guiding abilities and it'll show up in your score.

If the class comes down to two runs of equal quality, but one rider executes the pattern exactly and the other is all over the place, judges opt for the exact pattern every time.

The only time to deviate from the pattern is under adverse ground conditions. A good showman knows the kind of dirt in which he has to perform. He studies the dirt before and during a class to check for good and bad spots. Almost all arenas are wet down before a class to settle the dust. Sometimes, one area receives too much water or the dirt content in that spot holds too much moisture. The ground is sticky, which makes it difficult to slide or spin. Wet spots are darker in color compared to the lighter dry areas

next to them.

If possible, watch other runs to see what kinds of problems other riders are having. Often, after several runs, the ground develops holes where too many horses have stopped or turned around.

In either case, it is preferable to deviate from the pattern by five to 10 feet either side of the problem area rather than suffer the consequences of performing in bad dirt. Give yourself and your horse every chance possible to show the judge what you can do. In those situations, I find a different center as a reference point. Instead of keying on the middle of the in-gate as a center line, I look at the gate hinges as my new center point.

If you aren't able to study the ground as the class progresses, have someone you trust watch for you. He or she can then come out to the warm-up pen and tell you about any problems before it's your turn to go.

Since deviating from the pattern even slightly is cause for immediate disqualification, remembering the pattern is of the utmost importance. I do several things to help myself

A modern day horse with a lot of foundation breeding behind him, Two T Pachuco Wimpy is by Easter Gentleman and out of a daughter of Pachuco Wimpy. With Bob in the saddle, he was a finalist in the 1988 NRHA Futurity. Bob's daughter, Bobbie Jo, rode "Chuck" in the Freestyle Reining class at the 1989 NRHA Futurity show and impressed the crowd with a bridleless performance.

remember the pattern.

Thirty minutes before I show, I concentrate on nothing but the pattern and how my horse will run it. I don't like to talk to anyone and I want to be left alone. I leave any problems back at the stalls. If anything was bothering me earlier in the day, I make a mental dump of it, erase it from my mind.

I run every step of the pattern over and over in my mind. However, it is important how I do it. I allow nothing else in my thoughts except the pattern I am about to run and the run I am going to make on the particular horse I have. I run the pattern mentally the way it fits the horse I am riding. I focus on the places where this horse needs help and those where he is strong and I really want to show him off. I do this right up to the gate. On a walk-in pattern, I go over the pattern in my head for the final time as I walk from the gate to the middle of the pen. I fill my mind with nothing but the pattern until I have completed it.

If you let other things go through your mind, especially the last 30 minutes before you show, you will lose some of the effectiveness of your run. I actually talk myself through the run and draw an imaginary pattern in the air with my fingers. My fingers do the riding. It may look funny to someone who doesn't know what I am doing, but I don't care. It is an effective method for remembering things. It deeply instills the pattern in my brain.

Things that you have to count in a run, such as spins, are easier if you have done them in your mind first. You unconsciously count them in the pen while you are doing them. You won't even know it. You eliminate a lot of mistakes and going off pattern by having yourself mentally zeroed in on what you are doing.

Performing the required number of spins or turn arounds is usually one area where riders go off pattern easily. The trick I use to remembering how many spins I've done is to count the spin as I am completing it. For example, in the patterns that have four spins, I say to myself mentally, "one" during the first spin, "two" during the second spin and "three" during the third spin. When I say "four," I should be done with the fourth spin. If the pattern calls for four and one quarter spins, I say to myself "four and a quarter." On the word quarter, I am done.

The only times I have gone off pattern are times when I didn't prepare myself like this. I have never gone off pattern in 25 years when I properly prepared myself mentally.

Running through the pattern quickly in your mind allows other thoughts to leak into your thought pattern, destroying your concentration. Use mental imaging. The only way you can do that and block out everything else is to detail the run. Imagine each step your horse takes, prepare him for every maneuver, secure him where he needs it, show him off where he shines.

Also, a quick run down in your mind programs your brain to have you run the pattern that way as well, 100 miles an hour.

I am a high strung person. It is important that my mental

preparation is slow. It doesn't take much for me to speed up. I can get like an old-time movie. If I prepare myself quickly, I have a wreck. I can speed up mentally so fast that it is crucial for me to get laid back. I have to continually tell myself to "back off, back off."

Don't ever think you can't do some things with the human brain. You can program yourself to get beat. If you think you can't do it and you are going to screw up. you will.

To be a good showman, you must be a thinker and a planner. You have to know the pattern, carefully consider each part of your run and plan your strategy. You have to know the arena conditions, the ground, the markers and dead center. When you finish one maneuver, you need to know where you should be to get into perfect position for the next maneuver. A winning reining pattern is a well thought out and executed plan of action.

There are nine approved patterns in National Reining Horse Association competition. The following are current patterns as described in the NRHA Handbook as of the printing of this book. For up-to-date information, contact the NRHA. The organization's address is listed in the Appendix.

Here are some strategies to consider in negotiating each one. Many of the approaches to the maneuvers are similar, so there is some repetition in my guidelines. Helpful hints I mention in Pattern 1 apply throughout all the patterns.

NRHA PATTERN 1

1. Run at speed to the far end of the arena past end marker and do a left rollback — no hesitation.

Find the center of the arena lengthwise and head straight towards that spot. Go past the marker, but don't run into the wall. The judge won't mark you for fencing your horse. When you pass the marker, stop. Don't rush the rollback. Let your horse complete 95 percent of the stop. When he is almost stopped, ask your horse to flow into the rollback. Don't jerk him around. Leave the rollback at a lope, but not a hard, scrambling gallop. Build your speed to the next maneuver.

2. Run to opposite end of the arena past end marker and do a right rollback — no hesitation.

Run to the right rollback in the same tracks you did for the first one. Perform the same flowing rollback you did before.

3. Run past center of the arena, do a sliding stop, back straight to the center of the arena. Hesitate.

This is where you should be knowledgeable of how well your horse can back up. Legally, you have to back up 10 feet. If your horse is not a good backer, stop just past the marker and back up. If he can back up a mile, trust him and go 20 to 25 five feet past the center marker to really show him off. In either case, whether you back up a little or a long way, the important thing is to be in the center of the arena when you are finished backing.

Hesitate for three seconds and begin the next maneuver immediately.

4. In the center of the arena complete four spins to the right.

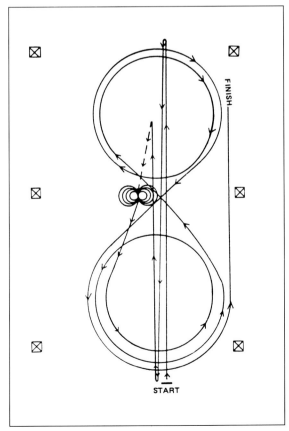

18 A — NRHA Pattern 1

The hard stops that Britton Princess made helped her win the 1972 NRHA Futurity.

When you approach your spins, do the first three steps slowly, softly and precisely. Three steps is usually somewhere between a quarter and a half a turn. Now start building speed. By the time you finish the first turn, you should be turning nicely. Your second turn should be quicker. By your third and fourth turns, you should be really spinning fast. This type of spin marks well. If you blurt into the first turn, you may get out of position and your horse's feet may get tangled up. Your last turn may be slower than the first one and you'll get a low mark.

A good way to remember how many spins you have done is to count them after each one is completed. Each time you pass your beginning point, count one, two, three, four or however many there are for that pattern. If you count at the beginning of the spin instead of after it is through, you can get confused and forget how many you have done.

5. Complete four and a quarter spins to the left so that the horse is facing left wall or fence. Hesitate.

When you finished your first set of spins to the right, you were facing the far end of the arena. Begin and end your left spins in the same manner you did the right ones, slowly building speed. Now, however, you must go another quarter of a turn and face the left wall. Remember to count the quarter of a turn after the fourth spin, by saying to yourself, "four and a quarter." By the time you've said "quarter," you're through. It is like taking a short breath. Stop after you say "quarter" or you'll over spin.

Your next maneuver calls for a left lead departure, so make sure you are perfectly straight to start.

6. Begin on left lead and complete two circles to the left. The first circle small and slow — the second circle large and fast.

Don't rush lead departures. First, get your horse's body

into the correct position for a left lead. Once you commit yourself to the lead. go. If it doesn't feel right. wait until it is. But when you do go. don't hesitate. If you pull up and start again. you'll get a penalty point.

Lope the small circle slowly. What you are demonstrating here is speed control. You must show a definite change in speed between the circles. When you go into your large. fast circle. don't jump into it at a full gallop. You'll scare your horse and next time. he might not give you another slow. small circle. Take the entire center of the arena and the first quarter of the large. fast circle to build speed. By the time you complete that first quarter of your large. fast circle. you reach a good speed.

7. Change leads at the center of the arena.

After you have completed your second large. fast circle. aim for the imaginary + in the center of the arena. One stride before you come to that +. ask for a lead change. By the time you reach that +. your horse should be changing in mid-stride and you'll be right on target.

8. Complete two circles to the right. The first circle small and slow — the second circle large and fast.

The instant you change leads after the second large. fast circle. sit down on your horse. drop the reins a little to indicate to him to slow down. Go into your small. slow circle. Again. when you reach the center of the arena. take the time to build to a large. fast circle. By the time you are into the last three quarters of the large circle. you are at top speed for that horse.

9. Change leads in the center of the arena. and begin a large, fast circle to the left. Do not close this circle. Run straight down the side of the arena past center marker and do a sliding stop approximately 20 feet from wall or fence.

Again, change leads right on the +. You will be on the left lead as you come around to the wall. Continue down the wall. Don't go to the middle to close the circle. Come to a sliding stop after the center marker. Remember to stay 20 feet off the wall.

10. Hesitate to demonstrate the completion of the pattern.

Count to three and then leave the pattern.

11. Rider must drop bridle to the judge.

NRHA PATTERN 2

1. Begin at center of the arena. Complete two circles to the right. The first circle small and slow — the second circle large and fast.

This is a walk-in pattern. Manners are important in a reining horse. Dancing and prancing horses who don't come to the center quietly start off on the wrong foot as far as the judges are concerned. Present a relaxed picture to the judge with your horse walking flat-footed and on a loose rein. The horse should look like he is happy to be there.

Walk down the wall. When you reach the center marker, make a left turn and walk straight to the center. Start your right lead departure exactly on the imaginary +, not before or after it. It's a nice touch to stop in the middle and hesitate for a few seconds and then begin your circles.

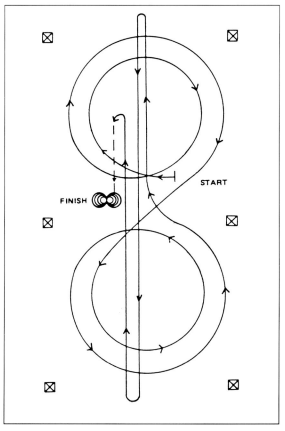

18 B — NRHA Pattern 2

Follow the suggestions in Pattern 1 for circles, speed differential and lead changes.

2. Change leads in the center of the arena.

3. Complete two circles to the left. The first circle small and slow — the second circle large and fast.

4. Change leads at the center of the arena.

5. Run to the far end of the arena — past end marker and do a left rollback — no hesitation.

This maneuver, where you change leads at the center of the arena out of a circle, then run down the far end and do a rollback is more difficult than changing leads during a circle and running down the wall. This maneuver can be made to look quite bad by going too far in the center to change leads, then having to veer back to the center to turn off and run down for a rollback.

To eliminate the problem, don't go near the imaginary + in the middle to change leads before heading down for a rollback. Go past the three quarter mark in closing the circle, but 10 to 15 feet before you get to the center of the arena where you would normally change leads, straighten your horse and change at that point. Give yourself room to smoothly turn the angle to run down the center of the arena. Hunt the center of the arena for this run down. Look at the in-gate or whatever marker you have chosen as your center width line.

If you go too far and are in the center of the arena to change leads, you are not going to be able to run straight to the rollback. You'll have to make a loop to get back into line for the rollback. This is one time when you shouldn't go to the center of the arena for a lead change. Look closely at the pattern diagram and see that it isn't necessary to do so to complete the pattern properly.

6. Run to opposite end of the arena — past end marker and do a right rollback — no hesitation.

7. Run past the center of the arena and do a sliding stop.

8. Back straight to the center of the arena. Hesitate.

For your stop, run past the center marker only as far as you want to back up. Again, if your horse is a poor backer, don't point this out to the judge with a long distance back up. On the other hand, if he is fancy, show him off at this maneuver. A good back up tells the judge how light your horse's mouth is. Back up to center marker. Hesitate for about three seconds.

9. Complete four spins to the right.

10. Complete four spins to the left.

The pattern doesn't say anything about hesitating, so go right into your left spin, but without rushing. Don't hurry your horse into your first set of spins or your second. Take time to position him for a smooth approach into each spin.

11. Hesitate to demonstrate the completion of the pattern.

12. Rider must drop bridle to the judge.

NRHA PATTERN 3

1. Begin approximately 20 feet from the left wall or fence on the right lead.

This is another walk-in pattern. Walk to your starting

point. Stop for a few seconds to indicate that you are ready to begin the pattern at the designated point. Begin right lead departure promptly. Don't trot into it or you will incur a penalty.

2. Lope straight down the side of the arena staying 20 feet from the fence, circle at the top end of the arena and run straight down the opposite end of arena past center marker and do a left rollback. *

This pattern requires that the horse be on the proper lead when it approaches the curve. If you are on the wrong lead, you will have to change leads on your run down to catch the curve in the proper lead.

Remember, it is okay to come out of your rollback on the right or left lead. However, it is a nice touch of showmanship to come out on the correct lead for the situation. In this case, the left lead.

However, if you are in the wrong lead, wait until you reach the curve to change. Then you can change comfortably and smoothly. If you change down the straightaway, it might not be as pretty if the judge sees you cuing your horse excessively.

On the straightaway after the curve, don't start building your speed for the run down until you have completed your curve. Be a couple of strides into the straightaway. Then start building your speed slowly. You want to be gaining speed at the stop. A horse that is loping at a constant speed won't stop as pretty as one that is gaining speed. A horse that is slowing down won't stop pretty at all and may even jam his front end into the ground. The elevation and the momentum of a horse that builds speed helps him tuck his hindquarters underneath for an impressive stop.

3. Continue straight down the other side at least 20 feet from the wall or fence and back around the top of arena (horse to be on left lead at this point) running straight down the other side of arena at least 20 feet from the wall, past center marker, and do a right rollback.*

Whenever the pattern says run down and do a rollback, it doesn't say stop and rollback. However, it is taken for granted that you have to stop in order to perform the rollback. Even though the pattern doesn't call for a sliding stop, most riders take the opportunity to stop that way to impress the judge.

4. Continue up the left side of the arena to center marker and at center marker horse should be on right lead; continue to center of arena on right lead.

Obviously, it helps to come out of that last rollback on the right lead. You don't have much time to change leads if you aren't already on the right lead. Make sure you turn right to go to the center of the arena at the center marker. Don't cut off that corner in a hurry to get to the center of the arena.

5. Complete two circles to the right; the first small and slow, the second large and fast. Change leads at the center of the arena.

Ask your horse to change leads at 10 to 15 feet or a stride before you hit the imaginary + in the middle (see Pattern 1 for circle and lead change suggestions). In this pattern the circles

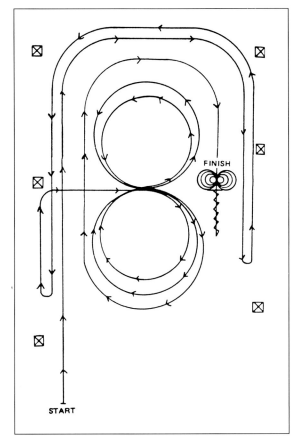

18 C — NRHA Pattern 3

and lead changes are marked as one maneuver, not two separate ones.

6. Complete two circles to the right, the first small and slow, the second large and fast. Change leads at the center of the arena.

7. Begin a large, fast circle to the right — do not close this circle.

8. Continue straight down the side at least 20 feet from the wall or fence, circle the end of the arena and run straight down the opposite side of the arena past center marker and do a sliding stop — at least 20 feet from the wall. Back up at least 10 feet. Hesitate.*

Here, it requires a minimum of 10 feet for the back up. Again, if you have a fancy backer, go a little farther. If not, stop right after you pass it.

In every maneuver in these patterns, it emphasizes staying 20 feet off the wall. That is for the rider's good and it is a rule. Breaking the rule will give you a 60 score or a penalty at the judge's discretion.

9. Complete four spins to the right and four spins to the left.

You approach this maneuver out of a back up. Don't confuse your horse and start turning him while he is still backing up. It looks terrible to the judge. After you have completed the back up, position your horse's body and then start into your spins slowly and methodically.

It's important that you shut spins off exactly in the middle of your imaginary + for the maneuver. An eighth or a quarter of a spin over or under causes you to lose points in any of your turnarounds. Anything beyond the quarter over or under spin is disqualification. Be precise. Don't ask for more speed in spins than you can handle.

10. Hesitate to demonstrate the completion of the pattern.

11. Rider must drop bridle to the judge.

*Horses may come out of rollback on either lead; however, they should be on correct lead when rounding the end of the arena.

NRHA PATTERN 4

1. Begin at the center of the arena. Complete two circles to the right. The first one large and fast — the second circle small and slow.

This is a walk-in pattern and manners are important as your horse walks down the right wall to approach the center of the arena. It doesn't matter if you take your right lead departure at a walk or if you hesitate and then begin. You start this pattern with a large, fast circle, which is an excitable maneuver to a horse. If you blurt this horse into a fast gallop as you start your lead departure, you are going to stir him up. The rest of his pattern might not be as pretty as it could have been. Instead, get into the right lead and take the first quarter of that circle to build your speed from a slow lope to a fast lope. Lope the last three quarters of the circle at a comfortably fast pace. Come to the center of the pen, sit down, relax and let your horse know it is time to shut down that speed. The

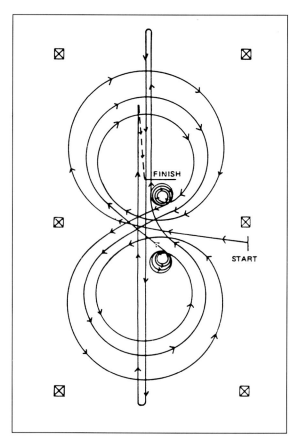

18 D — NRHA Pattern 4

quicker and the smoother your horse slows down from a fast circle to a slow one, the better you will score. Your speed control should be instantaneous.

2. At the center of the arena stop and complete four spins to the right — horse to be facing left wall or fence. Hesitate.

This pattern is much easier if you remember that you always spin to the inside of the circle. Forget left or right if it will help you. Just remember to spin to the inside of the circle and you will always be correct.

Don't rush into the spins. Ask your horse to stop and wait until he starts softly. Let him get three steps into the circle before you ask for speed in the spins.

Don't forget to hesitate. If you run right into the next maneuver, it will cost you in scoring.

3. Begin on left lead and complete two circles to the left. The first circle large and fast — the second circle small and slow.

Again, take the first quarter of your circle to build your speed and shut it down in the middle before you take the small, slow circle. There should be a definite size difference between the two circles. The small, slow circle should be at least from one half to two thirds the size of the large, fast.

4. At the center of the arena stop and complete four spins to the left — horse should be facing left wall or fence. Hesitate.

5. Begin on right lead and make a figure eight on top of the large circles.

Your figure eight should be a large, fast figure eight, as big or bigger than your large, fast circle. Obviously, you have a lead change. Do it in the center.

6. Close figure eight and change leads in the center of the arena. Run to the far end of the arena past end marker and do a left rollback — no hesitation.

Here again is that lead change that you don't go to the center of the pen to do. Instead, change leads 15 feet before you hit the middle, as your horse is changing directions. Turn and head straight down to the end of the pen for your rollback. The key to getting down to do the rollback is getting out of your circles and lead changes smoothly so you are loping up the center of the pen, not at an angle trying to get back to the center.

7. Run to the opposite end of the arena - past end marker and do a right rollback — no hesitation.

Remember, go past the end marker, but not so far past it you end up fencing your horse on the end wall. Stop comfortably between the marker and the wall.

8. Run past the center of the arena and do a sliding stop.

9. Back straight to the center of the arena or at least 10 feet.

10. Hesitate to demonstrate the completion of the pattern.

11. Rider must drop bridle to the judge.

NRHA PATTERN 5

1. Begin at center of the arena facing left wall or fence. Begin on left lead and complete two circles to the left. The

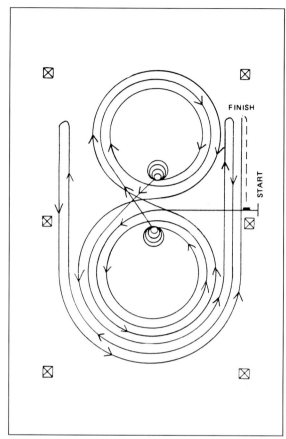

18 E — NRHA Pattern 5

first one large and fast — the second one small and slow.

Like Pattern 4, this pattern begins with a high pace maneuver. Don't jump into your left circle at a dead run. You may excite your horse and blow his mind for the rest of the pattern.

2. At the center of the arena stop and complete four spins to the left. Horse to be facing left wall or fence. Hesitate.

3. Begin on the right lead. Complete two circles to the right. The first one large and fast — the second one small and slow.

You are allowed to take two walking steps to get into a lead departure. Beyond that is a penalty. The best way to eliminate a penalty is don't use your two walking steps. Sometimes you may need them when you are out of position and in a tight bind, but don't use them purposely. If you plan on using two, you might end up using three and receive a penalty. A good showman takes all lead departures from a standstill.

4. At the center of the arena stop and complete four spins to the right. Horse to be facing left wall or fence. Hesitate.

Again, forget right and left. Remember to turn into the inside of the circle and you won't go wrong with the direction of your spin.

5. Begin on left lead and make a figure eight on top of the large circles.

Make the figure eight the same size or larger than your large circle and approximately the same speed.

6. Close figure eight and begin a large, fast circle to the left. Do not close the circle but run straight down the side past center marker and do a right rollback at least 20 feet from wall or fence, no hesitation.*

7. Continue back around previous circle, do not close the circle but run straight down opposite side of the arena past center marker and do a left rollback at least 20 feet from wall or fence, no hesitation.

8. Continue back around previous circle, do not close the circle but run straight down the side past the center marker and do a sliding stop at least 20 feet from wall or fence.

9. Back over slide tracks a minimum of 10 feet.

It doesn't look good and some judges will hurt you if you lope 50 feet past center and back only 10 feet. You will be 40 feet off center of completing your pattern. It's poor showmanship. Unless you are sure your horse can back straight for a long way, don't attempt it. It means your horse doesn't guide well in reverse. It also shows that after all the work you have done in the pattern, your horse doesn't have much mouth left at the end. It leaves a bad impression in the judges' minds.

10. Hesitate to demonstrate the completion of the pattern.

11. Rider must drop bridle to the judge.

*Horses may come out of rollback on either lead; however, they should be on correct lead going around end of arena.

NRHA PATTERN 6

1. Walk in to the center of the arena and complete four spins to the right. Hesitate.

2. Complete four spins to the left. Hesitate.

This is a pattern where you walk to the center of the arena and the first thing you do is turnaround. Knowing this is the first maneuver, don't make the mistake in the warm-up pen of really lighting a fire under your horse to make him turnaround. You may go to the pen, spin a blur and mark well on the spins. But when you finish the spins, you have a bunch of circles to lope. If you light too big a fire under your horse, he may be too chargey in the circles to follow.

Instead, ride quietly in the warm-up pen. If you practice spins, do them slowly and emphasize correctness, not speed. Then trust your horse to follow your commands to speed up once in the pen.

In any pattern, balanced spins look good to the judge. They should appear to be the mirror image of one another, same speed, same style. If your horse spins well to one direction and not the other, it says that your horse is bad or stiff in one direction.

3. Begin on the left lead, complete two large, fast circles to the left. One small, slow circle to the left, change leads.

This is a nice pattern because in the first two maneuvers you have got your horse really doing something. Now you have two large, fast circles. If your horse is broke, these two circles should relax him. It looks impressive if, after the fast maneuvers, your horse drops down in speed into a slow, casual lope for the small circle. Your horse is in hand if he can handle all the speed in a quiet, calm manner.

Changing leads is marked as part of this maneuver. Ask for your lead change one stride before you hit dead center.

4. Complete two large, fast circles to the right, and one small, slow circle to the right, change leads.

Your horse's speed control is on display here again.

5. Begin a large, fast circle to the left. Do not close this circle, but run down the side past the center marker and do a right rollback at least 20 feet from the wall or fence.

6. Continue back around previous circle, run down opposite side of the arena past center marker and do a left rollback at least 20 feet from the wall or fence.

7. Continue back around previous circle. Do not close this circle, but run down the side past center marker and do a sliding stop. Back straight to the center of the arena or at least 10 feet.

8. Hesitate to demonstrate the completion of the pattern.

9. Rider must drop bridle to the judge.

NRHA PATTERN 7

1. Run at speed to the far end of the arena past end marker and do a left rollback — no hesitation.

2. Run to the opposite end of the arena past end marker and do a right rollback — no hesitation.

3. Run past center of the arena, do a sliding stop, back straight to the center of the arena. Hesitate.

This is a fast-paced pattern in the beginning. You begin at a gallop, run practically the entire length of the arena, do three stops and two rollbacks. If your horse is all stirred up because you ran at break-neck speed, he may not handle well for the

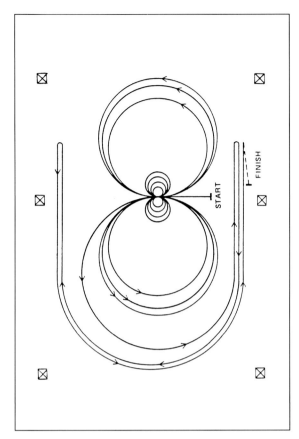

18 F — NRHA Pattern 6

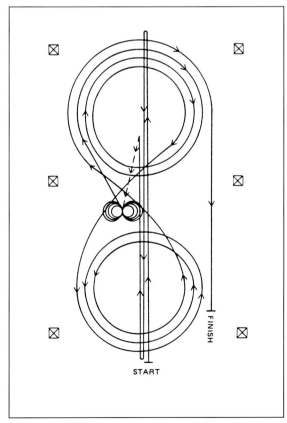

18 G — NRHA Pattern 7

following spins and circles. Control your gallop so you don't have a frantic animal to deal with in the rest of the pattern. You should know how your horse behaves under high speed maneuvers. Don't crowd him past the point that he won't come back nicely in hand.

4. Complete four spins to the right.

5. Complete four and a quarter spins to the left. Hesitate.

6. Beginning on the right lead complete three circles to the right, the first two circles large and fast, the third circle small and slow.

There is one salvation in this pattern. After your run downs, stops, rollbacks and spins, you now have a chance to get your horse back in control if he is too excited. You have three circles in which to calm him. If you had only one circle to do it, you might not get it done. By having two large circles before you have to lope a small, slow one, you have time to get his mind right again.

7. At the center of the arena — change leads.

8. Complete three circles to the left, the first two circles large and fast, the third circle small and slow.

9. At the center of the arena — change leads.

10. Begin a large fast circle to the right. Do not close this circle but run straight down the side of the arena past the center marker and do a sliding stop approximately 20 feet from the wall or fence.

There is a chance here for the rider to forget the pattern and back up after the last sliding stop. Remember, you have already completed a back up in the middle of the arena. Many patterns have a back up after the last stop and it is easy to forget which one you are doing.

11. Hesitate to demonstrate the completion of the pattern.

12. Rider must drop bridle to the judge.

NRHA PATTERN 8

1. Begin at center — horse should be facing left wall or fence.

2. Complete four spins to the left.

Although the pattern does not call for a "hesitate," don't be in a hurry going into your right spins. Take the time to get into the approach slowly.

3. Complete four spins to the right. Hesitate.

4. Begin on the right lead and complete two circles to the right. The first circle large and fast - the second circle small and slow.

5. Change leads in the center of the arena.

6. Complete two circles to the left. The first circle large and fast — the second circle small and slow.

7. Change leads in the center of the arena.

8. Begin a large fast circle to the right. Do not close this circle but run straight down the side past center marker and do a left rollback at least 20 feet from wall or fence, no hesitation.*

9. Continue back around top half of previous circle, do not close this circle but run straight down opposite side of the arena past center marker and do a right rollback at least

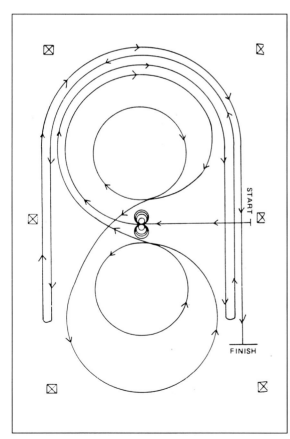

18 H — NRHA Pattern 8

20 feet from wall or fence — no hesitation.*

10. Continue back around previous circle, do not close this circle but run straight down opposite side of the arena past center marker and do a sliding stop at approximately 20 feet from wall or fence.

11. Back straight to center of arena or at least 10 feet.

12. Hesitate to demonstrate the completion of the pattern.

13. Rider must drop bridle to the judge.

*Horse may come out of rollback on either lead; however, they should be on correct lead when rounding the end of the arena.

NRHA PATTERN 9

1. Run past center marker and do a sliding stop.

2. Back straight to the center of the arena. Hesitate.

3. Complete four spins to the right.

4. Complete four and a quarter spins to the left. Hesitate.

5. Begin on left lead. Complete two circles to the left. The first one small and slow — the second one large and fast.

In this maneuver, use the "hesitate" to get your horse's body into the correct position for the lead departure. There is no reason to blurt into a sloppy lead departure when you have the time to execute a proper one. Two walking steps into a lead departure are allowed, but don't use the steps unless you must. It looks better to start into the lead departure from a standstill.

6. Change leads in the center of the arena.

7. Complete two circles to the right. The first one small and slow — the second one large and fast.

Right after you change leads from a large fast circle, you must go immediately into a small, slow one. It is impressive if your horse can go quickly into a slow lope from a fast lead change.

8. Change leads in the center of the arena.

9. Begin a large, fast circle to the left. Do not close this circle but run straight down the side past center marker and do a right rollback at least 20 feet from wall or fence, no hesitation.*

10. Continue back around top half of previous circle. Do not close this circle but run straight down opposite side of the arena past center marker and do a left rollback at least 20 feet from wall or fence, no hesitation.*

11. Continue back around previous circle, do not close this circle but run straight down the side past the center marker and do a sliding stop at least 20 feet from wall or fence.

This is another pattern where there is no back up after the last stop. Remember, you did your back up in the center of the pen.

12. Hesitate to demonstrate the completion of the pattern.

13. Rider must drop bridle to the judge.

*Horse may come out of rollback on either lead; however, they should be on correct lead when rounding the end of the arena.

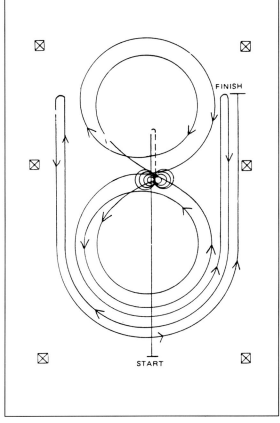

18 I — NRHA Pattern 9

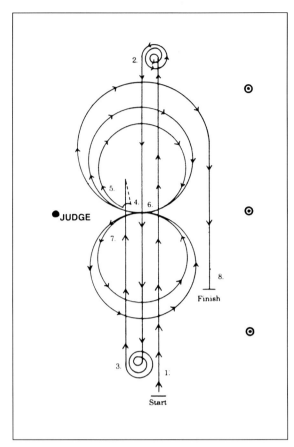

18 J — AQHA Pattern 1

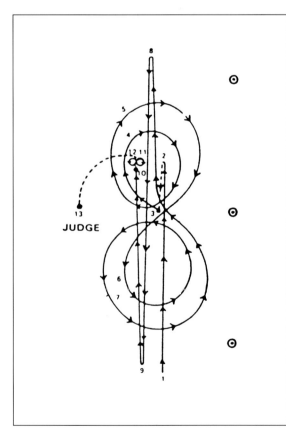

18 K — AQHA Pattern 2

No matter which pattern you run, the way to win is to have a penalty-free pattern (see Chapter 17 "Judging Reining"). It is poor showmanship to push your horse beyond his capabilities of staying penalty free. If you are getting a lot of penalties in your runs, either you are over-riding your horse or he isn't broke.

AQHA REINING PATTERNS

There are six AQHA approved open reining patterns plus one youth pattern. The same tips for handling the maneuvers I detailed in the NRHA patterns apply here as well. Be sure to contact the AQHA for its current handbook since rules and patterns change from year to year.

Scoring of AQHA patterns is similar to that of NRHA patterns, although you should check the AQHA handbook for specific penalties. Like NRHA, AQHA patterns are scored on the basis of 60 to 80, with 70 denoting an average performance.

There are faults against the horse and rider in AQHA competition that are scored accordingly, but do not cause disqualification.

Faults against the horse include opening the mouth excessively (when wearing a bit); excessive jawing, open mouth or head raising on stop; breaking gaits; lack of smooth, straight stop on the haunches (bouncing or sideways stop); refusing to change leads; anticipating signals; stumbling or falling; backing sideways; or knocking over markers.

Faults against the rider include losing a stirrup or holding on; any unnecessary aid (such as talking, petting, spurring, quirting, jerking of reins); or failure to go beyond markers on rollbacks and stops.

AQHA PATTERN 1

1. Run to the far end of the arena, stop and do 1/2 spins to the left — no hesitation.

2. Run to the opposite end of the arena, stop and do 1/2 spins to the right — no hesitation.

3. Run past center of arena, do sliding stop, no hesitation, back over slide tracks to center, hesitate.

4. Make a 1/4 pivot to the left to face left wall — hesitate.

5. Begin on right lead and make two circles to the right, the first small and slow, the second large and fast. Change leads at center of arena.

6. Make two circles to the left, first small and slow, the second large and fast. Change leads at the center of the arena.

7. Begin a large fast circle to the right. Do not close this circle, but run straight down the side past the center, do a sliding stop (Stop to be at least 20 feet from wall or fence).

8. Walk to judge and stop for inspection until dismissed.

9. The bridle may be dropped at the judge's discretion.

AQHA PATTERN 2

1. to 2. Run with speed, past center marker.

2. Stop and back up to center of pattern.

3. Settle horse for approximately 10 seconds. Start lope.

Circles should be made inside the end markers.

4. & 5. Ride two circles to the right, first circle small — should be slow — and second circle larger and faster.

6. & 7. Ride two circles to the left, first circle small and slow, second circle larger and faster.

8. Left rollback over hocks (should be made past far end marker).

9. Right rollback over hocks (should be made past near end marker).

10. Stop (should be made past center marker). Let horse settle, then in approximate area of stop, do the spins.

11. Do one 360 degree spin either right or left.

12. Do one 360 degree spin in the direction opposite that done in 11.

13. Walk to judge and stop for inspection until dismissed.

14. The bridle may be dropped at the judge's discretion.

AQHA PATTERN 3

1. Run past center of arena and do a sliding stop.

2. Back immediately to center of arena — hesitate.

3. Do two spins to the right.

4. Do two and 1/4 spins to the left — hesitate.

5. Beginning on left lead, make a small, slow circle, then begin a large fast circle. Do not close this circle, but run straight down the side past center marker and do a right rollback, (at least 20 feet from fence or wall).

6. Continue back to center of arena, horse should be on right lead at center. Make a small slow circle to the right, then begin a large fast circle. Do not close this circle, but run straight down the side past center and do a left rollback, (at least 20 feet from fence or wall).

7. Continue back to center of arena, horse should be on the left lead at center.

8. Make a large fast circle to the left at center of arena. Change leads and make a large, fast circle to the right, at center of arena. Change leads and begin a large, fast circle to the left. Do not close this circle, but run straight down the side past the center marker and do a sliding stop (at least 20 feet from the fence or wall).

9. Walk to the judge and stop for inspection until dismissed.

10. The bridle may be dropped at the judge's discretion.

AQHA PATTERN 4

1. Begin at center of the arena facing left wall or fence. Begin on left lead and complete two circles to the left. The first one large and fast — the second one small and slow.

2. At center of arena, stop and complete four spins to the left. Horse to be facing left wall or fence. Hesitate.

3. Begin on the right lead. Complete two circles to the right. The first one large and fast — the second one small and slow.

4. At the center of the arena stop and complete four spins to the right. Horse to be facing left wall or fence. Hesitate.

5. Begin on left lead and make a figure eight on top of the

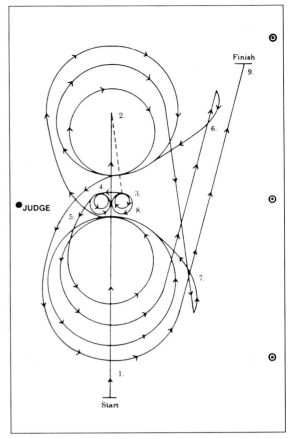

18 L — AQHA Pattern 3

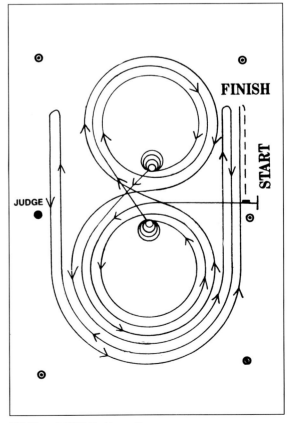

18 M — AQHA Pattern 4

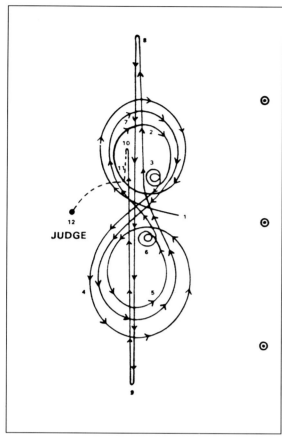

18 N — AQHA Pattern 5

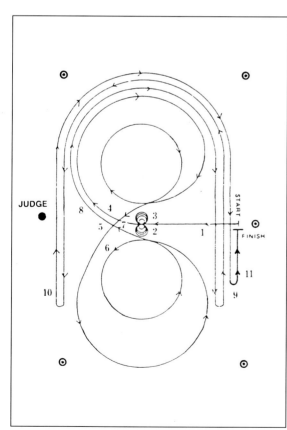

18 O — AQHA Pattern 6

large circles.

6. Close figure eight and begin a large fast circle to the left. Do not close this circle but run straight down the side past center marker and do a right rollback at least 20 feet from wall or fence, no hesitation.*

7. Continue back around previous circle, do not close this circle but run straight down opposite side of the arena past center marker and do a left rollback at least 20 feet from wall or fence, no hesitation.*

8. Continue back around previous circle, do not close this circle, but run straight down opposite side of the arena past center marker and do a left rollback at least 20 feet from wall or fence.

9. Back over slide tracks a minimum of 10 feet.

10. The bridle may be dropped at the judge's discretion.
*Horse may come out of rollback on either lead; however, he should be on correct lead when rounding the end of the arena.

AQHA PATTERN 5

1. Starting in the center of the arena make a large fast circle to the right.

2. Draw the circle down to a small circle until you reach the center of the arena — stop.

3. Do a double spin to the inside of the small circle in the center of the arena — at end of spins horse should be facing the left wall — slight hesitation.

4. Begin on left lead and make a large fast circle.

5. Then a small circle, again drawing it down to the center of the arena — stop — no hesitation on these stops.

6. Do a double spin to the inside of the circle — slight hesitation — horse to be facing left wall.

7. Begin on right lead and make a fast figure eight over the large circles — close the eight — and change leads.

8. Run to far end of arena and do a left rollback.

9. Run to opposite end of the arena and do a right rollback.

10. Run back past center of the arena and do a sliding stop. Hesitate.

11. Back over slide tracks.

12. Finish — Walk to judge for inspection and dismissal.

13. The bridle may be dropped at the judge's discretion.

AQHA PATTERN 6

1. Walk to center of the arena, stop, horse should be facing left wall or fence.

2. Complete four spins to the left.

3. Complete four spins to the right. Hesitate.

4. Begin on right lead and complete two circles to the right. The first circle large and fast — the second circle small and slow.

5. Change leads at center of the arena.

6. Complete two circles to the left. The first circle large and fast — the second circle small and slow.

7. Change leads at center of the arena.

8. Begin a large fast circle to the right. Do not close this circle but run straight down the side past center marker and

do a left rollback at least 20 feet from wall or fence, no hesitation.

9. Continue back around top half of previous circle, do not close this circle but run straight down opposite side of the arena past center marker and do a right rollback at least 20 feet from wall or fence — no hesitation.*

10. Continue back around previous circle, do not close this circle but run straight down the side past the center marker and do a sliding stop at approximately 20 feet from wall or fence.

11. Back straight to center of the arena.

*Horse may come out of rollback on either lead. However, it should be on correct lead when going around the end of the arena.

AQHA PATTERN 7 (YOUTH)

1. to 2. Run with speed past center marker.

2. Stop and back up to center of pattern.

3. Settle here for approximately 10 seconds. Start lope to the right. Figure eight should be made inside the end markers.

4. & 5. Ride small figure eight at a faster lope.

6. & 7. Ride a larger figure eight at a faster lope.

8. Left rollback over hocks (should be made past far end marker).

9. Right rollback over hocks (should be made past end marker).

10. Stop, (should be made past center marker), let horse settle, and in approximate area of stop, do the pivots.

11. Pivot, right or left, no more than 90 degrees.

12. Pivot opposite direction, no more than 180 degrees.

13. Walk to judge and stop for inspection until dismissed.

Docs Sail Win, a stallion by Topsail Cody, sold to Michele La Torre of Italy.

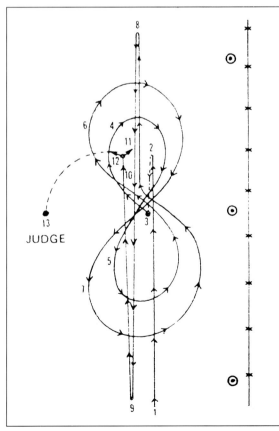

18 P — AQHA Pattern 7

19

History and Evolution of the Reining Horse

As in any form of competition, reining horse contests evolved because of a need to prove which horse was best. The degree of difficulty in riding a reining horse is high. While all horsemen want their horses to go forward, stop, turn around and back up, reining horse riders insist their mounts perform those movements at the highest level. They require their horses to run fast, stop hard, slide long and turn quickly with a combination of power and finesse. Any activity with the degree of difficulty demanded of a reining horse is highly competitive

The reining horse class, as we know it today, emerged when people with good handling horses wanted to have them tested against other horses.

REINING IN AQHA

In the 1950's, the American Quarter Horse Association approved the addition of reining in its show system. The class was called the reining contest. In that decade, the class evolved from one with simple requirements to one with more in-depth rules and horse and rider faults.

The first Reining Contest Course (see illustration 19 A) appeared in the 1950 AQHA handbook. A horse was judged on "neatness, dispatch, celerity, ease and calmness with which he performs the pattern. Any unnecessary aid given by the rider to the horse (such as unnecessary talking, petting, spurring, quirting, jerking of the reins, etc.) to induce the horse to perform in accordance with the above salient attributes will be considered a fault."

The first pattern consisted of a series of directional changes, lead changes, figure eights and circles. Sliding stops and a sharp, right angle turn were added for excite-

(previous pages) *A milestone in Bob's career was the year he won his first of six NRHA Futurities. In 1976, he rode Benito Paprika for C.T. Fuller of Willow Brook Farms, Catasauqua, PA.*

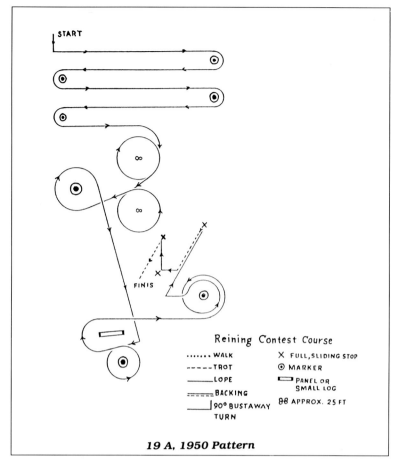

19 A, 1950 Pattern

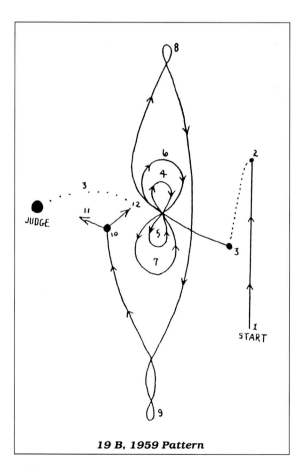

19 B, 1959 Pattern

ment. All three gaits were included in the pattern.

In 1954, the AQHA divided the class into hackamore and bit reining divisions and expanded its patterns to six. (see illustration 19 C). Specific faults showed up in the rules: "Excessive jawing, open mouth or head raising on stop, lack of smooth sliding stop on haunches, breaking gaits, refusing to change lead, anticipating signals, stumbling or falling, wringing tail, backing sideways, knocking over stakes and kegs, changing hands on reins, or losing stirrup, or holding on, or two hands on reins...failure to follow and execute the pattern as set forth."

The rule went on to say that the horse "shall rein and handle easily, fluently, effortlessly and with reasonable speed throughout the pattern."

Apparently from the beginning, reining meant finger-tip control of a horse at all gaits, speeds, directions and maneuvers.

In 1959, the rulebook returned to one standardized pattern. (see illustration 19 B). The format of the pattern and the maneuvers were starting to take shape.

1. to 2. Run at full speed.
2. Stop and rollback.
3. Settle horse for 10 seconds.
4. & 5. Ride small figure eight at slow canter.
6. & 7. Ride large figure eight fast.
8. Left rollback over hocks.
9. Right rollback over hocks.

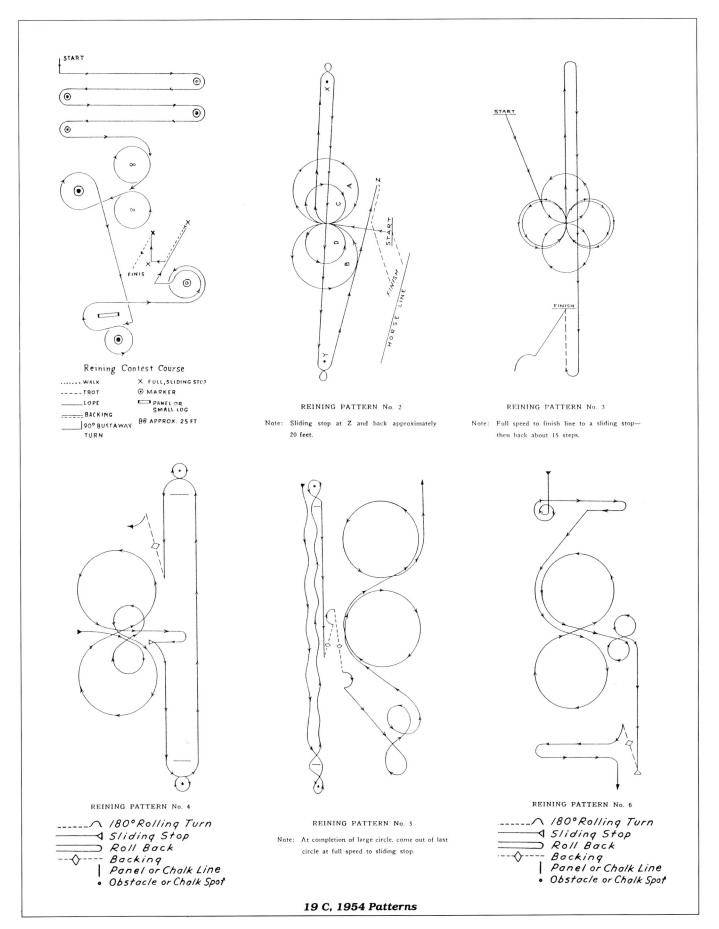

Reining Contest Course

...... WALK   X FULL, SLIDING STOP
----- TROT   ⊙ MARKER
_____ LOPE   ▭ PANEL OR SMALL LOG
-=-=- BACKING   ∞ APPROX. 25 FT
⌐ 90° BUSTAWAY TURN

REINING PATTERN No. 2

Note: Sliding stop at Z and back approximately 20 feet.

REINING PATTERN No. 3

Note: Full speed to finish line to a sliding stop—then back about 15 steps.

REINING PATTERN No. 4

⌢ 180° Rolling Turn
◁ Sliding Stop
⊐ Roll Back
◇ Backing
| Panel or Chalk Line
• Obstacle or Chalk Spot

REINING PATTERN No. 5

Note: At completion of large circle, come out of last circle at full speed to sliding stop.

REINING PATTERN No. 6

⌢ 180° Rolling Turn
◁ Sliding Stop
⊐ Roll Back
◇ Backing
| Panel or Chalk Line
• Obstacle or Chalk Spot

19 C, 1954 Patterns

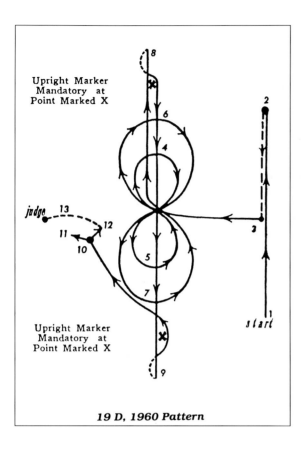

Upright Marker
Mandatory at
Point Marked X

judge

Upright Marker
Mandatory at
Point Marked X

19 D, 1960 Pattern

10. Stop.

11. Pivot left.

12. Pivot right.

13. Walk to judge and stop for inspection until dismissed.

By 1960, the class was becoming even more defined, obvious by the fact that it took up almost three pages of rules and definitions. The pattern contains many of the elements of a modern day reining pattern (see illustration 19 D).

1. to 2. Run at full speed (should be run at least 20 feet from any existing fence or wall).

2. Stop and back.

3. Settle horse for 10 seconds.

4. & 5. Ride small figure eight at slow canter.

6. & 7. Ride large figure eight fast.

8. Left rollback over hocks. Upright markers are mandatory at points marked X on the pattern.

9. Right rollback over hocks.

10. Stop.

11. Pivot left.

12. Pivot right

13. Walk to judge for inspection until dismissed.

REINING IN NRHA

Reining as a sport developed with the conception of the National Reining Horse Association in 1966. With the advent of the NRHA, maneuvers and patterns became more stylized and perfected. The class is strictly a handling horse class, with no bearing whatsoever on the work performed by ranch horses. The typical stock horse class today is working cowhorse, where horses are expected to handle cattle as well as run a reining pattern.

The definition of "reining" and its philosophy are embodied in one statement. "To rein a horse is not only to guide him, but also to control his every movement." That sentence is in the NRHA Handbook and has been in the rulebook since 1966.

The birth of the NRHA is best described by Pat Feuerstein, a long-time friend of mine, editor of "The Reiner" magazine and NRHA Historian.

"A 1965 AQHA show in Dayton, Ohio, was the spark that lit the NRHA fire. $50 in added money was up for grabs and when the judge, Carroll Bromley, saw the quality of reining horses present, he called a meeting of the contestants. They decided to make up their own, more difficult pattern. Bill Horn, who is to this day a bonafide NRHA superstar, won the event on Continental King. The class caused quite a stir. Excited reining enthusiasts gathered to see if perhaps they could put together an organization to promote reining - a single event association. People like Mickie Glenn Carter (owner of Continental King), Dale and Lucy Wilkinson, Stretch Bradley and his son Clark, Jim Cotton, R.D. Baker, Bill and Paul Horn, C.T. Fuller, Bob Anthony, Pat Faitz, all these people got together, formed the National Reining Horse Association and in 1966 offered the first NRHA Futurity for 3-year-old reining horses.

"The first NRHA Futurity was held in Columbus, Ohio. There was no great plan. There were no long range plans. Many thought that first futurity would be the 'one and only.' But some people had a dream. Through the years, they worked to give the reining horse earning power and recognition. Today, reining is appreciated world wide and the annual futurity, with a purse exceeding $500,000, is the heart of the National Reining Horse Association."

The program from the 1966 futurity shows exactly just how far reining has come. It said:

"What is a Reining Horse?

"A top reining horse can be compared to a famous athlete in any sport. He must have the proper training, conditioning and innate athletic ability. His most important qualities are balance and complete coordination. The three basic maneuvers a Reining Horse must do are stop and slide correctly, change leads fluidly and turn responsively. These are incorporated in pre-determined patterns that each horse must perform.

"The circles and figure eights in the pattern are used to demonstrate the horse's over-all movements and lead changes. In a circle to the right, a horse should lead with his right front leg and right hind leg and in a circle to the left

The first NRHA Futurity was won by Dale Wilkinson riding Pocorochie Bo for Miles Chester of Ohio. The pair earned $2,400 for the history making run.

(above) *The judges for the 1967 NRHA Futurity were (left to right) Jack Peek, J.D. Craft and Tommy Manion.*

(below) *The youngest reiner to win an NRHA Futurity was Sid Griffith of Columbus, Ohio. The 21-year-old rode Red Ant's Snort for Patty Middleswart of Ohio.*

the left front and hind legs must lead. In changing from right to left both front and hind legs should be changed simultaneously and smoothly. The lead change is performed at a canter and is an important part of the score for each horse. If the horse is not on the correct lead, he is not balanced and not in position to execute other necessary movements.

All horses entered in the Futurity are three years old and they do not have to be registered. Each horse will be judged on the neatness, ease and controlled speed with which it performs the patterns."

The horses were scored back then, as they are now, on a basis of 60 to 80, with 70 denoting an average score.

Faults were divided between horse and rider. Faults against the horse included breaking gaits, refusing to change leads, backing sideways, anticipating the next maneuver, excessive jawing or opening the mouth, knocking over the kegs and excessive stumbling or slipping.

Faults against the rider included changing hands on the reins, two hands on the reins at any one time, any unnecessary aid given to horse such as spurring, more than one finger between the reins, spurring forward of the cinch and running off pattern.

Pat's description of the first futurity told of the winner, Dale Wilkinson, who marked a 227 beating out 30 other entries.

"Dale Wilkinson will forever be associated with NRHA as the first futurity winner. He rode a horse named Pocorochie Bo and won $2,400. The total purse for the 1966 NRHA Futurity was $10,500 and at the time, reining enthusiasts thought they had died and gone to heaven.

"In 1967, the first All American Quarter Horse Congress was held in Columbus. The NRHA Futurity was on the show bill and it proved to be a big draw. Performance horse fans gathered in the coliseum to see Bill Horn win his first futurity on Mr. Poco Luis.

"For the next four years, our futurity was held in conjunction with the Congress. Clark Bradley, Dean Smith, Sid

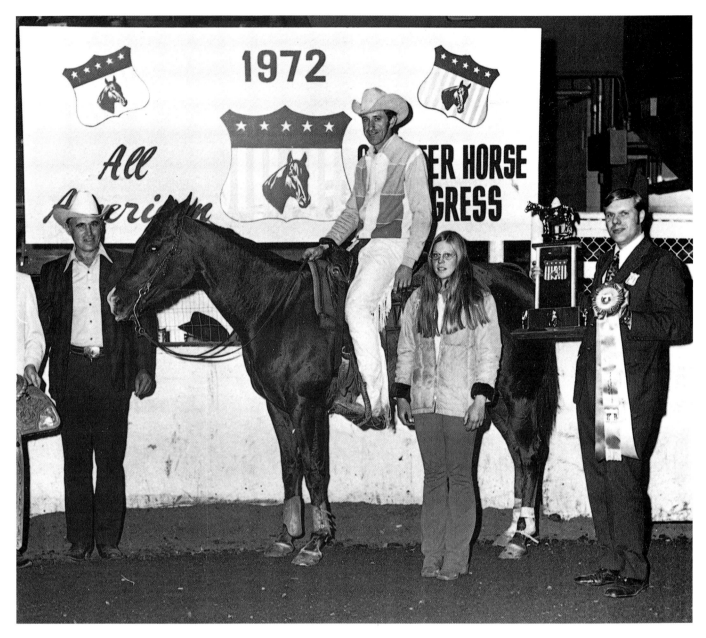

Griffith and Jim Willoughby all made the NRHA record books as futurity champions. And the total purses had climbed to the $20,000 range.

"In 1972, the futurity was held in Sedalia, Missouri. Bill Horn won his second title on Eternal One. In 1973 NRHA went back to the Congress and Paul Horn rode King Jay Bar to the futurity championship.

"The Futurity itself grew to include the Non Pro division in 1976 and the Limited Open division in 1983. The NRHA Sire and Dam Program, currently run by Wil Thomas, has been in existence since day one and is considered one of the finest breeding programs in the business, catering to the needs of breeders, trainers and exhibitors.

In 1968, when professionals decided they needed a place to go with their horses after the Futurity, the NRHA Open division came to be. Dr. John Mehaffey and Hickory Bomber won the first official NRHA Non Pro class offered in 1972 in

Four-time winner of the NRHA Futurity, Bill Horn, shown here winning the 1972 futurity on Eternal One.

Sedalia. The first reiner to win the NRHA Non Pro at Congress was Mike Greer on She Supreme."

Since its inception in the '60's, NRHA has grown tremendously. Besides having a strong membership in the United States, it serves as the parent organization for thirty affiliate organizations all over the world, including Canada, Great Britain, Italy, West Germany and Japan. The NRHA has instituted a movement to include reining as an Olympic event.

Along with numbers, the earnings have increased extraordinarily. The winner of the NRHA Futurity today takes home a guaranteed paycheck for $100,000. That is a far cry from Wilkinson's $2,400 check in 1966. The NRHA began guaranteeing the $100,000 first place money in 1983, when Craig Johnson won the futurity on Lucky Bay Glo.

Styles have changed as much as everything else. The way a reining horse performs has gone through as much of an evolution as the organization has.

Back in the early days, if you had a horse that could stop hard and turn fast, you could win almost any reining you wanted. All of that changed when High Proof hit the scene in 1975. He changed the style of reining horses from that of a stock horse to the show ring maneuvers we see today. He started a turning point in the industry. Before High Proof,

Craig Johnson won the 1983 NRHA Futurity the first year it paid $100,000 to the winner. He was on board Lucky Bay Glo, owned by Barbara Gerken of Florida.

the only things that were important were how hard you ran, how deep and long you stopped and how fast you spun.

Bob Anthony rode High Proof for C.T. Fuller of Willow Brook Farms, Catasauqua, Pennsylvania, in 1975 and I rode him in 1976. The Joe Cody gelding would run into the pen at a high rate of speed, stop effortlessly, slide 35 to 40 feet and do it with a relaxed, docile appearance. His turn arounds weren't necessarily lightning fast, but they were fluid, pretty and extremely correct. He didn't do things hard; he did them elegantly. Reiners liked that look so much that a new style of reining horse evolved. That was the end of the bad moving horse that could run, stop and turn around hard, but did it without class.

In today's tough reining contests, you've got to have a horse that not only performs well, but moves beautifully and profiles pretty.

A reining horse today has to have it altogether - a tremendous mind, outstanding ability, handsome looks, good movement and a gorgeous profile.

Reining horses and reining horse competition have come a long way in 40 years. Through the efforts of dedicated breeders, promotional organizations and skilled riders, we enjoy the sport we have today.

Dr. Jim Morgan, Eldersburg, MD, is one of the NRHA's top non-professional riders. He is a three-time, back-to-back winner of the NRHA Non-Pro Futurity. He captured the event in 1984, 1985 and 1986 and was reserve champion in 1987 and 1988. He is shown here on Boss Super Fly winning the 1985 Congress Non Pro Championship.

"THE KING P-234 LINE IS THE HEART BLOOD OF REINING."

20

Great Reining Horses I Have Known

OKIE'S BAMBOO

Okie's Bamboo was the first outstanding reining horse I ever rode. I didn't train her myself. She was trained by Bobby Bassinger in Nebraska. A good friend of mine purchased her when she was three and I showed her as a 3 and 4-year-old. She was an incredible athlete and had an excellent mind. It was unbelievable what she could do. A lot of the things she did and the things I felt in her were things I strived for in the horses I rode after her.

Okie's Bamboo, nicknamed Brown, was a natural. Everything was effortless for her. She was trained in a little, soft cotton rope hackamore that was nothing more than a rag. She was so soft in the nose a regular hackamore was too rough and abrasive for her.

Brown was one of those horses that made you think you were a horse trainer. The opportunity to ride her as a young man was an inspiration to me. I learned a lot from her.

I never showed Brown anywhere but in Nebraska. But I think I won every reining that I entered with her. I might have been second once or twice. The National Reining Horse Association wasn't in existence yet. I rode mainly in AQHA and saddle club shows.

Brown was by Okie Leo. Naturally, when I didn't have her to ride any more, I looked for more horses sired by Okie Leo. I found out that Dick Robey of El Reno, Oklahoma, owned the stallion. I immediately visited Robey. In time, he became a close friend of mine and was one of the people that encouraged me in my career. He helped me find some of the best colts Okie Leo ever sired. I feel fortunate to have been able to ride those horses.

Okie Leo actually got my reining career rolling.

(previous pages) *Topsail Cody was by far the most dynamic horse Bob ever rode.*

(above) *Monika was Bob's first great horse. She won all the major stock shows in reining and then become his wife Joyce's barrel horse. Also pictured is co-owner Owen Beach.*

MONIKA

Monika, by Okie Leo, was the first great horse that I trained myself. I got her from Robey as a filly. She was a goosey, flighty thing. The first few months riding her was like riding a water bug, she would jump around so much. Getting her broke wasn't easy. She was not a bronc, but she was jumpy. With everything she did, she jumped 20 feet here and 20 feet there. She was scared of everything. To help her get over her fear, I rode her hundreds of miles on the trails near my barn. I did no training on her out on the trails. We just enjoyed the rides. When she finally relaxed, she was probably as solid a horse as I've ever ridden. That mare never let me down.

She won all of the major stock shows and the Nebraska Futurity. We were in the top 10 in the 1969 NRHA Futurity. That was the first time I ever made it to that level.

I showed Monika for years. My wife Joyce barrel raced her and put barrel and pole bending points on her. After

Joyce rodeoed her for several years, I found myself needing a senior reining horse again. I had sold the horse I entered in the San Antonio Stock Show. When Joyce got back from a rodeo, I put Monika in the trailer and headed for Texas. I hadn't ridden the mare in two years. Four days later she won a six point reining at San Antonio and two weeks later she won a six point senior reining at the Houston stock show. The following year I ran her for the high point horse in Nebraska and she won that. After that, Joyce went back to rodeoing on her.

We did everything on Monika. She is in her 20's and still in my broodmare band.

BRITTON PRINCESS

Britton Princess, another daughter of Okie Leo, had the same outstanding qualities as Monika. However, both mares looked different. Monika was a nice, little, flop-eared mare. Britton Princess had a gorgeous body and neck, but she had a plain head. Both mares were great crowd pleasers. They were relatively ordinary looking until under saddle. When they moved, they were eye catchers.

Britton Princess was quite different to train than Monika. She was lazy. The summer I trained her for the futurity, I didn't know if she would ever turn around. She would flip and flop around like a dead fish. She always had a ton of stop and a beautiful mouth, great circles and she could run backwards. I worked and worked on her.

One day in July when I was schooling her, she stepped on both back shoes and ripped them off. I poked her in the shoulder with a spur and she turned around 5,000 miles an hour. From that day, she was a fancy spinning mare. I found out she could turn hard and pretty. She was such a sweet horse to train, I had put off getting after her hard as long as I could. But when I reached up and poked her one, she woke up. Even though I really didn't need spurs, she had to know I had them before she would turn hard.

She was a nice mare to show. I rode her in the 1972 NRHA Futurity. Back then, the futurity was four go rounds. She won the first three, but slipped on her last rollback in the finals and finished second.

I continued to show Britton Princess for years. She won all the stock shows. One year I rode Monika as my senior horse and Princess as my junior horse. That was a neat pair.

I sold her to a little boy in Nebraska and he made her the youth all around horse in the state four years in a row, winning nine events. After he was done with her, I bought her back and she is in my broodmare band.

Benito Paprika and High Proof were the first two horses C. T. Fuller of Willow Brook Farm, Catasauqua, Pennsylvania, sent to me to train. This was an important part of my career. Up to that point, Okie Leo had the largest influence on me. Now Joe Cody horses entered my life.

The Joe Codys have such stamina. They stay with you. They have hearts bigger than the whole world. They don't know when to quit. Joe Cody and Okie Leo were both out of

Britton Princess was reserve champion of the 1972 NRHA Futurity. Like Monika, she won all of the stock shows. One year, Monika was Bob's senior reining horse and Britton Princess was his junior reining horse. The two of them were tough to beat.

daughters of King P-234, the heart blood of reining. My broodmare band is founded on King blood.

I've never ridden a family of horses that could stop like the Joe Codys. They have a natural way of breaking in the loins, going to the ground and keeping the shoulders and front end loose. One thing about a Joe Cody, when you are in the finals and everybody's horses are getting tired, the Joe Codys act like the party has just begun.

BENITO PAPRIKA

Benito Paprika was by Doc's Benito Bar by Doc Bar and out of a Joe Cody mare named Paprika Cody, an AQHA honor roll reining horse. She was a big, gorgeous, sorrel mare that could move like a gazelle. She was an outstanding loper.

I didn't get Benito Paprika until May of her 3-year-old year. She had about 60 days of riding. To get a horse with only 60 days riding ready for the futurity is crowding it. Dick Herr, the manager at Willow Brook broke her and did a beautiful job. Her fabulous mind helped her train so easily.

It was on Benito Paprika that Bob won his first NRHA Futurity. That was in 1976 and in 1977 they placed third in the NRHA Derby and won the AQHA World Championship title in junior reining.

Her circles were beautiful and her turnarounds were absolutely effortless. Stopping came a little harder for her. She stopped every time you said "whoa." Her hindquarters went to the ground and she never picked up a hind foot to fall out of it. But it was hard for her to learn to release the front end. It took a long time for her front end to break loose. At the end of her stops, I tipped her nose back and forth, then rolled her back over her hocks and went the other direction. What that did was keep her front end moving and she learned to step with her front feet instead of jam them into the ground hard. Just before the futurity, she finally loosened up.

If Benito Paprika hadn't been such a golden-minded mare, it would have been impossible to get her ready. When I took her to the 1976 NRHA Futurity at the All American Quarter Horse Congress in Columbus, Ohio, she had never been off the ranch, had never gone anywhere to be seasoned. The first couple of days she was scared of everything, the pen, the crowd. To get her over her fear, I took it easy on her. She did enough to get into the finals, but she was at the low end of the point scale. At that time, there was a four to five day layover between the go-rounds and the finals. By finals night, I showed her as if she wasn't scared of anything and she wasn't. She won the futurity.

From then on, she was never afraid of anything again. As a 4-year-old, she won several NRHA bronzes at open reinings and was third in the 1977 NRHA Derby. That year she was the AQHA World Champion Junior Reining Horse. The next year we bred her to Boss Nowata Star and took her back to the world show seven months in foal. She was the reserve champion senior horse.

She went back to Willow Brook after that.

HIGH PROOF

High Proof is one of my all time favorites. Bob Anthony trained High Proof as a 3-year-old and rode him in the NRHA Futurity placing fifth. As a 4-year-old, he was not shown

1976
1ST PLACE
All American QUARTER HORSE CONGRESS

until Anthony took him to the Congress, where they won the NRHA Open reining. The next year, 1975, he was the NRHA World Champion Open Horse. He was magnificent that year. In 1976, C. T. Fuller gave me Benito Paprika and High Proof at the same time. I campaigned High Proof that fall, won the senior reining title at the AQHA World Show, the NRHA Open reining at the Congress and the Big Event in New York. The following year I rode him at the Versatility Class at the Congress and also won several pleasure classes on him. I would take him to AQHA shows in between reinings and show him in Western pleasure classes. I wanted him to know that every time we went to a show we weren't going to make a hard run. He did well in pleasure classes and won many big ones, such as the senior pleasure at the Nebraska State Fair.

High Proof was a turning point in the NRHA. He was a big, athletic, extremely beautiful horse. He was 15.2 and a big, long-necked, long-legged, gorgeous moving horse. He could stop so hard, yet soft and pretty. If he were showing under the current judging system, nine out of 10 of his stops would be plus 1 1/2 stops. He didn't spin real fast, but he did it correctly. High Proof wrote a book on correctness in every maneuver.

He was another one of those Joe Codys with a golden

High Proof was a big, gorgeous horse whose style in reining left its mark in NRHA history. He was the NRHA World Champion Open Horse in 1975. In 1976, Bob won the AQHA World Show and the Congress Open Reining on him.

195

mind. His dam was a big, pretty Scharbauer's King mare named Liz Five. You could run him as hard as you wanted and stop him with just a rope around his neck. You could pull on his mane and say "whoa." It was that easy for him and he enjoyed his work.

High Proof's style, with all of its correctness and finesse, was a direct contrast to the hard-riding, "run fast and stop anyway you can" style that had characterized reining competition to that point.

The gelding didn't have any quirks, but I do think he was half human. If you tuned High Proof before you showed him and got after him a little bit, made him turn hard and stop hard, excite him a little, you wouldn't have a good run. Instead, when I was ready to show High Proof, I just loped him and worked him quietly. I never asked him for anything hard. When I did walk into the pen and trust him, he gave me a 76, 77 run every trip. When he walked through that gate, he knew what he was there to do. If I kept him relaxed beforehand, he would give me the best run I could want. But if I had him a little nervous before the class, I would be in trouble. That was the only thing about him. It's as if he would say, "You treat me nice and I'll treat you nice." That was his attitude.

High Proof is still at Willow Brook Farm. Mr. Fuller and I are a lot alike in the respect that we take care of the horses that have been good to us. Mr. Fuller retires the old horses that won a lot for him. They spend their days on grass pastures and live the rest of their lives in comfort.

LADY ELDORADO

Lady Eldorado was another one of my favorites. She is by a son of Doc Bar, named Doc's Eldorado, which was out of a daughter of Hollywood Gold. Her mother is a direct daughter of Poco Birthday, a son of Poco Bueno.

When Lady came to the ranch, she was a pretty, little, baby doll mare that was easy to train. By March she was way ahead of my other futurity horses. Because things were so easy for her, I didn't notice her potential or think she would ever become a great reining horse.

When I went to the futurity with her, I thought to myself that I was taking an extremely broke horse. If the best futurity horses made a mistake, she could beat them by being so broke. She wouldn't make any mistakes. At home, everyday I rode her, she was better than the day before. It was a real pleasure to ride her. I didn't realize how pretty she was because no one rode her but me. I had never seen her go since I was always on her back.

Lady was another one that had never been anywhere except on the ranch. The NRHA Futurity at the Quarter Horse Congress was her first show experience. In the go-rounds, I came out of the arena scratching my head. She would run and circle and stop like I could never make her do at home. She was a show horse. All a horse can give you is a 100 percent effort with anything. When Lady walked in the pen, she'd give you 125 percent. She'd dig up stuff I didn't know she had and she did it every time. She'd walk through

(above and opposite above) *Lady Eldorado was a real "show horse." She would do more in the show pen than she did at home. The 1978 NRHA Futurity winner gave Bob 125 percent every time he showed her. The palomino mare went on to become a top youth reiner, winning 19 out of 20 classes she was entered in.*

that gate, guide better, run faster, stop harder and turn prettier than she ever did at home. She loved the show pen. When she got in the arena, she tried her little heart out.

Lady won the 1978 NRHA Futurity as a 3-year-old and the NRHA Derby of Canada and a lot of open reinings as a 4-year-old. The people that owned her, Darrell and Arlene Keener, had a pre-teenage daughter named Dolena, who was an extremely talented little rider. She took Lady to 20 AQHA shows and won 19 of them. The only class she lost, she went off pattern. She took her to the 1980 American Junior Quarter Horse Association World Show. In the reining finals, the pair marked four 77's under four judges. The closest competitor to her marked four 75's. She won the youth world champion reining title by eight points.

After that show, I bought Lady from the Keeners. She has been in my broodmare band ever since and has had several nice foals for me.

CASSANDRA CODY

Cassandra Cody is by Joe Cody and out of a world champion 2-year-old halter mare named Dude's Baby Doll. She is a full sister to Corona Cody, a son of Joe Cody that stands at Willow Brook Farms. Mr. Fuller sent Cassandra to me when she was a yearling. I showed her in some halter fu-

(below) Cassandra Cody won the 1979 NRHA Futurity and was reserve in the 1980 NRHA Derby. Besides reining, Cassandra Cody was a top Western pleasure horse.

turities and was second in the Nebraska and Pennsylvania futurities. She also won several AQHA shows in yearling halter classes.

When Cassandra was a 2-year-old, I showed her in both halter and pleasure classes. She earned 25 AQHA Western pleasure points and seven halter points.

Cassandra won the NRHA Futurity in 1979. We were second in the NRHA Derby in 1980. She was a gigantic stopper with beautiful circles and good lead changes. Not the fanciest turn around horse, but she turned around adequately. She took a little more riding than some of my horses, but was a superb athlete.

She is still at Willow Brook Farm in the broodmare band. She has produced several good performance foals.

TOPSAIL CODY

Topsail Cody is by far my favorite. He is the most dynamic horse I have ever ridden. I showed horses for Willow Brook for several years and all the time that I rode those Joe Codys, I knew that I wanted to wrap my breeding program around a son of the great stallion. Every year when I went back to Catasauqua, Pennsylvania, I looked at all his colts. There would be one or two that I liked real well, but the one that would dazzle me just wasn't there. Some were close, but

Topsail Cody is closest to Bob's heart. The sorrel son of Joe Cody has never been beaten in the arena. He is the only horse to win all go rounds of the NRHA Futurity, which he won in 1980. At the 1981 AQHA World Championship show, he won all the eliminations and finals of the junior reining division. Topsail is now one of the reining industry's top siring stallions, with world and futurity champion offspring. Pictured from left to right: Ed Loomis, Opie Burk, Bobbie Jo Loomis on Topsail, Bob and Joyce Loomis.

not quite good enough. Then in March of 1978, when I was on my way home from the derby, which was in Canada, I stopped at Willow Brook and looked at the colt crop as I usually did. Nobody knew it at the time, but that was the last crop that Joe Cody would ever sire. The stallion was 26 years old.

While I looked at the yearling stallions, a little chestnut colt with a blaze face loped up to the fence. He was by Joe Cody and out of a direct daughter of Doc Bar. He is the first and only stud colt with that cross in his pedigree. When I watched him lope around the pasture, I looked at him and knew that he was the one. I bought him and took him home with me. A week later, it was discovered that Joe Cody was sterile.

When Topsail was old enough to break, my niece, Chris Loomis, who was a quiet rider, did the job. She rode him his entire 2-year-old year. She lived next door to a beautiful park with lots of bridle paths. The two spent many hours on the trails. Besides trail riding, Chris rode Topsail in junior pleasure classes, such as the Nebraska State Fair. They didn't place, but it was good experience for Topsail.

I started riding him January 1 of his 3-year-old year. He was unbelievable from the beginning. Chris put a lot of quiet miles on him and had him riding beautifully. Everything came easy to him. He could stop like a dynamo. His turn arounds were effortless and his circles perfect. There was never a problem in his training. By the first of May, he was ready to go to the futurity. This was the first time in my life that I had this problem. Here it was the first of May, this horse is ready to compete and the hardest thing I've ever had to do in my life is ride him everyday and keep him at that same level from May 1 to October 15.

When I was training Topsail for the futurity in 1980, I took him to two AQHA shows, both had six point reining classes, which he won.

Topsail is the only horse to win all the go-rounds and the finals of the NRHA Futurity during the Quarter Horse Congress. Until the 1988 futurity, he was the only stallion to win the futurity since its inception in 1966.

To this point, Topsail has marked the highest scores awarded in the futurity or in any NRHA competition. He ran a 230 in the first go-round, 232.5 in the second and a 234.5 in the finals. A 234.5 score is two 78's and one 78 1/2. An 80 is perfect.

When Topsail was four, I took him to two more AQHA shows with six point reining classes. He won both of them as well and qualified for the AQHA World Championship Show. There, he won the eliminations and the finals. After that, I retired him and never showed him again. He had proved himself.

Training and showing Topsail Cody was one of the greatest thrills of my career.

Topsail's outstanding show career has been followed by an outstanding breeding career. He has had more horses in the finals of the NRHA Futurity than any other stallion. He has sired world champions and futurity champions.

(top) *Miss Della Doc had a heart greater than all outdoors, which helped her in the show arena. The winner of the 1984 NRHA Futurity also placed well at the 1985 NRHA Derby and was reserve champion junior reining horse at the AQHA World Show.*

(above) *Diamonds Ms Sparkle was a reserve world champion in senior reining at the AQHA World Show and champion of the open reining at the Congress.*

MISS DELLA DOC

Miss Della Doc is by Docs Poco Bueno, a full brother to Lady Eldorado. Della's mother was also a daughter of Poco Birthday, but a different dam than Lady has. Her dam is Tama's Sue Skip by Sir Skip and out of Tama, by Poco Birthday. Darrell and Arlene Keener own Miss Della Doc too.

Although nice to train, Della was not what I would call a great athlete. Things didn't come that easy for her. Della was an average athlete with a great mind. Where she wasn't physical, she made up for it in her disposition and try. She was so trainable and had a big heart. She always did much more than she was capable of because she would try so hard.

It was hard for her to learn to turn, to stop and do the other maneuvers. Once she learned them, she did them well, but it took some doing to get her there. She did guide beautifully and was "deadly leaded." I would have to categorize her as a mental sweetheart with average ability. But that kind of horse can win a lot of money for you.

I won the 1984 NRHA Futurity on Della. Her good mind came through in the finals. When the money was up, the chips were down and the pressure was on, she gave me all she had. She never tried to speed up or slow down. She stayed between the reins, did everything she was asked to do to the very best of her ability.

There are a lot of different things that make a horse great. But I think horses with great minds and limited ability have won a lot more than great athletes with limited minds.

Of course, the ultimate is to have an animal with both. However, you rarely get that. I'll take one on my string like Della any day. The bay mare has never been mad a day in her life. No matter what the circumstances, she tried and tried and tried all she was worth and it was good enough.

In her 4-year-old year, she placed well at the NRHA Derby and was reserve world champion reining horse at the AQHA World Show. As a 5-year-old, Mrs. Keener showed her and did quite well on her as did her youngest daughter, Dana. The Keeners still have Della.

DIAMONDS MS SPARKLE

Diamonds Ms Sparkle was originally broke by Sonny Jim Orr, an outstanding hand who rode her in reining and working cowhorse. She went from Sonny Jim to Al Dunning, who also showed her in those two events. When she came to me, she had been ridden by very good people.

I got Sparkle early in 1984. She won several open reinings for me including the Quarter Horse Congress. At the AQHA World Show, she was Reserve World Champion Junior Senior Reining Horse that same year.

Sparkle is a big, beautiful, palomino mare. She stands 15.2 and moves as graceful as a swan. She was an incredible stopper, had gorgeous circles and was deadly leaded. I've never seen a big horse turn as dynamically as she did. Usually, big horses can turn pretty and correct, but rarely can they turn fast. Diamonds Ms Sparkle could turn like a little horse despite the fact that she is a long-necked, long-legged, elegant thing. When I asked her to turn around, she'd drop her nose down and turn as hard and fast and with as much authority as a smaller, typically more athletic horse. She could do all the physical things any little horse ever thought of doing, but yet had all the elegance of a big horse.

But, this is not a surprise. All throughout this book, I have talked about breeding. When talking about breeding and great families, Sparkles' family is one of the greatest broodmare families in the world. She is a full sister to Diamonds Sparkle, which was a Copenhagen-Skoal Super Horse. Her produce have been great. She is the mother to Sparkles Rosezana, the 1985 NRHA Futurity champion and an AQHA World Champion Reining Horse. She is also the dam of Zans Diamond Sun, fourth in the NRHA Futurity and another AQHA World Champion Reining Horse. Another of her foals, Sparkles Suzana, was fourth in the NRHA Futurity and an NRHA Derby Champion.

Sparkle's father is Mr. Diamond Dude, which is a full brother to Dude's Baby Doll, the mother to Cassandra Cody, my 1979 futurity winner. Both Mr. Diamond Dude and Dude's Baby Doll are direct sons and daughters of Blondy's Dude, an outstanding sire of performance horses.

At the time I showed Sparkle, both she and her sister were owned by Richard Stewart of Colorado. Shortly after I finished showing her, I purchased her and Carol Rose, Gainesville, Texas, purchased Diamonds Sparkle. I sold Diamonds Ms Sparkle to the Arcese family in Italy, but she stays on my ranch in the broodmare band.

SOPHIE OAK

Sophie Oak is a daughter of Doc's Oak, who is by Doc Bar, and out of a daughter of Mr. Gun Smoke. Her mother is a mare named Life Saver, a full sister to Gun Smoke's Dream, the horse Dale Wilkinson rode to win the 1972 NCHA Futurity.

In early summer 1986, top cutting horse trainer Tom Lyons had Sophie in training for the NCHA Futurity. He called me up and described her to me over the phone. He said she had a beautiful mind and he didn't think it was possible to make her mad. She was making a nice cutting horse and had a lot of cow. However, she was short of having the ability to do all the fancy stuff in the middle of the pen outstanding cutting horses have to do to compete in the futurity. He thought she'd make a better reiner.

I have a tremendous amount of respect for Tom's opinion of a horse. When I rode Sophie, she was everything Tom said she was. She was a pretty mover, but a wild looking one, with her bald face, glass eye and four white stockings. She stuck out in a crowd. She wasn't a Paint Horse, but almost. She was barely legal to register as a Quarter Horse. If she had an inch more white anywhere, it would have been too much.

Tom and I arranged to partner on her. I started her reining training June 1, which is extremely late to start reining maneuvers for the futurity. Tom had her nicely broke and that was my salvation. She was soft in both directions and loped well. When he said that you couldn't make her mad, he was right. She was a sweet horse. I only had five months to train her. Luckily for me, the futurity moved to Oklahoma City, Oklahoma, for the first time that year. I don't think I could have made the Quarter Horse Congress October date. We trained right to the first day of the futurity go-rounds.

Sophie wasn't an awesome athlete, but she was a good one. She was the kind of horse that you look forward to riding. Everyday I got on her, she was a better horse than she was the day before. Things were easy for her. Turn arounds and stops were a snap. She was quite soft in the poll. With the shortage of time we had, I spent a good deal of time on her everyday to get her ready. I probably put a year's riding on her in five months. Despite that, she was never sour. She would come out of the stall happy and eager to go everyday. She never pinned an ear or made a face. If we had any bad days, we never would have been ready.

I took Sophie everywhere I went that year just to school her. I've had futurity horses that never left the ranch until I took them to the main event, but they were well broke. They were solid on the maneuvers by the time we got there. But Sophie didn't have that advantage. She learned through

Sophie Oak was an ex-cutter turned reiner that became the 1986 NRHA Futurity winner. After her win, she placed in the NRHA Derby and captured the Italian Reining Futurity for owner Eleuterio Arcese of Italy. Also pictured are Rich McDonald and Joyce Loomis holding trophy and Bobbie Jo in the saddle.

experience on the road.

The first time I showed her was at the Southwest Reining Horse Association Futurity in Ardmore, Oklahoma. She wasn't quite ready, but close. She was green, but she won it. That was about a month prior to the big futurity. In those last weeks, she came on strong. After showing her once, it was unbelievable how fast she came along. At the Southwest Futurity, I saw exactly where we were weak and that gave me 30 days to work on those areas. By the time we got to the NRHA Futurity, she was on target. She tied to win the first go-round. I backed off of her the second go-round and was fifth. She came back in the finals with her best run.

That was the way Sophie was. If you wanted to have a nice, easy run, you could. If you wanted to pull the hammer back, you could. She didn't care. Whatever I wanted to do suited her fine.

I sold Sophie to Eleuterio Arcese of Italy. I wanted a foal out of her badly. Before I sent her overseas, I bred her to Topsail Cody using the embryo transfer process. They produced a crop-out Paint filly.

I showed Sophie to a fifth in the NRHA Derby and won the Italian Reining Futurity, which is an event for 4-year-olds. Since then, she has won several open reinings in Europe.

In the spring of 1989, Dick Pieper and I were invited to Essen, Germany, to give a demonstration at Equitana, Europe's largest horse exposition. Mr. Arcese let Dick and I use Sophie and Spirit Of Five, the 1987 NRHA Futurity champion he purchased a few days before the finals of that event. We did our demonstration bridleless to show the European crowd what reining horses could do. Neither mare had been ridden in a while, but they performed beautifully. Sophie stopped and turned and circled just as good as she did in a bridle. She was just that kind of horse.

SURPRISE ENTERPRISE

Surprise Enterprise is a horse that has it all. He is similar to Topsail Cody in that he is mentally and physically outstanding. He has everything; conformation, power, fabulous mind and a world of talent.

Bill Horn trained and rode the bay stallion in the 1988 NRHA Futurity. He won the first go-round on him and tied for sixth, seventh and eighth in the finals. Arcese bought him before the futurity and I got him right after that.

I showed Surprise at the Lazy E Reining Classic, won the first go-round and was second in the finals. At the NRHA Derby, we won the first go-round and were third in the finals. We won the NRHA Super Stakes after that.

Instead of going to Italy, Surprise stands at stud on my ranch. I believe he will be an excellent outcross on my Topsail Cody daughters. He is by Be Aech Enterprise, Horn's stallion whose sire is Squaw Leo and dam is Enterprise Lady, one of the all time great reining horses. She was a big, black, gorgeous mare that Bill showed for years. Surprise's dam, Jimmy's Valentine is by Roper's Jimmy and out of a daughter of Poco Bueno who is out of a daughter of Beaver Creek. Surprise's pedigree holds a strong dose of King P-234.

Surprise Enterprise was a finalist in the 1988 NRHA Futurity, reserve champion of the Lazy E Reining Classic, finalist in the NRHA Derby and winner of the NRHA Super Stakes. Surprise, a stallion by Be Aech Enterprise, belongs to the Arcese family of Italy.

Glossary

All American Quarter Horse Congress — termed the world's largest horse show. An annual Quarter Horse show held in October at the fairgrounds in Columbus, Ohio. Organized by the Ohio Quarter Horse Association. Former site of the NRHA Futurity for many years.

AQHA, American Quarter Horse Association — breed organization responsible for registering Quarter Horses, recording the sale and transfer of Quarter Horses, monitoring activities in which Quarter Horses are involved and approving shows and races.

AQHA World Championship Show — annual competition for Quarter Horses which have qualified throughout the year in AQHA approved shows. Horses with the specified number of points are eligible to compete against other horses of the same caliber to determine the world champion in each event. Takes place in Oklahoma City, Oklahoma each November.

Balance on the bridle — phrase used to describe when the rider takes the slack out of the reins. The horse is "on the bit." However, the rider does not pull on the reins.

Bars of the mouth — portion of the horse's lower jaw which is devoid of teeth, space between the tushes (long, pointed teeth) and molars where the bit lies in the mouth.

Behind the bridle — phrase used to describe what a horse does when he overreacts to the bit or the actions of the rider's hands controlling the bit. Horse tucks his nose past vertical, almost to his chest, in an effort to evade or avoid the bit.

Bell boots — protective boots which cover the horse's coronary band.

Bend-counterbend — an advanced suppling exercise done in a circle where the horse's body is bent in one direction, but the horse is moving in the opposite direction. For example, the horse's body is in an arc to the right while the horse moves in a circle to the left.

Body alignment — arrangement or position of the horse's body in a straight line. Through the use of hand and leg cues, the horse's body is adjusted correctly for the maneuver the rider wants.

Bosal — thick nosepiece made of braided leather, part of a hackamore bridle.

Broodmare — a female horse used for breeding purposes.

Cadence — each stride a horse takes is exactly the same distance as the rest.

Cannon bone — that part of the horse's leg between his knee or hock and pastern.

Cantle — the rear of the seat of the saddle

Capturing the horse's face — phrase used to describe when a horse flexes at the poll.

Caslicks operation — female horses have their vulvas sutured shut by veterinarians in an effort to prevent infection and keep the vulvas from sucking air. Sutures are removed prior to breeding.

Cavesson — leather noseband which helps to keep a horse's mouth from opening.

Center marker — dead center of an arena lengthwise.

Chasing — technique used in speed control to regulate the horse's rate of speed. In galloping, the rider leans forward from the waist running his hand up the horse's neck encouraging him to go faster.

Cheeking a horse — technique used in mounting an unbroke horse. A rider grabs the horse's halter cheek piece and turns the horse's head toward the rider before he gets in the saddle.

Chin strap — also called "curb strap." A leather strap that attaches to the cheek pieces of a curb bit. It fits under the horse's jawbone and works in conjunction with a shank bit to exert leverage on the horse's mouth. There are also curb chains. They are made of metal links that lie flat against the horse's jawbone.

Cinch — the strap around the horse's belly which attaches the saddle to the horse's back. See also "Girth."

Colt — a male horse under the age of four, called a foal prior to weaning. As he matures, referred to as a stallion if left entire, or a gelding if castrated.

Conditioning – an equine exercise program designed to develop musculature and wind power.

Conformation – the general shape and size of a horse, the way in which a horse's body is put together.

Counter-canter – the horse lopes a circle on the wrong lead. For example, the horse lopes a right circle on the left lead.

Cow-hocked – hocks that turn in and point towards one another instead of straight ahead. Cows are similarly shaped, hence the name. The hind legs of cow-hocked horses toe-out.

Cow sense – a horse is said to have "cow sense" or "a lot of cow" when he demonstrates his ability to handle cattle in a competitive or work situation. Whether on a ranch or in a horse show, a good cutting horse with "lots of cow" outwits his opponent under any circumstances.

Crockett-Renaulde – a particular type of bit no longer manufactured. The bit had a copper mouthpiece with a low port and an aluminum shank. This type of bit is now made by other bit manufacturers.

Crossfiring – refers to the horse being on two different leads as he lopes. Horse travels on one lead with his front legs and another lead with his hind legs.

Crop-out – a horse born to two Quarter Horse parents, but which has too much white to register as a Quarter Horse. If there is a sufficient amount of white hair with underlying pink skin, the horse is usually registered with the American Paint Horse Association.

Crow hopping – another term for bucking.

Cutting – In a cutting horse contest, the horse "cuts" two to three cows from a herd, one at a time, and prevents them from returning to the herd.

Daisy clipping – phrase used to describe movement of a horse whose legs barely skim the earth, as opposed to gaited horses which raise feet high. For a Western performance horse, a "daisy clipper" is considered a pretty mover, an efficient mover who wastes little time

and energy in the air.

Dam – female parent of a horse.

Deadly leaded – horse that is a natural lead changer is said to be "deadly leaded."

Direct rein – direct pressure resulting from a pull on the reins; i.e. horse responds to a tug on the right rein by turning right in the direction of the direct pull.

Disposition – a horse's attitude towards his handlers and other horses.

Dragging a hind lead – phrase used to describe when a horse does not complete a lead change with his hind legs. For example, when changing from the right lead to a left lead, the horse changes to the left lead in front, but remains on the right lead behind.

Driving the horse up into the bridle – phrase used to describe when the rider uses leg pressure to move the horse forward while the rider's hands remain in a fixed position. As the horse moves forward and the slack is taken out of the reins, the horse is "driven up into the bridle." The horse bends or flexes at the poll in response to pressure on the bit.

Dropped noseband – leather noseband which fits just below the bit. Prevents a horse from opening his mouth and evading bit pressure.

D-shaped circle – a circle in the shape of the letter "D." One side of the circle is in a straight line, which resembles the flat part of the letter "D."

Equitana – Europe's largest equine exposition, occurs every other year in Essen, Germany.

Farriery – the practice of shoeing horses.

Fencing – running a horse up to a gate, wall or some barrier and asking him to stop. Fencing gates are standard equipment on reining horse trainers' slide tracks. They aid in teaching horses to stop properly.

Fill up with air – phrase comes from letting the horse's lungs fill with air. After strenuous exercise the rider allows the horse to stop and catch his breath, to resume normal respiration and heart rate. Running or working a horse until he is out of air damages the animal physically.

Filly — a female horse under the age of four. Called a foal prior to weaning.

Flat spin — a horse is said to be "flat" in his spin or turn around when his head, neck, back and hindquarters are reasonably level in performing the maneuver.

Flexing the poll — phrase used to describe when a horse tips his head down, making it perpendicular to the ground. A horse flexes his poll when the rider exerts pressure on the bit to bring the head into line.

Floating — in equine dental work, the sharp points of the horse's teeth, usually molars, are filed down to prevent the horse from injuring himself.

Foal — term for a horse (male or female) prior to weaning.

Free longeing — a method of longeing or working a horse without a longe line. Horse is maneuvered around the longeing or round pen by the use of body language and voice cues.

Futurity — a competition for which entry fees are paid well in advance of the event. As it relates to horse contests, it means a test of young horses to determine future suitability for a particular event.

Gelding — a castrated male horse.

Girth — in reference to a horse's body, the circumference of the horse's body as measured from behind the withers and around the horse's barrel. In reference to equipment, the strap around the horse's belly which attaches the saddle to the horse's back; also called cinch.

Green — a horse that is barely broke is said to be "green."

Guiding — the ability to put the horse wherever the rider wants, accomplished with the use of hand and leg aids.

Hackamore — a bitless bridle of Spanish origin (la jaquima) consisting of a simple headstall, bosal or rawhide noseband, heel knot and hair ropes (mecate) used as reins. Pressure points used in control of the horse are the nose and jaw.

Headstall — leather strap that goes around the top of the horse's head to secure the bit.

Heat — estrus in mares, a short period of time, five to seven days, when mares are receptive to breeding.

Heavy in the face — phrase used to describe a horse that is pulling on the reins, the horse pulls against the rider's hands.

Hip displacement — the ability to control the movement of the horse's hips, being able to make them move to the right or to the left using leg cues.

Hobbles — restraining devices made out of rope or leather consisting of two loops which fasten together around the horse's front legs. Prevent horse from straying.

Hot horse — phrase used to describe an excitable horse, one that has a lot of energy to move forward.

Indirect rein — the horse is guided by pressure on his neck instead of mouth, as in direct or plow reining. When rein is placed on horse's neck, he moves in the opposite direction. See also "neck rein."

In-skirt rigging — indicates that the front rigging, which includes the latigo straps and the cinch, is located in the skirt of the saddle. As opposed to on-the-tree rigging, which has rigging attached to the saddle tree.

Interval training — a type of conditioning program for horses where the animal is put through alternate periods of stress. The handler brings the horse to a peak level of stress, then backs off, followed by another period of increased stress. The increased loads, followed by slack time, develop strong bones, tendons, ligaments, muscles and lung capacity.

Jointed mouthpiece — mouthpiece of a bit is jointed in the middle, often associated with snaffle bits. Such bits have a nutcracker effect on the horse's jaw.

Jump horse up in bridle — phrase used to describe when the rider pushes the horse up into the bridle by squeezing his legs to propel the horse forward. At the same time, the rider holds his hands in a fixed position so that horse flexes at the poll.

Keg shoe — standard, manufactured steel shoe. Keg shoes are not hand-made by blacksmiths. They are factory-made.

Knee guards — protective covering over the horse's knees.

Leads — a horse is said to be on the right or left lead depending upon which front leg is leading in a lope. For example, in a right lead, the horse's right foreleg strides forward farther than does the left foreleg.

Mare — a female horse over the age of four.

Markers — cones or pylons that designate the boundaries in which a reining pattern is to be run.

Mullen mouth — a mouthpiece with a low, slightly curved port.

NCHA, National Cutting Horse Association — organization dedicated to the activities of the cutting horse, approves shows for cutting horse competition, records earnings of cutting horses, sponsors cutting horse events, such as the NCHA Futurity and Derby.

NRHA, National Reining Horse Association — organization devoted to the interests of reining horse riders, approves shows for reining horse competition, sponsors reining horse events, such as the NRHA Futurity.

NCHA Futurity — annual event for 3-year-old horses which have never been shown in cutting competition. Has open and non-pro divisions. Takes place in Fort Worth, Texas, each December.

Neck rein — the horse is guided by pressure on his neck instead of pressure on his mouth, as in direct or plow reining. When rein is placed on horse's neck, he moves in opposite direction. See also "indirect rein."

New mouth — phrase which means the rider releases any bit pressure on the horse's mouth before he picks up the reins again to ask the horse to do something.

NRHA Derby — annual event for 4-year-old reining horses. Once held in Raleigh, North Carolina. Now takes place in St. Paul, Minnesota, each spring.

NRHA Futurity — annual event for 3-year-old reining horses. Has open, non-pro and limited open divisions. Once held at the Quarter Horse Congress in Columbus, Ohio. Now takes place in Oklahoma City, Oklahoma, every December.

NRHA Super Stakes — annual event for the get of subscribed stallions. Takes place in Columbus, Ohio, each summer.

Offspring — a stallion's progeny.

Over-bent — horse is too radical in moving his head or his body. In the case of head carriage, horse tips his nose past vertical and is said to be "behind the bit." With respect to body, the horse moves off the rider's leg too far and bends body in an arc.

Packing a bridle — phrase used to describe when a horse picks up his bit and holds it in his mouth.

Palate — roof of the horse's mouth.

Pattern — a prescribed diagram of direction and maneuvers. There are nine approved patterns in NRHA competition.

Pedigree — a horse's parentage. The sire and dam bloodlines combine to form the horse's family tree. In breed organizations, pedigrees usually trace as far as the association records go back in time. They indicate which families were bred to form certain lines or strains of horses.

Pivot foot — the hind leg which remains stationary on the ground as horse's body turns around it, either 180 degrees in a rollback or 360 in a turn around.

Poll — an area of the horse's head located between the ears, joins the skull with the spinal cord of the neck.

207

Port — the upward curve of the mouthpiece in the center of a curb bit. Ports can be called "high" or "low" depending upon the degree of the curve.

Produce — a mare's progeny

Progeny — offspring, descendants

Prospect — a horse, which by its breeding, conformation and disposition, appears to be suited for a particular event.

Pylons — cones or markers that designate the boundaries in which a reining pattern is to be run.

Reining — To rein a horse is to guide and control his every movement. In a reining horse contest, the horse must complete a specified pattern which includes circles, stops, rollbacks, lead changes, turn arounds and back ups.

Rollback — a stationary turn on the haunches. A 180 degree turn on the hocks accomplished when a horse stops, pivots on inside hind leg and moves off in the other direction.

Round pen — small circular enclosure for exercising horses.

Running martingale — equipment which regulates head carriage, consists of straps which attach from the girth or breastplate to the reins. Divided into two branches, each with a ring at the end through which the reins pass. It prevents a horse from raising his head past a certain point.

Sacking out — rubbing the horse's entire body with a cloth, blanket, sack or some object. A desensitizing process used most often on a spooky or young horse in order to get the animal over the fear of being handled or of particular objects.

Shank — the long cheek pieces of a bit. Shank bits are to be used with chin or curb straps and allow the rider to exert leverage on a horse.

Sickle-hocked — phrase used to describe weak hock conformation. Sickle hocks are bent in the shape of a sickle, hence the name. Cannon bones are often at an angle to the ground instead of coming straight down as in normal conformation.

Sire — male parent of a horse.

Skid boots — protective boots which cover the fetlocks on the horse's hind legs.

Slide plates — special shoes worn by reining horses, designed to facilitate long, sliding stops. Plates are much wider than the normal shoe. They cover more of the surface of the horse's foot. In a stop, when the slick surface of the shoe hits the dirt, the horse literally slides on top of the ground.

Slide track — large, open area, with no fence lines, that reining horse trainers use to school their horses. The ground is prepared to keep the surface level and of good consistency for galloping and performing maneuvers, such as sliding stops and turn arounds.

Sliding Stop — horse comes to a complete halt after sliding a distance of several feet over the surface of the ground; horse's hindquarters drop toward ground as his hind legs lock up for stability, front legs continue to pedal as hind legs remain stationary in the dirt.

Snaffle bit — a true snaffle bit which exerts no leverage on the horse's mouth. Consists of a jointed or unjointed mouthpiece and 0-rings or D-rings as cheek pieces. True snaffles have no shanks. Also see "Western snaffle."

Softly in hand — also "softly in the bridle." Phrase used to describe a horse which does not pull on the reins. Such as horse is light and responsive to the rider's commands.

Speed control — the ability to adjust speed at a gallop. Through the use of cues, the rider controls the speed at which the horse moves.

Spin — a 360 degree turn on the hocks accomplished when a horse places a hind pivot foot on the ground and turns completely around it. Also called a turn around.

Splint boots — protective boots which cover the horse's front cannon bones from the knees down to and sometimes including the fetlocks or ankles.

Spurs — metal devices that attach to the heels of riding boots. They have shanks with a blunt point or rowels which poke into the horse to encourage movement, used to accentuate leg aids.

Stallion — a male horse, used for breeding purposes.

Supple — to soften or make flexible the horse's body parts through various exercises.

Swells — forks of a Western saddle that form the front of the saddle and provide security for the rider's seat.

Teamster — a horseman who drives horses, handles the reins of horse hitches which pull heavy loads in wagons.

Toe-in — phrase used to describe conformation of horses that have front or hind legs turned inward instead of straight ahead.

Toe-out — phrase used to describe conformation of horses that have front or hind legs pointed outward instead of straight ahead.

Trailers — extensions of the horseshoe which add stability to sliding stops.

Trapezoid — In mathematics (geometry), a plane figure with four sides, two of which are parallel to each other. In reference to horses, the term describes the structure of a horse's body denoting the shoulder and hip angles in relation to the length of the back and underline.

Turn around — a 360 degree turn on the hocks accomplished when a horse places a hind pivot foot on the ground and turns completely around it. Also called a spin.

Twisted wire — mouthpiece, usually jointed, made of twisted wire. Bit is considered more severe as it has more of a bite on the horse's tongue.

Weanling — horses, of either sex, from weaning to one year old.

Western snaffle — a bit with a jointed mouthpiece and a loose-jawed shank is often referred to in Western horsemanship circles as a snaffle.

Wolf teeth — small teeth that have no function in a horse's mouth. They develop in front of a horse's molars. Pulling them is usually a simple operation and prevents a horse from injuring himself when there is a bit in his mouth.

Working cowhorse — a horse that can handle cattle as well as run a reining pattern. Working cowhorse competition is divided into dry work, herd work and fence work. In the dry work, the horse runs a reining pattern. In the herd work, the horse cuts a cow from a herd and prevents it from returning to the herd. In the fence work, the horse maneuvers the cow by running the animal along a fence line, stopping and turning it, then forcing it to change directions by running it in a figure eight pattern.

Yearling — horses, of either sex, from January 1 of the year after they were foaled until January 1 of the next year, at which time they are considered 2-year-olds.

Appendix A: Alphabetical and Numerical Indexes to Horses

ALPHABETICAL

Appendix B: Training Program Outline

AGE	MAINTENANCE AND HEALTH CARE	TRAINING PROCEDURES	TRAINING GOALS
Weanling	Inoculations, de-worming and farriery work every 60 days	Halter breaking Hobble breaking Grooming Free longeing in round pen	Create a bond between horse and man. Gain horse's confidence Teach horse to come to handler Teach voice commands and meaning of "whoa"
Yearling	Inoculations, de-worming and farriery work every 60 days	N/A	N/A
2-year-old Program Round Pen (1st week)	Inoculations, de-worming and farriery work every 60 days Teeth floated, wolf teeth pulled Fillies sutured Front feet shod, only if necessary	Repeat free longeing from weanling lessons Sacking out First saddling	Get horse used to equipment and weight on his back Teach horse to give his nose to right and left, to move forward and stop Introduce lead cues
2-year-old Program Arena (2nd week)	N/A	Repeat round pen procedures, except no sacking out	Repetition of cues reinforces basic training concepts to horse
2-year-old Program Slide Track (from first two weeks to 90 days)	Inoculations, de-worming and farriery work every 60 days	Basic training principles of neck reining, suppling of nose, neck and rib areas, circling and backing up Change leads a couple of times	Build solid foundation for reining maneuvers See how horse changes leads
3-year-old Program (December of 2-year-old year to January of 3-year-old)	Inoculations, de-worming and farriery work every 60 days Shod with keg shoes on front feet and 1" slide plates on hind feet	A refresher course of basic suppling exercises and riding skills first in round pen, then on slide track Build lung capacity and body strength through interval training conditioning techniques	Reintroduce horse to having a rider on his back and following basic commands Condition equine athlete for the year's work
3-year-old Program January through February	Inoculations, de-worming and farriery work every 60 days	Continue refresher course and interval training Horse should be able to lope 10 minutes each way with a 10 minute walk in between	Repeat basics until they are solid Horse's body should be supple
3-year-old Program March through May	Inoculations, de-worming and farriery work every 60 days	Advanced suppling exercises including poll flexion and hip displacement Simple maneuver work on circles, lead changes, stops, rollbacks, turn arounds and back ups Begin speed control	Transition phase from snaffle bit or hackamore to shank bit and from simple to advanced suppling exercises
3-year-old Program June through August	Inoculations, de-worming and farriery work every 60 days	Emphasis on maneuver work Concentrate on perfecting circles, lead changes, stops, rollbacks, turn arounds and back ups Speed control program now includes hard galloping	Horse is performing all maneuvers confidently Horse has settled into a comfortable training routine
3-year-old Program September to December	Inoculations, de-worming and farriery work every 60 days	Finish work Polish transitions from one maneuver to next Bring horse to peak level of performance prior to competition	Final preparation before competition All parts of horse's body are supple and response to commands is instantaneous Performing all maneuvers with speed and a high degree of difficulty

EQUIPMENT	APPROXIMATE LENGTH OF TIME	OBJECTIVES	CHAPTER
Halter Lead rope Hobbles	2-4 weeks	Turn out to pasture with horse understanding walk, trot, lope and stop on command. Horse has a pleasant association with people	5
N/A	1 1/2 years	Turned out to pasture to grow up	N/A
Halter Lead rope Saddle Splint boots	1 week	Horse understands leg and rope pressure for moving forward, stopping and turning Horse can guide well enough to go to arena	6
Saddle Hackamore or snaffle bit Splint boots	1 week	Rider should feel secure that horse is reasonably broke enough to go outside to slide track or pasture	6
Saddle Hackamore or snaffle bit Splint boots	2 1/2 months	Initial breaking period should solidify concepts of walk, trot, lope and back up on a loose rein before horse is turned out to pasture until December	7
Saddle Hackamore or snaffle bit Splint boots	1 month	Prepare horse, mentally and physically, for the year's work	8
Saddle Hackamore or snaffle bit Splint boots	2 months	Prepare horse, mentally and physically, for the year's work	8
Saddle 7" shank snaffle bit (jointed mouthpiece) Splint boots Bell boots Knee guards, if necessary	3 months	Horse is in good condition by this time and prepared for advanced maneuvers	9-13
Saddle 7" shank snaffle bit/solid bar grazing bit Splint, bell and skid boots Knee guards, if necessary	3 months	Horse is ready to accept the pressure of being asked to perform all maneuvers correctly and with speed	9-13
Saddle 7" shank solid bar grazing bit Splint, bell and skid boots	3 months	Finished reining horse	9-13

Appendix C: NRHA Judges Score Card

JUDGE_____

EVENT_____ DATE_____ CLASS_____

MANEUVER SCORES   -1.5 = EXTREMELY POOR   -1 = VERY POOR   -.5 = POOR   0 = AVERAGE   .5 = GOOD   1 = VERY GOOD   1.5 = EXCELLENT

Draw #	Entry #	Maneuvers	1	2	3	4	5	6	7	8	Composite	Penalties	Score
		Penalty 70 Score										↓	
		Penalty 70 Score										↓	
		Penalty 70 Score										↓	
		Penalty 70 Score										↓	
		Penalty 70 Score										↓	
		Penalty 70 Score										↓	
		Penalty 70 Score										↓	
		Penalty 70 Score										↓	
		Penalty 70 Score										↓	
		Penalty 70 Score										↓	
		Penalty 70 Score										↓	

Appendix D: Recommendations for a Feeding Program

I follow two separate feeding programs, one for my show horses and one for my broodmares and pasture horses. After much research and experience, I have found that these programs meet the energy and nutritional requirements of my stock. You can tailor a feeding program to suit your needs using some of these guidelines.

SHOW HORSES

I feed my show horses a diet of alfalfa hay and oats. I use a general guideline as to how much feed every horse gets. However, once a week, I walk down the barn aisle and inspect each horse. Depending upon how they look, I increase the feed for horses that need it and decrease it for those that look overweight.

Oats: Feed one gallon morning and night using a gallon measuring can. I feed cleaned racehorse oats that weigh over 40 pounds per bushel. Oats that are under 40 pounds per bushel are more hull than they are grain.

Hay: Feed two flakes alfalfa hay morning and night. I feed alfalfa hay that has 20 percent protein. Be careful to buy alfalfa from parts of the country that don't have a blister beetle infestation problem. When the hay is harvested, blister beetles can be trapped in a bale of hay. They produce a poison called cantharidin, which causes irritation to the gastrointestinal and urinary tracts of horses.

Horses can experience severe colic and even death.

BROODMARES AND PASTURE HORSES

I feed my broodmares and pasture horses grass hay and a specially formulated grain ration. I had the feed developed for me by a nutrition expert, Jim Pumphrey of The Noble Foundation.

Grain Ration: Feed, which has corn, ground alfalfa and soybean meal as the main ingredients, is ground up and made into a two inch range cube. The cubes fed from September to May contain 18 percent protein. The cubes fed during the hotter months of June through August contain only 12 percent protein. 18 percent protein is too much to feed when the temperatures reach 90 to 100 degrees. Horses don't gulp the large cubes. Instead, they pick them up one at a time and chew them slowly. Since the feed is already ground, when it enters the horse's stomach, the acids act on the food, digesting it easier. This feed is not recommended with alfalfa hay because the protein levels would be too high.

Hay: Bermuda grass and prairie grass hay. Good pasture grass is also available.

Appendix E: Address List

American Paint Association,
PO Box 18519, Fort Worth, Texas 76118

American Quarter Horse Association,
2701 I-40 East, Amarillo, Texas 79168

Greg Darnall Bits,
Rt. 2, Box 78 A3, Lone Oak, Texas 75453

Hackamore Reinsman, c/o Connell,
PO Box 718, Tomball, Texas 77377

National Cutting Horse Association,
4704 Highway 377 South, Fort Worth, Texas 76116

National Reining Horse Association
448 Main St., Suite 204, Coshocton, Ohio 43812

The Reiner
PO Box 36, Minster, Ohio 45865

Index

LIST OF ILLUSTRATIONS AND DIAGRAMS

Photo Credits

With the exception of the following pages, all pictures in this book, including the front and back covers, were photographed by Kathy Kadash.

VIII, Linda Blake-Caddel, courtesy of Horseman Magazine

Profile XVII (top), Jim Keeneland Photography

Profile XVII (bottom), Williams Photography

Introduction, Joleen Wiseman

Chapter 3
14	Courtesy of American Quarter Horse Association
15	(Doc Bar) Anna Robertson, courtesy of Horseman Magazine
16	(Joe Cody) Linda Blake-Caddel, courtesy of Horseman Magazine
17	(Okleos Sail Win) Joyce Loomis

Chapter 16
150-151	Don Trout Photography
152	Doug Leahy Photography
153	Don Trout Photography

Chapter 17
159	Joyce Loomis

Chapter 18
160-161	Bonnie Lindsey, courtesy of Horseman Magazine
163	Waltenberry Photography
166	Lesky and Matacale Photography

Chapter 19
180-181	Harold Campton Photography
185	Dalco Photography
186	Dalco Photography
186	Dalco Photography
188	Harold Campton Photography
189	Harold Campton Photography

Chapter 20
192	Ed Holmgren Photography
195	Harold Campton Photography
196	Janssen Photography
197	(Lady Eldorado) Waltenberry Photography
197	(Cassandra Cody) Harold Campton Photography
198	Harold Campton Photography
200	(Miss Della Doc) Harold Campton Photography
200	(Diamonds Ms Sparkle) Harold Campton Photography
202	Pat Hall Photography
203	Jeff Kirkbride Photography